Alla memoria della mia madre e mio padre,
con riconoscente affetto.

Contents

Acknowledgments

During the years from 1990 to 1995 when I was researching and writing this book, I benefited from the sponsorship of several organizations. The National Endowment for the Humanities (Travel to Collections), the American Philosophical Society, the University of Pennsylvania Center for Italian Studies (Salvatori Research Grant), and a University of Pennsylvania Research Foundation Grant funded trips to Italy in the summers of 1990, 1991, and 1992. In Italy, Doctor Marina Giannetto, director of the Sala di Studio of the Central State Archives in Rome, was unfailingly courteous and helpful. The staffs of the National Libraries in Florence, Rome, and Verona fulfilled my innumerable requests for microfilms and photocopying.

I wrote this book while I was a member of the Sociology Department of the University of Pennsylvania. Junior Faculty Leave for the academic year 1992–1993 provided the free time to draft Chapters 3, 4, and 6. During that period, I was a Visiting Fellow at the Minda De Gunzberg Center for European Studies of Harvard University and the Sociology Department of Harvard. Guido Goldman, director of the Center, and Abigail Collins, associate director, provided office space and resources during the summers of 1992 and 1993. Peter Marsden, chair of the Harvard Sociology Department, facilitated access to departmental resources and made it possible for me to have a Widener Library card for the entire period. I thank all of them for making my time at Harvard rewarding.

I completed the revisions of the manuscript in the summer of 1995 supported by a grant from the German Marshall Fund of United States. I corrected the copyedited manuscript while I was a Visiting Fellow in the Department of Social and Political Sciences at the European University Institute in Florence, Italy. I thank Professor Christian Joppke for arranging my stay at the Institute.

In Philadelphia, my colleagues Paul Allison, Antonio McDaniel, Samuel Preston, and Herbert L. Smith patiently gave advice on the graphs in Chapter 5. Paul Allison was particularly generous with his time. My graduate student Deborah McIlvaine, in consultation with Professor Allison, produced numerous versions of what I have come to think of as the "ritual waves," and I am thankful to her for her diligence. Herbert L. Smith and Ian Lustick read drafts of Chapter 3, and Paul Lichterman read a draft of Chapter 6. Their comments helped in the revisions process. Another graduate student, Mori Insingher, aided me in assembling the photographs as well as serving as my library assistant in the summers of 1994 and 1995. During the years that I was researching and writing, an army of undergraduates fetched and carried books from libraries in Cambridge and Philadelphia; among this group, Yulia Miteva deserves special mention. The secretarial staff of the Sociology Department at Penn helped to produce several copies of the manuscript. Tina Nemetz arranged for endless photocopying and Federal Express mailings.

During the writing process, I had the good fortune to present parts of the book as "work in progress" at several university seminars where I benefited enormously from the discussion and criticism of colleagues and graduate students. Among these were David Kertzer's graduate seminar on ritual in the Department of Anthropology at Brown University (spring 1993) and Gene Burns's graduate seminar on culture in the Department of Sociology at Princeton (spring 1994). Samuel Cohn invited me to speak to the Italian Study Group at the Harvard Center for European Studies in the spring of 1992. A highlight of my pilgrimages with the evolving manuscript in hand was the "ritual" presentation that David Laitin has established for Wilder House authors at the University of Chicago. My visit to Wilder House at an early stage in my writing challenged me. In addition to Laitin, I particularly wish to thank George Steinmetz and William Sewell, Jr., as well as the assembled graduate students for their contributions to that event.

After I completed the first version of the manuscript, Marta Petrusewicz invited me in the autumn of 1994 to the Columbia University Seminar in Modern Italian Studies. That session was invaluable for clarifying and refining the Italian dimension of the argument. In February 1995, I presented Chapter 5 at Wendy Griswold's Culture and Society Workshop, Department of Sociology, University of Chicago, where her lively and talented graduate students pushed me to clarify and refine arguments.

While I was writing the book, I also taught a yearly graduate seminar on sociological approaches to the study of culture. The University of Pennsylvania graduate students who took that course were a source of continual intellectual stimulation as I thought through the design of the book. I thank all the students who enrolled in Sociology 561 between 1992 and 1995.

The ever permeable boundary between the public and private is one of the book's central themes. During the writing of it, I myself lived through an unusual series of public and private events. I could not have written this book, or any book for that matter, if I had not enjoyed the friendship and support of a remarkable group of people who cheerfully crossed the public/ private divide on my behalf. During the spring of 1993, friends in Cambridge, Abigail Collins, Samuel Cohn, Nerys Patterson, George Ross, Joseph Soares, Mary Vogel, Genevieve Warner, and Mary Waters, provided fellowship, humor, and emergency housing. Jeanette Valentine and Alonzo Plough continually opened their home to me—although their children, Julian and Lewis, probably wondered why I always seemed to visit with my computer! Back in Philadelphia in the fall of 1993, a trio of colleagues were unfailingly supportive. Diana Crane repeatedly asked when the book would be done; Linda Aiken was a source of general enthusiasm and a vast number of dinners; and Magali Sarfatti Larsen amused me with social narratives, constant exhortations to "take a walk" or "see a movie," and even memories of fascist Italy. Most important, Magali read and copyedited the entire first draft of the manuscript. Not only did I benefit from her sociological acumen, but she also saved me from numerous errors of Italian grammar and spelling. In the spring of 1995, Lynn Hunt and Michele Lamont were especially generous with their time and advice. During the entire period, Lucia Benaquisto, Alice Holmes Cooper, Robert Fishman, and Ted Perlmutter were sustaining forces. Despite the ups and downs of their own public and private lives, all four were always "there," and I am deeply appreciative of their friendship.

But books, no matter what instrumental purposes they may serve, are ultimately intellectual products, and my most deeply felt debts are intellectual in the broadest sense of the word. In contrast to many first books, this work did not originate in my dissertation—a more restricted study of art and politics in fascist Italy. Yet I could not have conceived of this project if I had not studied as a graduate student at Harvard with Daniel Bell, Orlando Patterson, Alessandro Pizzorno, and Theda Skocpol; this book is a measure of the enduring influence that all four have had on my work and my sociological imagination. Theda Skocpol especially has been exceedingly kind and generous, as well as unfailingly responsive and supportive, in the years that I have known her. Her indirect contributions to the completion of this manuscript were enormous.

David Laitin's infectious enthusiasm when the book was only an idea and his belief that I would actually write it, when I myself had doubts, kept me going in what he did not know were difficult times. I am deeply appreciative of the commitment that he displayed to me and my project. Michael Burawoy devoted a part of his 1994 Christmas holiday to the manuscript and

Making the Fascist Self

Post-Fascism/Fascism:
Italy 1994/1922

Two Rallies and a Mass

On March 28, 1994, a coalition of right-wing parties swept the Italian elections. A month later, neo-fascists (or "post-fascists," as they prefer to label themselves) held positions in the Italian government for the first time since 1943 when Benito Mussolini's fascist regime crumbled. On April 25, 1994, the forty-ninth anniversary of the Allied liberation of Italy, "Liberation Day" as the state holiday is known, post-fascists and reconstructed communists appropriated public space to debate the meaning of fascism— old and new.

The public piazza once more became the arena of cultural contestation over the meaning of fascism. The public piazza, the center of every major Italian city and town, resonates deeply with Italian society, culture, and politics. In the pre-fascist period, the piazza had been the site of bloody clashes between socialists and fascists; during the fascist period, it was the site of parades, rallies, and public political rituals. The defeat of fascism did not signal the end of the piazza's cultural and political significance. From labor strikes and student protests to the terrorist bombings of the Piazza Fontana in Milan in 1974, the piazza was, and is, a vital component of the Italian public sphere and civic life.[1]

On April 25, three hundred thousand persons led by a coalition of parties that had lost the March elections marched to Piazza del Duomo in Milan.

[1] For the cultural and social significance of the Italian piazza, which dates to the Renaissance, see Peter Burke, "The Historical Anthropology of Early Modern Italy," in *The Historical Anthropology of Early Modern Italy* (Cambridge: Cambridge University Press, 1987), 3–14. For a discussion of the piazza during the modern period, see Mario Isnenghi, *L'Italia in piazza: I luoghi della vita pubblica dal 1848 ai giorni nostri* (Milan: Mondadori, 1994).

They labeled the demonstration a nonpartisan effort to dramatize commitment to "pride in democracy," and their marching slogan was "Don't you dare [*Non ci provate*]."[2] In Rome, Gianfranco Fini, leader of the reconstructed post-fascist party, attended a mass in the Basilica of Santa Maria degli Angeli to celebrate a "feast of reconciliation" and "national pacification." Standing on the steps of the church, Fini proclaimed, "We think of the future—enough of the fences and hatreds of the past!"[3] If the piazza is the secular space of Italian political life, the church is the sacred space of Italian civic and cultural life. Fini exploited this widely perceived distinction to contrast an image of post-fascists at prayer with an image of post-communists and others marching against the results of a legally constituted election.

Less than a month later, in Piazza San Lorenzo in Vicenza, Italian youth belonging to the "Skin-head Front of the Veneto" demonstrated to celebrate the return of fascism. Declaring themselves "heirs of the fascists of Salo," the Nazi puppet regime set up in northern Italy after Mussolini's regime crumbled, they dressed in black, gave the fascist salute, and called for a resurgence of fascism in its most extreme and brutal form. Chanting "Honor, Fidelity, and Courage" and shouting "We are hard, no one will stop us," they proclaimed that "fifty years of democracy and pluralism had changed social structure for the worse."[4] A *La Stampa* journalist described the scene in the piazza as an inevitable outcome of the March election: "I saw Italian naziskins march. They were some months early, but we knew that sooner or later they would return: they advanced decisive, brutal in dress and face, lined up like a military company, with flags raised high, garish, unmistakable: even those who see them for the first time understand what they symbolize, who invented it, what they recall."[5]

The piazza, the church, the piazza—the sites of these three public ritual events were temporally proximate but politically distant. The piazza and the church represent two poles of a calculated political battle over the memory and meaning of the old fascism. The Vicenza rally was a spontaneous outpouring of disaffected youth from which the Italian post-fascist leader had been trying to disassociate himself. The Vicenza rally and the images it produced—Italian skinheads in black shirts—were consonant with popular understandings that have equated fascism principally with violence. Even a scholar as distinguished as Zeev Sternhell, in a recent reinterpretation of

[2] Mino Fuccillo, "La storia siamo noi," *La Repubblica* (Rome), 26 April 1994, 3. Unless a translator is named, all translations from the Italian are my own.
[3] Quoted in Paolo Boccacci, "Fini, una messa per dimenticare," *La Repubblica*, 26 April 1994, 5.
[4] Quoted in Gabriele Romagnoli, "Reportage nel covo degli skin," *La Stampa* (Turin), 19 May 1994, 7.
[5] Ferdinando Camon, "Perche proprio oggi," *La Stampa*, 16 May 1994, 1.

European fascism, concludes: "Fascism, therefore, was not content to criti-
cize the existing state of affairs; it also sought to provide the nucleus of a
comprehensive, heroic, and violent political culture."[6]

The neo-nazis of Vicenza and the "post-fascists" of the Basilica Santa
Maria degli Angeli together evoke conflicting emotions of artificial comfort
and false alarm. The artificial comfort derives from the relative ease with
which politicians, "post-fascist" and other, can reject the implicit illegality of
skinhead political practice. The low probability that skinheads will ever assume control of the Italian state—or any state, for that matter—means that
the alarm they generate is false. Violence is not the defining feature of fascism, old or new.

Contested and partial understandings of the European fascism of the
1920s and 1930s drive the current Italian conflict over meaning and memory. Historians and social scientists confronted with the diversity of national
variations of "old" fascist practice declared the attempt to find a common
thread futile. Rather than elevating fascism to the status of a new political
ideology, they viewed it as a historical aberration (to invoke Benedetto
Croce, "a parenthesis") best understood by careful analysis of its various
national manifestations.[7] At its most benign, fascism was a political exercise
in "developmental dictatorship"; at its worst, it was a temporary exercise in
irrational violence.[8]

New political developments in continental Europe that include the emergence of Italian "post-fascism" as an electoral power force a revision of fascism as a political idea. Fascists or "post-fascists" (the name is irrelevant)
have an understanding of their political projects even if social analysts do
not. The locations chosen for the events of April 25, 1994, the church
versus the piazza, are suggestive of the meaning of the new and old fascist
projects.

The piazza and the church have a formal similarity that is constitutive of
much of the analysis that follows. In both, one loses one's private self in the
public community. But when one leaves the piazza, one becomes a private
citizen again, whereas when one leaves the church, the community leaves
with one—that is, the space between public and private self evaporates. In
rallies in liberal democracies such as contemporary Italy, citizens have multiple identities or selves that they espouse at different moments. In contrast to
their relationship to the church, where public and private selves merge, citi-

---

[6] Zeev Sternhell, *The Birth of Fascist Ideology*, trans. David Maisel (Princeton: Princeton
University Press, 1994), 252.

[7] For Croce's assertion, see Renzo De Felice, *Interpretations of Fascism*, trans. Brenda Huff
Everett (Cambridge: Harvard University Press, 1977), 14.

[8] A. James Gregor, *Italian Fascism and Developmental Dictatorship* (Princeton: Princeton
University Press, 1979).

zens reassume their private identities when they leave the piazza. The piazza reinforces the boundary between the public self of political engagement and the private self of ordinary life.[9]

The Italian Fascist Project

The Italy of 1922, the year Benito Mussolini's fascist movement assumed control of the state, appears at first glance worlds apart from the Italy of 1994. Pluralist democracy, free markets, and universalism—political inventions of the Enlightenment—seem finally to have triumphed in the world. But instead, the opposite has occurred. In Italy, the wave of political scandals referred to as *tangentopoli* toppled postwar political arrangements and gave way to the electoral success of post-fascism and the proliferation of right-wing violence embodied in the rise of neo-nazi and skinhead cadres.

In 1922, the First World War had finally destroyed Europe's old regimes. In Italy and Europe, statesmen and citizens, ordinary men and women, perceived themselves as "Wandering between two worlds, one dead, / the other powerless to be born."[10] The unborn world of 1922 included increasing worker militancy, economic recession, and widespread fears of socialist revolution, all of which seemed to threaten an already precarious social stability. Roberto Vivarelli suggests that the fascist impulse which overtook Italy and Europe in the early twentieth century, and which in reconstituted form threatens contemporary Europe, "speaks Italian."[11] Vivarelli's broader point that Italy in 1922 is useful as an entry to understanding Europe's present as well as its past is congruent with themes I advance in this book. The similarities, and not the differences, between 1922 and 1994 lend wider cogency to my analysis.

Popular fascist idiom described Benito Mussolini's takeover of the Italian state as a "revolution." The fascist revolution did not topple the Italian state, however, and it did not change underlying class relations in Italian society.[12] What sort of revolution did Mussolini and his supporters have in mind? The Italian fascist regime that governed Italy from 1922 to 1943 aimed to create new men and women, a new ethos, a new culture. In con-

[9] Cf. Charles Taylor, *Sources of the Self: The Making of the Modern Identity* (Cambridge: Harvard University Press, 1989).
[10] The lines are from Matthew Arnold, "Stanzas from the Grande Chartreuse."
[11] Roberto Vivarelli, "Interpretations of the Origins of Fascism," *Journal of Modern History* 63 (March 1991), 30.
[12] I follow Theda Skocpol's definition of social revolution. *States and Social Revolutions: A Comparative Analysis of France, Russia, and China* (Cambridge: Cambridge University Press, 1979), 4–5.

temporary parlance, the regime sought to forge new identities. Although it is highly unlikely that either regime intellectuals or ordinary Italians conceived of their selves in the language of identity, the term serves as a convenient way to encapsulate the fascist revolutionary project.[13] Fascism in general, and Italian fascism in particular, was a political project that aimed to recreate the self, to create new identities as citizens of fascist Italy.

The "fascist project" was the set of actions and programs the regime undertook to accomplish its desired cultural ends. The regime "fascistified" Italy's principal cultural and social institutions. It reorganized schools, took over popular and elite artistic institutions from cinema to theater to publishing, controlled the press, and created a web of voluntary organizations that mobilized men and women of all ages. It made peace with the Catholic Church in the Concordat of 1929 and instituted demographic policies that redefined the nature of the Italian family.[14]

Public spectacle was the favored expressive vehicle of the fascist identity project. Public political spectacles or rituals (I use the words interchangeably), such as the events of April 25, 1994, are not simply arenas for the exegesis of political symbols but venues for addressing broader theoretical issues concerning the nature of nondemocratic politics. Political rituals—rallies, parades, commemoration ceremonies, holidays—are cultural prisms that I analyze to advance an argument about how politics, culture, and identity intersect.

By taking the fascist project on its own terms, I seek to understand a remarkably persistent modern political force. This book plows two distinct yet interconnected fields. The first involves demarcating the boundaries of fascism itself; the second concerns how public political rituals served as vehicles of the fascist political idea. This double focus reflects the tension between two senses of culture that underlie my analysis.

The first sense concerns culture in the broad ethnographic understanding of the term, what Clifford Geertz has captured with his method of "thick

---

[13] "Identity" is historically specific, but this in no way obviates its use if we are cautious. On the transcultural use of the term, see Richard Handler, "Is 'Identity' a Useful Cross-cultural Concept?" in *Commemorations: The Politics of National Identity*, ed. John R. Gillis (Princeton: Princeton University Press, 1994), 27–40. On the analytic use of historically specific terms, see Craig Calhoun, "'New Social Movements' of the Early Nineteenth Century," *Social Science History* 17 (Fall 1993), 385–427.

[14] The best general introductions remain Philip V. Cannistraro, *La fabbrica del consenso* (Bari: Laterza, 1975); Edward R. Tannenbaum, *The Fascist Experience* (New York: Basic, 1972); and Victoria De Grazia, *The Culture of Consent: Mass Organization of Leisure in Fascist Italy* (New York: Cambridge University Press, 1981). For a recent capsule summary of regime demographic policies, somewhat overburdened by its theoretical apparatus, see David G. Horn, *Social Bodies* (Princeton: Princeton University Press, 1994).

description" and his definition of culture as "webs of significance that [man] himself has spun.[15] This sense of culture reveals what is "Italian" in fascist culture, and the mapping of historical context re-creates it. The second sense of culture is captured in the detailed analysis of objects and practices—in this case fascist political ritual. William Sewell's distinction between a schema and a resource elegantly summarizes the dualities embedded in this second sense. According to Sewell, a schema is a society's "fundamental tools of thought," consisting of "conventions, recipes, scenarios, principles of action, and habits of speech and gesture."[16] Resources are the capacities human agents have to recraft social structure, or culture writ large, depending on their manipulation of the available schema. Neither schemata nor resources are independent of each other. They mutually reinforce each other and limit and enhance the capacity for action as well as for cultural and political transformation.

In trying to create a fascist identity or new conception of the self, the regime continually relied on the available schema and was ultimately a prisoner of it: what was "Italian" about Italian culture and identity limited and constrained what was fascist about fascist identity. Just as the regime was constrained by the exigencies of the particular, so too my path in this book constantly glides among the abstraction of theoretical generality, the schema of fascism, and the empirical specificity of Italian fascist public events.

Orienting Questions

Three questions structure my analysis of public political ritual. First, I ask a broad theoretical question about the nature of fascism that abandons old and dead-end categories and reconceptualizes fascism in terms of citizenship, state, nation, and the construction of the self. In this task, I pay close attention to fascist narratives that reject liberalism as political ideology and democracy as a form of government. I argue that Italian fascism rejected the split between the public and private self, the cultural core of liberal democracy. Political movements and parties which reject this split on cultural grounds are more likely to gain political ascendance during those historical moments when diverse social groups perceive the cultural bifurcation of a public and private self as untenable. I suggest that movements and parties that reaffirm the self as a totality might be fruitfully redefined as fascist.

---

[15] Clifford Geertz, "Thick Description: Toward an Interpretive Theory of Culture," in *The Interpretation of Cultures* (New York: Basic, 1973), 5.

[16] William H. Sewell, Jr., "A Theory of Structure: Duality, Agency, and Transformation," *American Journal of Sociology* 98 (July 1992), 8, 10–13.

Second, I ask whether states, even reputedly totalitarian states, can impose meaning or identities on their citizens. This analytic question addresses current debates about the role of symbols, images, and language in political practice and challenges the assumption that representations of power equal realities of power. Internal colonization is the governing metaphor of the political process that underlay the Italian fascist cultural project.[17] Just as colonial administrators encountered resistance from indigenous cultural practices, fascist cultural bureaucrats encountered resistance from prior Italian cultural forms with strong institutional buttresses.

"Ritual" is the analytic term that most appropriately captures the numerous public spectacles which occupied public space in fascist Italy. In contrast to the usual scholarly practice of analyzing ritual as text, my analysis focuses on the formal properties of ritual action as constitutive of meaning. In so doing, I conceptualize rituals as emotive practices or actions whose meaning lies in the repetition of patterns.

A third, historical, question merges my theoretical and analytic propositions. I ask how Italian fascism attempted to reconstitute the nature of political identity through redefinitions of community and self. Using empirically grounded case studies, I demonstrate that the Italian fascist regime attempted to create a fascist political community and identity by merging the public and private self in rituals—communities of feeling—in the public piazzas. The new fascist political community, dramatized in the public piazzas of Italy, created fascist citizens—men and women whose identities were bound to the regime—to the extent that these new identities articulated with earlier identities buttressed by preexisting social institutions, most salient among them the popular cultural practice of Catholicism and the sacredness of the family embodied in the figure of the mother.

The Italian fascist regime, in competition with the church and the family, wanted its citizenry to find its total self, public and private, in the piazza. Ideal fascist citizens would carry the piazza with them wherever they went. The piazza was the community, the temporary community of fascist feeling, that would define the fascist self or identity in much the same way the Roman Catholic Church defined the Italian religious self. I argue that in the polyvalence of the piazza and the univalence of the church, we can approach a new understanding of the "old" fascism that has contemporary social and political salience.

---

[17] The literature on colonization, though it tends to focus empirically on former territorial colonies of European empires, has become an area where issues of culture and power are analyzed. See, for example, Timothy Mitchell, *Colonising Egypt* (Berkeley: University of California Press, 1991), and Jean Comaroff and John Comaroff, *Of Revelation and Revolution* (Chicago: University of Chicago Press, 1991).

Mapping the Terrain Ahead

This book attempts to re-create the social experience of fascist ritual by analyzing the patterns of ritual events. What meaning lay in the fascist identity creation project, lay in the disruption and appropriation of familiar patterns. Patterns of ritual events across time and space serve as my principal methodological frame. Because I focus on the reconstruction of experience, I do not emphasize the textual exegesis of fascist symbols such as the wearing of the black shirt, or the *passo Romano*, or the fasces or the eagle. These symbols were part of particular ritual actions, and I discuss them only when they affect the context in which they occurred.

The empirical analysis begins in 1923 with the first anniversary of the "March on Rome," the symbolic event that brought Italian fascism to power, and ends in the fall of 1938 as Italy was mobilizing for war. Background material presented in various chapters incorporates the pre-1923 period; Italian soldiers' letters written in 1941 from the battlefield subsumes the war period. The book bypasses the fall of the regime, the Salo Republic, and the Resistance, though popular memory in Europe and the United States tends to equate these events with fascist Italy. The war period is absent but war is not. Many of the public ritual events I describe were prolegomena for military action, and war is a subtext of the analysis.

Commenting on the rationale behind case selection in comparative history, historian Charles Maier has noted, "Flower arranging is not botany."[18] Maier's felicitous metaphor applies equally well to case selection and research design in studies that wed political to cultural analysis. The architecture of this book depends on three case studies that illustrate my theoretical, analytic, and empirical claims. These cases cohere internally, though they do not represent steps in a linear argument. Their juxtapositions are logical; their style is narrative. They produce a cumulative effect, underscoring my central empirical point that the meaning of fascist ritual lay in its practice and my central theoretical point that fascism as ideology sought to merge the public and private self in the community of the state. Each case uses different methods, from literary to quantitative, to interpret fascism and explain ritual action.

The case studies are, first, an analysis of how the regime redesigned the annual commemoration of the March on Rome over the period between 1923 and 1938; second, an analysis of daily ritual life in Verona spanning twenty years; and third, an exploration of what Italian fascism meant to its most dedicated adherents—a group of fascist "heroes," soldiers who died

---

[18] Charles S. Maier, *Recasting Bourgeois Europe* (Princeton: Princeton University Press, 1975), 5.

fighting for Italy on the Greek Albanian front. The third case relies on textual exegesis of dead soldiers' letters. These "voices from the grave" allow me to extend previous studies of politics and culture and to discuss the extent to which fascist identities formed.

Internal and external comparisons structure each case. The story of the March on Rome examines its commemoration at key temporal intervals to map change and continuity. Chapters 3 and 4 focus on how the annual staging of the March appropriated public space in the name of the regime. Radiating outward from the Roman center, the annual holiday commemoration filled the cities and towns of Italy. Pilgrimage is the leitmotif that united the bodies of mothers, soldiers, fascist leaders, dead heroes, and Mussolini himself as they boarded the trains that carried them to ceremonies dotting the Italian landscape.

The appropriation of time structures Chapter 5, the story of ritual life in Verona. Based on a Fascist Party calendar that recorded all fascist events in the city of Verona for a twenty-year period, the chapter describes how fascism re-created civic life and to what extent it met with resistance from preexisting cultural forms, particularly the strong Veronese Catholic culture that looked dubiously at fascism and socialism. I map change in ritual genres and in local/national ritual interaction over time to examine the issue of ideological production in the Italian periphery.

Chapter 6 addresses the question of how committed fascists articulated, reinterpreted, and lived their identities. I contrast public narratives of fascist heroism with personal narratives of fascist heroes by juxtaposing obituaries as popular cultural texts with soldiers' letters from the battlefield. The three cases lie on a continuum. Space and time unite the March and Verona cases; the internalization of fascism assesses the effects of the appropriation of space and time. Because each story exists in real time, I explore the effect of exogenous regime events such as fascist colonial aggression and internal state economic and social policies on ritual outcomes.

Note on Sources

The empirical and analytic arguments presented in this book are based on systematic reading of primary historical materials. Sources vary widely; they include newspaper accounts, state documents, police records, propaganda narratives, and plays and novels. What unites them is that they are all "fascist" in origin. This is a strength and a limitation. With the exception of data taken from police files, there are no counternarratives or alternative constructions of events. Thus, the data force us to take the fascist project on its own terms.

It is possible, however, to construct counternarratives from these fascist sources. For example, I take newspaper accounts as neither true nor false representations of political events but simply as narratives that convey the emotions the regime hoped to engender in its participants. Thus, they are real representations of hoped-for emotions but not necessarily pictures of emotional attachment to the regime. They convey intention but not reception. The journalists who wrote these accounts were trapped by an Italian language of sentimentality that is not particularly fascist but that the fascist regime mobilized to its advantage.

Similarly, the analysis of public events in Verona tells us much in terms of sheer magnitude but little directly about Veronese reception of these events. At the same time, the sheer fact that they occurred tells us something about the fascist project. The letters from the front provide the best available evidence of an authentic voice of the fascist self articulated in the language of the quasi-educated petite bourgeoisie—the lower middle class—whose cultural and social aspirations drew its members to the regime. Those voices teach us much about the political and social appeal of fascism that kept it in power for twenty years and also explain the transience of that appeal as the war came.

CHAPTER I

Interpreting Fascism/
Explaining Ritual

Fascism as Political Idea

Defining the Undefinable

Parsimony eludes past and current exegeses of fascism. Attempts to theorize fascism have mined specific historical instances for generalities and yielded catalogs of characteristics.[1] Even a cursory reading of this scholarship suggests that it is impossible to generalize across cases and leaves the impression that Benedetto Croce was correct when he described fascism as a "parenthesis" in European history. Yet an analysis of the process of Italian fascist identity creation demands a conceptualization of fascism, no matter how provisional, as political idea.

Existing studies of fascism fall into two schools. The first tries to answer the "what," or definitional question. Frequently, this is articulated in a discussion of whether or not fascism is a "generic" concept or a national variation of historically specific political instances. Of those who try to define fascism, the central theme is the impossibility of definition. For example, fascism is the "vaguest of political terms"; and "a general theory of fascism must be no more than a hypothesis which fits most of the facts."[2] The sec-

---

[1] The literature on fascism written roughly between 1945 and 1976 is as voluminous as it is inconclusive. My discussion is highly selective and makes no claim to completeness. *Fascism: A Reader's Guide*, ed. Walter Laqueur (Berkeley: University of California Press, 1976), Renzo De Felice, *Interpretations of Fascism* (Cambridge: Harvard University Press, 1977), and Stanley G. Payne, *Fascism: Comparison and Definition* (Madison: University of Wisconsin Press, 1980), provide useful introductions to that literature.

[2] Payne, *Fascism*, 4–5; George L. Mosse, "Towards a General Theory of Fascism," in *International Fascism*, ed. George L. Mosse (London: Sage, 1979), 1.

ond approach bypasses definition and tries to establish the characteristics of regimes and constituencies.[3]

Seymour Martin Lipset's classic account of the class composition of fascist movements attributes fascism's success to the political disaffection of the middle classes. Juan Linz's approach to constituency formation starts from the premise that an independent "phenomenon" of fascism existed, defined as a "hyper-nationalist, often pan-nationalist, anti-parliamentary, anti-liberal, anti-communist, populist and therefore anti-proletarian, partly anti-capitalist and anti-bourgeois, anti-clerical, or at least, non-clerical movement, with the aim of national social integration through a single party and corporative representation not always equally emphasized: with a distinctive style and rhetoric, it relied on activist cadres ready for violent action combined with electoral participation to gain power with totalitarian goals by a combination of legal and violent tactics."[4]

Linz's definition rests on his assumption that fascism occupies a residual political field. As a late-comer to the political scene, fascism had to capture whatever "political space," in the form of ideological doctrine and political constituencies, was available to it. His argument is dependent on an analysis of the social bases of fascism's political competitors.[5] Linz recognizes the importance of national case studies, and the characteristics he outlines are applicable in various combinations to a broad range of fascist movements and regimes. In general, studies of institutions and constituencies display greater analytic precision than those that wrestle with definition.

Historian Gilbert Allardyce's frequently cited, and somewhat strident, analysis, published in 1979, appeared to have closed the question of "generic" fascism. Allardyce asserts that fascism had no meaning outside Italy and that it was neither an ideology nor a mental category. Comparing fascism to romanticism (and curiously obtuse about fascism's other ideological kin—modernism), he states that both terms "mean virtually nothing." Resigned to the fact that "fascism [as a political term] is probably with us for good," Allardyce maintains that the proper analytic task is to "limit the

[3] Again, the literature is vast. Alberto Aquarone's study of the Italian fascist regime, L'organizzazione dello Stato totalitario (rpt., Turin: Einaudi, 1974), and Karl Dietrich Bracher, The German Dictatorship, trans. Jean Steinberg (New York: Holt, Rinehart and Winston, 1970), serve as examples of the first category; in the second, see Seymour Martin Lipset, Political Man (rpt., Baltimore: Johns Hopkins University Press, 1981), 87–179, and Gino Germani, "Fascism and Class," in The Nature of Fascism, ed. Stuart J. Woolf (London: Weidenfeld and Nicolson, 1968), 65–95.

[4] Juan J. Linz, "Some Notes toward a Comparative Study of Fascism in Sociological Historical Perspective," in Fascism: A Reader's Guide, ed. Laqueur, 12–13.

[5] Juan J. Linz, "Political Space and Fascism as a Latecomer," in Who Were the Fascists: Social Roots of European Fascism, ed. Stein Ugelvik Larsen (Bergen: Universitetsforlaget, 1980), 153–89.

damage"; he concludes: "Placing it [fascism] within historical boundaries at least provides a measure of control, restricting the proliferation of the word in all directions, past and present, and preventing it from distorting political rhetoric in our own time. Fascism must become a foreign word again, untranslatable outside a limited period in history."[6]

Fascism refuses to go away. Its death knell has not sounded either in the real world of political practice or in the relatively cloistered world of academic discourse. Recent scholarship signals a resurgence of interest in fascism and conservative ideology.[7] Much of it appears similar to its predecessors. For example, Roger Griffin argues that the term "fascism" has undergone an "unacceptable loss of precision." He proposes a new "ideal type" of fascism based on the following definition: "Fascism is a genus of political ideology whose mythic core in its various permutations is a palingenetic form of populist ultra-nationalism."[8] A revival of the "social interpretations" of fascism, particularly nazism, has also occurred.[9] Heirs of Lipset's mode of analysis, these studies are less deterministic and grounded in a more nuanced notion of class and political action.

A central weakness in much of the writing on fascism, past and present, has been a failure to draw a sharp distinction between fascist movements and regime action, between fascism as ideology and fascism as state, between political impulse and political institution. In general, analysts elide the question of culture and ideology or simply deal with it in a descriptive manner. The forces that enable a political movement to assume state power are different from, but not unconnected to, the forces that define a new regime. During the 1920s and 1930s, virtually every country in Europe had a fascist movement, or a political movement that displayed the characteristics of the fascist impulse, but relatively few of them progressed to political regimes, that is, took control of the state.[10] Culture and ideology figure differently at both stages. In the movement phase, they act as powerful mobilizing devices that frame the political beliefs of committed cadres of supporters.[11] In the

[6] Gilbert Allardyce, "What Fascism Is Not: Thoughts on the Deflation of a Concept," *American Historical Review* 84 (1979), 388.

[7] See, for example, Zeev Sternhell, *The Birth of Fascist Ideology*, trans. David Maisel (Princeton: Princeton University Press, 1994), and Roger Griffin, *The Nature of Fascism* (New York: St. Martin's Press, 1991).

[8] Griffin, *Nature of Fascism*, 26.

[9] See Peter Baldwin, "Social Interpretations of Nazism: Renewing a Tradition," *Journal of Contemporary History* 25 (1990), 5–37; Gregory M. Luebbert, *Liberalism, Fascism, or Social Democracy* (Oxford: Oxford University Press, 1991); and the collection of essays in *Splintered Classes*, ed. Rudy Koshar (New York: Holmes and Meier, 1990).

[10] For a summary of these movements, see Peter H. Merkl, "Comparing Fascist Movements," in *Who Were the Fascists*, ed. Larsen, 752–83.

[11] Recent developments in social movement theory that take the role of culture into account are useful for analyzing fascist movements. For a summary, see Sidney Tarrow, "Men-

regime phase, they serve as conversion mechanisms to ensure the consent of a broad public constituency. This book focuses on the latter while not denying the importance of the former.

Totalitarian states are not necessary outcomes, and as my analysis suggests, they are as much fascist fictions as political realities. Mussolini declared that his regime was the first totalitarian state; and although recent historiography has shown that the fascist cultural project was highly fissured, the intention of, if not the reality of, coherence was a goal.[12] Hannah Arendt built terror into the definition of totalitarianism.[13] Her quasi-psychoanalytic approach to fascism, which paints a portrait of mass societies, mobs, and atomized individuals responding to the congeries of a police state, evokes the neo-nazis of Vicenza and the images of an Orwellian *1984*. Terror and violence as analytic frames may capture the political realities of Stalinist Russia and Holocaust horrors, but terror did not represent the quotidian experience of Italian fascism and distracts from historical and theoretical understanding.

In contrast to Nazi Germany and Stalinist Russia, the Italian fascist regime was relatively nonrepressive. Prominent socialist intellectuals did not fare well. Between 1922 and 1943, the regime banned politically dissenting groups and subjected the Italian population to an elaborate apparatus of social and cultural control administered by a state bureaucracy. Yet comparative reading of the historical evidence suggests that the social, economic, and even cultural practices of fascist Italy were not terribly different from those of other state bureaucracies during the 1920s and 1930s.[14]

Any pretext at democratic government was abandoned after the plebiscite of 1929. The regime instituted its racial laws in 1938 as a result of its alliance with Nazi Germany. Nonetheless, Italy for much of this period was a refuge for Jews fleeing nazism from other European countries. When the war started and the regime fell, the puppet government at Salo became ex-

---

talities, Political Cultures, and Collective Action Frames," in *Frontiers in Social Movement Theory*, ed. Aldon D. Morris and Carol McClurg Mueller (New Haven: Yale University Press, 1992), 174–202, and Sidney Tarrow, *Power in Movement: Social Movements, Collective Action, and Politics* (New York: Cambridge University Press, 1994), 118–34.

[12] For accounts of the malleability of the regime's policies, see Victoria De Grazia, *How Fascism Ruled Women: Italy, 1922–1945* (Berkeley: University of California Press, 1992); Mabel Berezin, "The Organization of Political Ideology: Culture, State, and Theater in Fascist Italy," *American Sociological Review* 56 (1991), 639–51; Gabriele Turi, *Casa Einaudi* (Bologna: Il Mulino, 1990); and Alexander De Grand, "Cracks in the Facade: The Failure of Fascist Totalitarianism in Italy, 1935–39," *European History Quarterly* 21 (1991), 515–35.

[13] Hannah Arendt, *The Origins of Totalitarianism* (New York: Harcourt Brace Jovanovich, 1973) esp. 460–79.

[14] See Diane Ghirardo, *Building New Communities: New Deal America and Fascist Italy* (Princeton: Princeton University Press, 1989).

tremely repressive. But the period of the Nazi occupation of Italy is a separate story from the one offered here.[15]

Scholars have argued that it should be possible to establish a "fascist minimum," by which they mean a set of criteria without which fascism could not
exist.[16] Yet they have been reluctant to ascribe greater or lesser degrees of
importance to the variables they view as characteristic of fascism. I believe a
fuller understanding of the "old" fascism emerges when we analyze the cultural features of democracy that it rejected. Italian fascism was anti-socialist
and anticlerical, despite its conciliation with the Catholic Church, but above
all it was anti-liberal as liberalism was understood in early-twentieth-century
Italy. The rejection of liberalism in Italy was deeper than a rejection of the
failures of the Giolitti regime.[17] A revision of previous discussions of fascism,
and Italian fascism as a historical case, in light of the rejection of liberalism,
suggests new and less restricting ways to think about fascism, by whatever
name one chooses to call it.

The Rejection of Liberalism

Discussions of Marxism have confounded discussions of fascism. Simply
positing that fascism is not Marxism, or is a form of "anti-Marxism," fails to
address salient features of both ideologies.[18] Many fascists, including Mussolini himself, began their political careers as socialists. Few fascists (I cannot
identify one) began their careers as liberals, and few liberals converted to
fascism. What were the differences and points of confluence between fascism
and Marxism which made the transition from one to the other possible?

[15] Interpretations of this period are highly contested among Italian historians. For a recent
account, see Claudio Pavone, *Una Guerra civile* (Turin: Bollati Boringhieri, 1991).

[16] Payne, *Fascism*, 196, citing De Felice, *Interpretations of Fascism*.

[17] Roberto Vivarelli, *Il Fallimento del Liberalismo: Studi sulle origini del Fascismo* (Bologna: Il Mulino, 1981), attributes the rise of Italian fascism to the failure of liberalism. In
this respect his argument is congruent with mine; he locates his analysis in the economic
dimensions of Italian society, however, whereas I focus on the cultural climate. According to
Vivarelli, Italy in 1922 was an agrarian society with a quasi-literate populace that did not
generate the economic resources and social capital conducive to liberal government (see 33–
36).

[18] Ernst Nolte's controversial interpretation of fascism as a "meta-political phenomenon"
that manifests a "resistance to transcendence" begins as a form of "Anti-Marxism." "Transcendence" has a theoretical and practical dimension that, despite the highly abstract philosophical language, suggests an affirmation of the cultural dimensions of liberalism. "Theoretical transcendence" implies a capacity to imagine a world outside the local or the particular, a
world outside the self; "practical transcendence" represents an ability to engage in multiple
social relations or intersect with diverse networks. Transcendence is an overly abstract way of
talking of universalism and impartiality, the core of liberal values and the hallmark of the
democratic state (*Three Faces of Fascism*, trans. Leila Vannewitz [New York: New American
Library, 1969], 537, 542).

The beginning of an answer lies in Zeev Sternhell's analysis of fascism as an "independent cultural and political phenomenon" representing a "*revision*" of Marxism. According to Sternhell, fascism was a political hybrid that rejected, first, the liberal ideals of rationalism, individualism, and utilitarianism, and second, the materialistic dimensions of Marxism. From Marxism, fascism borrowed a concept of communitarianism embodied in a new form of revolutionary syndicalism; and from liberalism, it borrowed a commitment to free markets.[19] Sternhell's contention that market economies are compatible with fascist ideology and regimes forecloses purely economic interpretations of fascism.[20] Sternhell's analysis lends support to the importance I ascribe to fascism's disavowal of liberal political culture, but it is too dependent on the writings of national, and sometimes obscure, avant-garde intellectuals to serve as a fulcrum for generating new theories of fascism.

Stephen Holmes's critique of nonmarxist communitarianism as a form of "anti-liberalism" is most congruent with the arguments I advance. Marxism is a form of communitarianism whose commitment to science identifies it as an Enlightenment ideology distinct from fascism. "Anti-liberalism" is a third form of modern political ideology which Holmes explicitly, although guardedly, relates to fascism. Anti-liberalism is a "mind-set" that Holmes identifies by what it is against: "individualism, rationalism, humanitarianism, rootlessness, permissiveness, universalism, materialism, skepticism, and cosmopolitanism." Anti-liberals long for the restoration of lost community, which liberalism destroys in the name of Enlightenment claims to science.[21]

Liberalism as political ideal was a product of the French Revolution's call for "personal security," "individual liberty," and "democracy." "Equality," the fourth feature of liberalism, was not a fundamental concern of its initial exponents. Holmes distinguishes liberalism as ideal from liberalism as political institution. Individualism and freedom are the liberal cultural ideals that democratic states institutionalize. According to Holmes, anti-liberals equate the failures of the democratic state with the failures of liberalism.[22]

Holmes is concerned principally with contemporary anti-liberals, such as Alasdair MacIntyre and Roberto Unger, whom he is careful not to label fascists. He traces the roots of anti-liberalism to the eighteenth century and explicitly draws a connection between contemporary theorists and fascist in-

[19] Sternhell, *Birth of Fascist Ideology*, 4–5, 7.

[20] Marxist scholarship has been the principal source of economic interpretations of fascism. For an empirical study of structures of production under fascism and nazism written from a neo-liberal perspective, see Charles S. Maier, "The Economics of Fascism and Nazism," in *In Search of Stability* (Cambridge: Cambridge University Press, 1987), 70–120.

[21] Stephen Holmes, *The Anatomy of Antiliberalism* (Cambridge: Harvard University Press, 1993), 4–6.

[22] Holmes is writing a defense of liberalism and takes the position that the failure of the democratic state is not sufficient justification for the rejection of liberalism as a political ideal.

tellectuals such as Giovanni Gentile.[23] Holmes's conception of anti-liberalism has greater theoretical cogency as a framing device than theories of fascism that are wed to early-twentieth-century Europe. His concept is transcultural and transhistorical. First, Holmes identifies anti-liberal communitarian ideology in diverse cultural and historical milieus from eighteenth-century France to the contemporary United States. Second, he posits no necessary connection between the form of state or political movement that follows this ideological persuasion. Among the authors he analyzes, Carl Schmitt became an architect of Nazi legal theory, Alasdair MacIntyre has become the cultural icon of groups seeking to revitalize American democracy, and Leo Straus has remained an esoteric figure known principally within the academy. History and culture, as well as opportunity for political engagement, have circumscribed, and circumscribe, the practical influence of these thinkers.

Liberalism, as ideal and political organization, institutionalized the central cultural chasm of modernity—the fractionalization of individual and collective identities into public and private selves.[24] Identity is an issue of modernity that is connected to an ideological conception of individualism. Individualism as well as fascism, to invoke my earlier reference to Vivarelli, "speaks Italian." Jacob Burckhardt suggested the modernity of individualism and dated it to the Italian Renaissance: "at the close of the thirteenth century Italy began to swarm with individuality."[25] From our vantage point, in which the Enlightenment division of subject and object is under scrutiny, Burckhart's observation is contestable. Nevertheless, it was a given of two hundred years of intellectual history and is the Archimedean point of eighteenth-century philosophy.

Liberalism incorporates a multiplicity of identities—political, social, national, gender; the list is potentially endless and subject to ever greater refinements. Public and private as a broad categorization schema captures all possible identities. As an analytic frame, it has an intellectual history that usually incorporates a discussion of the differences among the state, civil society, and the market. I advocate a slightly less conventional use of this distinction as a convenient shorthand for what we term private or "ordinary" life—family, gender, love, religion, arenas of deeply felt identities that are beyond the purview of the liberal democratic state.[26]

[23] Holmes, *Anatomy of Antiliberalism*, xii–xiii, 9.

[24] Jürgen Habermas, *The Structural Transformation of the Public Sphere*, trans. Thomas Burger (Cambridge: MIT, 1989) contains the paradigmatic statement of the genesis of the separation between the public and private and its relation to liberal democracy currently prevailing in social science discourse.

[25] Jacob Burckhardt, *The Civilization of the Renaissance in Italy*, vol. 1 (New York: Harper, 1958), 143.

[26] "Public/private" is a term used with more frequency than precision. Much of the current thinking on it derives, as previously mentioned, from Habermas, *Structural Transforma-*

Democratic contractualism, which upholds the integrity of individualism and multiple identities, sometimes has a political effect that diverges from its theoretical intent. In his discussion of totalitarianism, Claude Lefort suggests the alienating potential of democracy when he notes, "Number breaks down unity, destroys identity." He locates the weakness of democracy in its desacralization of politics represented in its rejection of a sacred center, which the monarchy symbolizes in pre-liberal forms of government. Democracy leaves an empty symbolic space that totalitarian forms might fill: "Democracy inaugurates the experience of an ungraspable, uncontrollable society in which the people will be said to be sovereign, of course, but whose identity will constantly be open to question, whose identity will remain latent."[27] Lefort's analysis suggests that the split between public and private self is the historical exception rather than the historical norm, a split that became structurally tenable in the caesura known as modernity. It is precisely this aspect of liberal democracy that communitarians reject, and it is the void that fascism attempts to fill when it repudiates the liberal democratic state.[28]

Italian fascism's rejection of the liberal bifurcation of identity made it similar to other forms of pre-Enlightenment social and political organization such as aristocracies and tribes. Fascism departed from older organizational forms in its attempt to re-create a public/private version of the self in the political arena, or the fascist community of the state. A. James Gregor argues, "Fascism as an ideology was a far more complex and systematic intellectual product than many of its antagonists (and many of its protagonists as

---

tion. See for example, Margaret R. Somers, "What's Political or Cultural about Political Culture and the Public Sphere? Toward an Historical Sociology of Concept Formation," *Sociological Theory* 13 (1995), 115–43, and the essays in *Habermas and the Public Sphere*, ed. Craig Calhoun (Cambridge: MIT Press, 1993). But the distinction also has roots in legal and feminist theory. For one early example among many, see Jean Bethke Elshtain, *Public Man, Private Woman* (Princeton: Princeton University Press, 1981). For an overview of recent uses of the term, see Jeff Weintraub, "Varieties and Vicissitudes of Public Space," in *Metropolis*, ed. Philip Kasinitz (New York: New York University Press, 1995), 280–319, and Jeff Weintraub, "The Theory and Politics of the Public/Private Distinction" in *Public and Private Thought and Practice: Perspectives on a Grand Dichotomy*, ed. Jeff Weintraub and Krishan Kumar (Chicago: University of Chicago Press, 1996). For a discussion that delves into the personal and comes closest to my sense of the distinction, see John Brewer, "This, That and the Other: Public, Social, and Private in the Seventeenth and Eighteenth Centuries," in *Shifting the Boundaries—Transformation of the Languages of Public and Private in the Eighteenth Century*, ed. Dario Castiglione and Lesley Sharpe (Exeter: University of Exeter Press, 1995), 1–21.

[27] Claude Lefort, *The Political Forms of Modern Society*, trans. John B. Thompson (Cambridge: MIT Press, 1986), 303–4.

[28] On the relative novelty and cultural particularity of democracy, see Giuseppe Di Palma, *To Craft Democracies: An Essay on Democratic Transitions* (Berkeley: University of California Press, 1990), 16–26.

well) have been prepared to admit."[29] According to Gregor, Giovanni Gentile, the Italian philosophy professor who was Mussolini's first minister of education and general cultural adviser, was the intellectual architect of the new "third way." Gentile's collected works fill many volumes, but the salient point of his political analysis was that the fascist citizen found his or her self in the community of the state.[30] Gentile's own words best capture the spirit of this argument: "The State is itself a personality, it has a will, because it knows its aims, it has a consciousness of itself, a certain thought, a certain program, it has a concept which signifies history, tradition, the universal life of the Nation, which the State organizes, guarantees, and realizes."[31]

Gentile's conception of the "ethical" state represents an inverted Hegelianism that links, as it confounds, fascism and Marxism. Historian George Mosse notes, "At the turn of the century, the radical left and the radical right were apt to demand control of the whole man and not just a political piece of him."[32] A belief in community unites fascism and Marxism; a commitment to an Enlightenment vision of science unites liberalism and Marxism. Fascism rejected the social, cultural, and political dimensions of modernity while accepting its economic and technological features.[33] Antiliberalism offers the most parsimonious theoretical frame in which to analyze the broad cultural issues that fascism as ideology poses.

Community, public/private self, identity, and citizenship are commonly invoked to discuss democratic practice but rarely to discuss fascism. I argue that the terminology of liberalism can be fruitfully employed to understand fascism as political ideal. Applying these terms to fascism as ideal and institution opens the black box of endless categorization and provides conceptual tools for making sense of what otherwise appears an inchoate mass of contradictory ideas and actions.

The Political Construction of Identity

Self and Culture

Identity and cultural meanings are intimately connected. Part of the cultural understanding of the self, identity is central to the participation in

[29] A. James Gregor, *The Ideology of Fascism* (New York: Free Press, 1969), 26.
[30] Ibid., 216.
[31] "L'organizzazione scientifica dello stato e l'istituto di finanza," in Giovanni Gentile, *Politica e cultura*, ed. Herve A. Cavallera, vol. 2 (Florence: Le Lettere, 1991), 86.
[32] "Towards a General Theory of Fascism," 4.
[33] It is a truism that Italian fascists were attracted to technology. There is no study of Italy similar to Jeffrey Herf, *Reactionary Modernism: Technology, Culture, and Politics in Weimar and the Third Reich* (Cambridge: Cambridge University Press, 1984). For a comparative analysis of futurism, fascism, and technology, see Charles S. Maier, "Between Taylorism and Technocracy: European Ideologies and the Vision of Industrial Productivity in the 1920s," *Journal of Contemporary History* 5 (1970), 27–61.

meaningful patterns of social action. We all have identities, no matter how
narrowly construed, from the moment the infant realizes that a world apart
from itself exists. Self and other, subject and object—the recognition of
difference begins from earliest life. The self, embodied in the person, is neither wholly constructed nor wholly essential. Both these notions are under
scrutiny today, but for purposes of this analysis I assume the idea of a self.[34]

Psychological theories of identity focus on individuals. Social theories of
identity focus on the formal matrix of relations, or networks, in which
individuals are enmeshed. Social identities are first steps to political identities
and are customarily prior to political identities. In contrast to liberalism,
which holds these identities separate, fascism tries to reverse or obliterate the
boundaries between the two. Who we are, how we define and conceive of
ourselves, how we recognize others who are one of us and who are not are
connected to how we construct ourselves in public and private space.

Political theorists tend to conceptualize identity in terms of difference.
Anne Norton begins an essay on political identity with the aphoristic statement, "Meaning is made out of difference."[35] William Connolly maintains
that "an identity is established in relation to a series of differences that have
become socially recognized. These differences are essential to its being. If
they did not coexist as differences, it would not exist in its distinctness and
solidity." Difference, as Connolly argues, implies "otherness"—a word that
has distinctly negative connotations. Modern identities have a tendency to
assume an essential and rigid character that appears as truth: "The maintenance of one identity (or field of identities) involves the conversion of some
differences into otherness, into evil, or one of its numerous surrogates. Identity requires difference in order to be, and it converts difference into otherness in order to secure its own self-certainty."[36] Difference is a useful concept if one wishes to focus on groups that have been excluded from the
polity because of constructed otherness. It is less useful if one wishes to
understand the process of collective identity formation on which any political identity ultimately turns. Difference, as an analytic category, can be as
rigid as the "truths" it legitimates.

Identity is an inescapable dimension of social life. Even Connolly admits
that "each individual needs an identity; every stable way of life invokes
claims to collective identity."[37] Identity may also be conceived in terms of

[34] For social science theories of selfhood, see the collection of essays in *The Category of the Person*, ed. Michael Carrithers, Steven Collins, and Steven Lukes (Cambridge: Cambridge University Press, 1985).

[35] Anne Norton, *Reflections on Political Identity* (Baltimore: Johns Hopkins University Press, 1988), 3.

[36] William E. Connolly, *Identity\Difference* (Ithaca: Cornell University Press, 1991), 64.

[37] Ibid., 158.

similarities, or the communities of selves toward which individuals orient their actions. The social construction of identities involves the specification of a web of social relations or communities which envelop the self and through which individuals feel themselves identical with others.[38] Theories of identity tend to share a focus on language and narrative as communicative vehicles of identity. Common language is the dimension of identity providing the discursive cues that direct likeminded subjects to each other.[39]

The philosopher Charles Taylor's nuanced definition of identity that includes conceptions of ethics and community is a useful starting point for an analysis of the political construction of identity.[40] Taylor argues: "To know who I am is a species of knowing where I stand. My identity is defined by the commitments and identifications which provide the frame or horizon within which I can try to determine from case to case what is good, or valuable, or what ought to be done, or what I endorse or oppose. In other words, it is the horizon within which I am capable of taking a stand." "Horizon" suggests an ethos that guides behavior, but it is not sufficient to structure identities or selves, "One is a self only among other selves. A self can never be described without reference to those who surround it." Identity without community is incomplete: "The full definition of someone's identity thus usually involves not only his stand on moral and spiritual matters but also some reference to defining community."[41] If we put aside the ethical component of Taylor's theory, an admittedly large putting aside, his conception of identity provides a theoretical entry to the fascist project.

Hierarchies of Identity

Social, political, and economic institutions, the organizational forms of modern community, serve as arenas of identity. Institutions organize identities.[42] A matrix of identities exist that may be categorized as public and

[38] Much of the current sociological discussion of identity has been carried out at the level of theory and not empirical analysis. For example, see the essays in *Social Theory and the Politics of Identity*, ed. Craig Calhoun (Oxford: Blackwell, 1994).
[39] See Margaret R. Somers, "The Narrative Constitution of Identity: A Relational and Network Approach," *Theory and Society* 23 (1994), 605–49.
[40] For a discussion of the utility of Taylor to sociological analysis, see Craig Calhoun, "Morality, Identity, and Historical Explanation: Charles Taylor on the Sources of the Self," *Sociological Theory* 9 (Fall 1991), 232–63.
[41] Charles Taylor, *Sources of the Self: The Making of the Modern Identity* (Cambridge: Harvard University Press, 1989), 27, 35, 36.
[42] For a discussion of how institutions create meaning, see James G. March and Johan P. Olsen, *Rediscovering Institutions* (New York: Free Press, 1989), 39–52; and Roger Friedland and Robert R. Alford, "Bringing Society Back In: Symbols, Practices, and Institutional Contradictions," in *The New Institutionalism in Organizational Analysis*, ed. Walter W. Powell and Paul J. DiMaggio (Chicago: University of Chicago Press, 1991), esp. 247–56.

private. Public identities principally include citizenship and work identities that are institutionally buttressed by the legal organizations of the modern nation-state and the market. These identities are based on a conception of interest and rationality. Private identities originate in their purist forms as biology or kinship relations. Whether or not we acknowledge the social ties of kinship, by virtue of our existence we are mothers, fathers, sons, daughters. Family, whether absent or present, provides the institutional supports for our biological roles. Kinship identities have never escaped the legal system; for example, the law defines the parameters of marriage and inheritance. Nature, and not interest, structures these identities.

But there are other forms of identities that are more fluid and not as easily located on a public/private continuum. Cultural identities—religious, national, regional, and ethnic—may be either public or private, depending on the political regime. Liberalism tends to legislate religious, regional, and ethnic identities out of the public sphere and to invoke selectively the affective dimensions of nationalism to support the nation-state.[43] All these identities are based on meanings—of religious practice, homeland, and race—and they generate powerful public emotions and militancy.

Identities are neither essential nor purely constructed; they are multiple but not schizophrenic.[44] Individuals relate to and derive meaning from many communities of similar selves. This does not imply, however, that all identities carry equal meaning to those who participate in them. Many identities are, in Connolly's terminology, "contingent."[45] These identities are circumstantial and more or less given at will. Some identities are more vulnerable to contingency than others. For example, one's vision of oneself as politically engaged may have more to do with structural opportunity or immediate grievances than with any long-term commitment to social or political change. Similarly, certain private identities such as marital status or sexual orientation may likewise be subject to opportunity and interest as well as social reinforcement.

Identities belong to a category of objects Taylor has described as "hyper-goods," by which he means objects that are of relatively more value to us than others.

Even those of us who are not committed in so single-minded a way recognize higher goods. That is, we acknowledge second-order qualitative dis-

---

[43] There is a burgeoning literature on nationalism. E. J. Hobsbawm's discussion linking it to the development of the nation-state is most congruous to the issues I am raising (*Nations and Nationalism since 1780* [New York: Cambridge University Press, 1990], 14–45).

[44] Craig Calhoun, "Social Theory and the Politics of Identity," in *Social Theory and the Politics of Identity*, ed. Craig Calhoun (Cambridge: Blackwell, 1994), 9–36.

[45] Connolly, *Identity\Difference*, 173.

tinctions which define higher goods, on the basis of which we discriminate among other goods, attribute differential worth or importance to them, or determine when and if to follow them. Let me call higher-order goods of this kind "hypergoods," i.e., goods which not only are incomparably more important than others but provide the standpoint from which these must be weighed, judged, decided about."[46]

Identities are felt as hierarchies. There are some identities that we value more than others, that we experience as "hypergoods," and some we experience as essentially "contingent." The felt force of some identities is so potent that we might be willing to die for them. It is those identities that generate powerful emotions carrying political importance. Religious, national, and ethnic identities frequently fall into this category.

States and Identity

Political identities tread a difficult line because they require of their partisans a feeling that something exists outside the private self—the party, the state—that is worth dying for. War making, as Charles Tilly has argued, may be a major activity of the modern state, but conscription alone does not create soldiers.[47] The modern nation-state is the ideal type of modern political organization and a vehicle of mass political commitment. "Nation-state" is a dual concept, and a discussion of state and identity formation, in either liberal democratic or totalitarian states, requires that we uncouple this dyad. The "state" part is in the business of rule and focuses on bureaucratic efficiency and territorial claims;[48] the "nation" part is in the business of creating emotional attachment to the state, or noncontingent identities.

To borrow Benedict Anderson's familiar formulation, the modern nation-state is an "imagined community" that creates a spirit of "fraternity" that "makes it possible . . . for so many millions of people, not so much to kill, as willingly to die for such limited imaginings." A principal goal of the nation side of the equation is to create a feeling of "attachment" to the state in the form of "love for the nation." The "nature" of "political love"

can be deciphered from the ways in which languages describe its object: either in the vocabulary of kinship (motherland, *Vaterland*, *patria*) or that of home (*heimat* . . .). Both idioms denote something to which one is

[46] Taylor, *Sources of the Self*, 63.

[47] See Charles Tilly, "War Making and State Making as Organized Crime," in *Bringing the State Back In*, ed. Peter B. Evans, Dietrich Reuschemeyer, and Theda Skocpol (Cambridge: Cambridge University Press, 1985), 169–87.

[48] Gianfranco Poggi, *The Development of the Modern State: A Sociological Introduction* (Stanford: Stanford University Press, 1978).

naturally tied. As we have seen earlier, in everything "natural" there is always something unchosen. In this way, nation-ness is assimilated to skin-colour, gender, parentage and birth-era—all those things one cannot help. And in these "natural ties" one senses what one might call the "beauty of *gemeinschaft*."[49]

The nation side of the nation-state dyad, though it appears to be the product of natural emotions, is highly constructed. The success of individual nineteenth-century nation-state projects lies in the strength of constructed emotion, and some were more successful than others. France is the paradigmatic case. As Lynn Hunt has shown, a repertoire of political inventions, symbolic practices, and images constituted the culture of the French Revolution; it was not until the nineteenth century that "peasants" became "Frenchmen" and the process of creating a modern French political identity tied to a nation-state was complete.[50]

Historical and theoretical accounts demonstrate that nineteenth-century nation-states did not just come together as a result of the elective affinity of compatriots. They were forged from wars, the reorganization of cultural institutions (principally education), and the standardization of language. National cultures were made at the expense of local and regional cultures. Though it is impossible to have any form of modern political organization without either a state or a nation, it is possible to have a nation without a state, or a state without a nation. The Arab-Israeli conflict may be construed as a problem of nations without states; the former Eastern European bloc countries and Soviet Union fall into the category of states without nations, which suggests why these states crumbled with the Berlin Wall.

The uncoupling of nation and state forces a reexamination of the concept of totalitarian states. If states are simply the organizational and technological side of the nation-state dyad, then states may be conceived of as relatively neutral formal entities. Nation, in contrast, is a highly specific cultural construct tied to historical context. The nation side of the dyad introduces variance to the concept of state.

Standard definitions of totalitarian states do not make these distinctions. For example, Linz summarizes the characteristics of a totalitarian state as (1) a monolithic center of power, (2) an exclusive ideology to which all must subscribe, and (3) mandatory citizen participation in the form of active and continued mobilization. He distinguishes between totalitarian and authori-

---

[49] Benedict Anderson, *Imagined Communities: Reflections on the Origin and Spread of Nationalism*, rev. ed. (London: Verso, 1991), 7, 141, 143.

[50] Lynn Hunt, *Politics, Culture, and Class in the French Revolution* (Berkeley: University of California Press, 1984), and Eugen Weber, *Peasants into Frenchmen* (Stanford: Stanford University Press, 1976).

tarian regimes based on the instrumental versus expressive character of the state. He places Nazi Germany in the former category and fascist Italy in the latter.[51] What is lacking in Linz's formulation is any discussion of the etiology of the totalitarian state form.

If we accept historical accounts which suggest that nation-states are end products of a political process that bears greater resemblance to arranged marriage than to spontaneous coupling, we can think of totalitarian states as states without nations or states where the failure or weakness of the nation-state process has demanded a "hypernationalization" project. If we conceptualize fascism as a political ideal that denies the separation of the public and private self, then we can think of totalitarian states as the organizational form of that destroyed boundary. To the extent that all nation-states need to create citizens who will sacrifice some parts of their private selves to the state, whether their income in taxes or their bodies in war, then the terms "totalitarian" and "liberal-democratic" as demarcations of state forms start to appear as only differences of degree.

Totalitarian and democratic as nominal categories have limited capacity to elucidate the process of state identity formation, which requires a conception of agency. Colonialism, which evokes a strong nation-state's imposing of its identity on weakly bounded territorial groups or nations of lesser stature, provides a better approximation of the political processes involved in the Italian fascist project than the rubric of totalitarian/democratic. Timothy Mitchell's discussion of political identity captures the "normal" division between the public and private self. Mitchell argues:

> Political identity, therefore, never exists in the form of an absolute, interior self or community, but always an already-divided relation of self/other. Political identity, . . . is no more singular or absolute than the identity of words in a system of writing. Just as the particularity of words . . . is merely an effect of the differences that give rise to language, so difference gives rise to political identity and existence. There are no political "units," no atomistic, undivided selves; only relations or forces of difference, out of which identities are formed as something always self-divided and contingent.[52]

Mitchell's analysis, influenced by Michel Foucault and Jacques Derrida, would, carried to its logical conclusion, posit no difference between identity formation in a totalitarian state or in a democratic state. His analysis shifts

[51] Juan J. Linz, "Totalitarian and Authoritarian Regimes," in *Handbook of Political Science*, ed. Fred I. Greenstein and Nelson W. Polsby, vol. 3 (Reading, Mass.: Addison-Wesley, 1975), 191–92, 275.

[52] Timothy Mitchell, *Colonising Egypt* (Berkeley: University of California Press, 1991), 167.

when he takes up the issue of colonialism, however, and becomes congruent with my arguments about the Italian fascist project. According to Mitchell, colonialism affects identity by destroying the split between self and other, public and private: "Identity [under colonialism] now appears no longer self-divided, no longer contingent, no longer something arranged out of differences; it appears instead as something self-formed, and original."[53] The colonial or fascist state represents a noncontingent undivided form of identity.

Citizenship is the legal vehicle that codifies and solidifies national political identities. Citizenship, whether one accepts T. H. Marshall's definition of it as an attribute of persons living in a nation-state, or revisionist theories that view it as a boundary-making device or relational process, is minimally the mechanism that makes individuals feel as though they participate in the state.[54] Regimes, the constellation of political actors controlling the state at given historical moments, frequently resort to symbolic politics to orchestrate the affective dimension of citizenship. All regimes from democratic to totalitarian employ some form of symbolic politics. In democratic states, symbolic politics, practices, and objects are expressive entities that temporarily objectify the state; in totalitarian or fascist states, symbolic politics, particularly ritual actions, attempt to obliterate the distinction between self and other.

There is no necessary connection between the retreat to symbolic politics and its effects. The state fiction of totalitarianism should not be confused with the reality of totalitarianism. Representation captures the tension between fiction and reality. In Mitchell's analysis of colonial Egypt, colonialism by its existence defines reality—the world is the "exhibition."[55] Norton discusses representation:

A representation preserves things in their absence. The representation—or the representative—presents something prior to itself. Each act of representation is a re-presentation, a presentation of something that has appeared before. It is repetitive. Yet each representation, occurring in a different context, attaches additional associations to the act or individual that is recalled,

[53] Ibid.

[54] T. H. Marshall, "Citizenship and Social Class," in *Class, Citizenship, and Social Development: Essays by T. H. Marshall*, intro. Seymour Martin Lipset (rpt., Chicago: University of Chicago Press, 1964), 71–134; Rogers Brubaker, *Citizenship and Nationhood in France and Germany* (Cambridge: Harvard University Press, 1992); Margaret R. Somers, "Law, Community, and Political Culture in the Transition to Democracy," *American Sociological Review* 58 (October 1993), 587–620.

[55] Mitchell, *Colonising Egypt*, 7–15.

and disguises the significance of once-meaningful attributes. Thus representation shows itself to be at once endlessly repetitive and ever changing.[56]

My approach to representation borrows from, and significantly departs from, what might be loosely defined as postmodern approaches to the study of politics. What Mitchell and Norton are elaborating is the polysemic nature of representation or "exhibition." My analysis follows this feature of the postmodern approach. Where it departs is that I argue that, unlike Gertrude Stein's characterization of Oakland, there is a there, there—even if it is not always clear of what it consists. Returning to Norton, I contend, first, what is preserved in absence is by no means certain, and second, the meaning of the representation is reinvented with its repetition. Representations of ideological power do not equal realities of power.

Fascism as a political ideology and cultural program appears less protean if one redefines it as the fusion of the public and private self in the state. My redefinition suggests a rationale for the regime's reliance on public political rituals—the desire to create a new form of political community. The Italian fascist regime attempted to create a fascist political identity by merging the public/private self in public political rituals, or to create temporary communities of feeling in the public piazza in the absence of the democratic contractualism in the state. We now turn to those rituals.

Communities of Feeling and the Politics of Emotion

Nation-states may be imagined and felt as community, but the feelings and imaginings of national belonging are evanescent without an underlying structure of cultural institutions and symbolic practices. National languages and education systems as well as museums, monuments, and national anthems serve to keep the spirit of national belonging alive.

States, such as fascist Italy, that are engaged in what I have labeled "hypernationalization" projects need to institute immediate and drastic measures to foster feelings of national incorporation. The public political spectacle was the dramatic enactment of fascist community and the expressive crucible in which fascist identity was forged. Italian men and women did not become fascist in the public piazza. They became fascist to the extent that they assumed a fascist identity in the schools, Fascist Party organizations, and labor corporations. The public spectacle was an arena of political emotion, a community of feeling, in which Italians of all ages were meant to feel themselves as fascists.

[56] Norton, *Reflections*, 97.

Emotion is central to the politics of spectacle. Emotion obliterates identity. It fuses self and other—subject and object. The experience of public political spectacle is analogous to the experience of music, a comparison fascist functionaries did not hesitate to make. Music, in the words of Susanne Langer, is the "tonal analogue of emotive life." Music is a highly articulate language without vocabulary.[57] Like music, emotion has a cognitive dimension.

As Clifford Geertz argues in his discussion of the Balinese cockfight, ritual display can serve as a kind of "sentimental education" in its use of "emotion" for "cognitive ends": "What the cockfight says it says in a vocabulary of sentiment—the thrill of risk, the despair of loss, the pleasure of triumph. Yet what it says is not merely that risk is exciting, loss depressing, or triumph gratifying, banal tautologies of affect, but that it is of these emotions, thus exampled, that society is built and individuals are put together."[58] Geertz's analysis, while pointing to the cognitive ends of emotion, is too close-ended as to ritual outcome. Ritual, by acting out emotion, includes indeterminacy.

Political ritual creates a "liminal" space in which new identities may form.[59] Emotion may obliterate the old self, but there is no guarantee as to what form the new self or identity might assume. The fascist "communities of feeling" aimed to create fascist community and fascist identity. "Community of feeling" is my adaptation of Raymond Williams's concept of "structure of feeling." According to Williams, "structures of feeling" are "social experiences *in solution.*" In his attempt to articulate the nondiscursive elements of aesthetic emotion, Williams contrasts "feeling" with discursive elements such as "world-view" and "ideology," which are linguistic and textual in their import. His analysis diverges from Geertz's in that it suggests the indeterminacy of emotional politics: "We are concerned with meanings and values as they are actively lived and felt, and the relations between these and formal or systematic beliefs are in practice variable (including historically variable), over a range from formal assent with private dissent to the more nuanced interaction between selected and interpreted beliefs and acted and justified experiences."[60]

Scholars acknowledge the emotional dimension of fascist political practice and dismiss it as yet another feature of the politics of irrationality. Emotion as the basis of politics was not new. Emotion is the antithesis of modern political organization except when it is rigidly codified in the nation side of

---

[57] Susanne K. Langer, *Feeling and Form* (New York: Scribner's, 1953), 7.

[58] Clifford Geertz, "Deep Play: Notes on the Balinese Cockfight," in *The Interpretation of Cultures* (New York: Basic, 1973), 449.

[59] I borrow this well-known concept from Victor Turner.

[60] Raymond Williams, *Marxism and Literature* (New York: Oxford University Press, 1977), 133, 132.

the nation-state dyad. Emotion is nonrational, but it is not irrational and it is intimately connected to the Italian fascist rejection of liberalism—the essence of political rationality.

Italian fascism rejected discursive prose or linearity. It repudiated the word and the text. Argumentation, explanation, the scientific method were all aspects of modernity and rational discourse that fascism replaced with the primacy of feeling and emotion.[61] The fascist emphasis on feeling and emotion was a celebration of the nonrational, not the irrational, since fascist feelings aimed to communicate belonging and solidarity. The distinction Karl Mannheim makes between conservatism and liberalism is instructive regarding this point.[62] He discusses conservatism as valorizing the "qualitative" and the experiential and liberalism as valorizing the "quantitative" or cognitive dimensions of social life. According to Mannheim, "quantitative" encompasses a range of liberal values such as social equality and the belief in norms as a guide to action, whereas "qualitative" espouses the primacy of being or essences and a view of events as end points of the past. Although Mannheim's primary focus is Germany, his arguments are applicable to the distinctions I am drawing in the Italian case.

Fascist propagandists, journalists, artists, and intellectuals generated torrents of words in fascist Italy. Yet they were words without referents. Ignazio Silone made this point in his parody of fascist politics, *The School for Dictators*. When asked what the fascist cry *eia eia alala* means, the author's persona replies:

Nothing. It was a cry D'Annunzio invented during the war. You will find no trace of it in any language or dialect, and its own inventor gave it no rational meaning. . . . For the success of a fascist movement, such words are more valuable than any theoretical treatise on corporations. . . . The psalm-like chanting of incomprehensible texts has been a precious resource of mass religions in every age. Latin has never kept illiterate peasants from attending Catholic rites; on the contrary, it has always been a big help in attracting them.[63]

[61] Benedetto Croce makes this point in *A History of Italy, 1871–1915*, trans. Cecilia M. Ady (Oxford: Clarendon Press, 1929): "During the early years of the twentieth century, both in Italy and elsewhere, a reaction set in against the cult of science, or positivism" (237). Croce attributed this "reaction" to "the influence of foreign thinkers, Germans who were once more speculating over the conception of 'values'" (238).

[62] Karl Mannheim, "Conservative Thought," in *From Karl Mannheim*, ed. Kurt H. Wolff (New York: Oxford University Press, 1971), 132–33, 144, 166, 168–69. Croce's remark (see note 61) suggests that my evocation of Mannheim is not so far afield.

[63] Ignazio Silone, *The School for Dictators*, trans. William Weaver (New York: Atheneum, 1963), 112.

"Ideology" is a word I use in a specialized sense to connote the fascist cultural project. It is a convenient matrix for a set of political and cultural practices but not a body of discursive ideas. Fascists did not believe in abstract values such as liberty, equality, fraternity. They believed in action and style—ideas that specify means and not ends and that make the ends of fascist action extremely malleable. The fascist belief in style has derailed attempts to codify fascist ideology. Scholars' searches for doctrinal coherence have misread the issue of political style and drawn the incorrect conclusion that Italian fascism was inchoate.[64] The Italian fascist commitment to style and action makes ritual action an excellent venue for an analysis of the fascist project.

The rally and the parade have been interpreted as a sign of the destruction of the public sphere under fascism. I argue that public spectacle was the regime's attempt to create temporary fascist communities of emotional attachment that would create bonds of solidarity which would last long after participants left the piazza. The public piazza was the cathedral of fascist culture, a nonliberal public sphere based on performance and not text. What these performances "meant" was indeterminate. Historian David Cannadine points to the difficulties involved in studying the relation of politics, emotion, and ritual with a felicitous simile: "Ceremonial is like the snow: an insubstantial pageant, soon melted into thin air. The invisible and ephemeral are, by definition, not the easiest of subjects for scholars to study."[65] The next section discusses my methodological approach to capturing the "snow," or specifying the indeterminacy of fascist public spectacle.

Fascist Ritual and Political Communication

Ritual and Representation

From Foucault's spectacle of the guillotine to analyses of the political culture of revolutions, studies of cultural politics assume that public political rituals, such as the events that proliferated in fascist Italy, are potent vehicles of political communication and meaning.[66] Public political ritual is performance; and performance, whether it occurs in the tightly bounded world of

[64] For an articulation of this position, see Adrian Lyttelton, introduction to *Italian Fascism from Pareto to Gentile* (New York: Harper and Row, 1973), 36.

[65] David Cannadine, "Introduction: Divine Rites of Kings," in *Rituals of Royalty: Power and Ceremonial in Traditional Societies*, ed. David Cannadine and Simon Price (Cambridge: Cambridge University Press, 1987), 1.

[66] Michel Foucault, *Discipline and Punish*, trans. Alan Sheridan (New York: Pantheon, 1977), 47–57. For example, Hunt, *French Revolution*; Mona Ozouf, *Festivals and the French Revolution*, trans. Alan Sheridan (Cambridge: Harvard University Press, 1988); James Von Geldern, *Bolshevik Festivals, 1917–1920* (Berkeley: University of California Press, 1993).

the theater or the more permeable social space of a public piazza, is a highly elusive entity because its effects are experiential.

The experiential or performative nature of ritual, coupled with assumptions about the efficacy of political ritual, drives the methodological retreat to "thick descriptions" of unique ritual events. Geertz's study of Negara, the "theater state," is typical of this mode of analysis. Geertz argues that the state in nineteenth-century Bali was pure spectacle and concludes, "The dramas of the theater state, mimetic of themselves, were, in the end, neither illusions nor lies, neither sleight of hand nor make-believe. They were what there was."[67] Textual exegesis of political ritual frequently fails to uncouple the relation between ritual activity and political meaning, thus leaving assumptions about political efficacy unchallenged. Such exegesis suggests that representations of power equal realities of power, or that, to paraphrase Norton, what is preserved in absence is the power of the state. The analytic and methodological discussion that follows is an argument for complexity in the face of the surface transparency of the fascist public rituals that form the core empirical section of this book.

Theories of ritual focus on questions of definition that are inextricably linked to issues of meaning. How we draw the parameters of ritual circumscribes the range of interpretive methodologies we apply to the study of ritual. Durkheim's *Elementary Forms of the Religious Life* is the Archimedean point from which any theoretical study of ritual begins. Three features of Durkheim's analysis affected the development of theories of ritual: the equation of ritual with religion; the idea of collective representation, which pointed to the symbolic function of ritual practice; and the generalized classification scheme of sacred and profane.[68]

Although social scientists no longer treat ritual as necessarily bound to religious practice, they have retained their interest in the role of ritual symbols and the dichotomy between sacred and profane. The symbolic dimension of ritual encompasses a range of definitions and disciplinary orientations. Steven Lukes defines ritual as "rule-governed activity of a symbolic character." In *Ritual, Politics, and Power*, David Kertzer defines ritual as "action wrapped in a web of symbolism. Standardized, repetitive action lacking such symbolization is an example of habit or custom and not ritual. Symbolization gives the action much more important meaning."[69]

Anthropologists have criticized the sacred/profane distinction as a sim-

---

[67] Clifford Geertz, *Negara: The Theater State in Nineteenth-Century Bali* (Princeton: Princeton University Press, 1980), 136.
[68] Emile Durkheim, *The Elementary Forms of the Religious Life*, trans. Joseph Ward Swain (New York: Free Press, 1965), 17, 22, 26, 52.
[69] Steven Lukes, "Political Ritual and Social Integration," *Sociology* 9 (1975), 291; David I. Kertzer, *Ritual, Politics, and Power* (New Haven: Yale University Press, 1988), 9.

plistic dichotomy that replicates the value system of the observer.[70] Such criticism suggests three problems that underlie the semiotic and discursive analysis of ritual events. First, this method continues to elide the distinction between participant and observer as separate interpreting subjects; second, treating ritual as a text contributes to its conceptualization as an object rather than an action; and third, it focuses attention on the content rather than the form of ritual.[71] A plausible account of the meaning of political ritual requires the resolution of each of these problems.

The distinction between observer and participant is not as simple as it would appear at first glance. Within the anthropological literature, the distinction is predicated on a fieldworker who is an outsider venturing into a "foreign" culture to observe the social or religious ritual behavior of the "native" insiders. Typically, fieldworkers conduct their observation of ritual in the present.[72] Analysis of political ritual presents a level of complexity missing in religious or social ritual because the categories of observer and participant are multiple. Historical analysis offers the vantage point of distance in parsing these categories.

First, the social analyst in the instance of historical analysis of political ritual is not strictly speaking an observer; rather, he or she is the interpreter of the representations of multiple observers. I constructed my analysis of fascist political ritual from the representations of journalists, photographers, and regime propagandists. The citizens who lined the streets of Italy's cities and towns watching the fascists march by were observers whose voices go unheard. Second, the participant is not simply the person standing in the piazza forming part of the ritual display. Participants may be those who create or design the rituals, those who perform the political rites, or those who witness it from the outside. This last group might also constitute observers.

In the case of fascist ritual, the regime decided the scope and range of events, the local and national Fascist Party mobilized bodies to rally in the piazzas to perform the political rites, and the Italian citizens lined the streets for events that interrupted the daily rhythms of work, commerce, and lei-

---

[70] For example, Jack Goody, "Religion and Ritual: The Definitional Problem," *British Journal of Sociology* 12 (1961), 143, 149, 152. Sally F. Moore and Barbara G. Myerhoff, "Secular Ritual: Forms and Meanings," in *Secular Ritual*, ed. Sally F. Moore and Barbara G. Meyerhoff (Amsterdam: Van Gorcum, 1977), in a critique of Mary Douglas, argue that it is difficult to establish the boundaries of the sacred and profane independently of the cultural predispositions of the observer (19).

[71] Catherine Bell, *Ritual Theory, Ritual Practice* (New York: Oxford University Press, 1992), emphasizes the distinction between ritual as action and as object (42).

[72] On the problems of contemporaneous observation, see Sally Falk Moore, "Explaining the Present: Theoretical Dilemmas in Processual Ethnography," *American Ethnology* 14 (1987), 727–36.

sure. An analysis of fascist ritual that simply read the text of the available representations, or described it as the sacralization of public space in the name of the regime, would fail to capture the meaning of the ritual to its participants broadly defined and would skim the surface of the official meanings of the event.

Ritual as Cultural Action

In the *Elementary Forms*, Durkheim did not ignore the action dimension of ritual. He distinguished between the "rite" and "belief" components of religion. Beliefs were the repository of representations or symbols, whereas rites were the locations of "determined modes of action."[73] Although analysts have tended to elide this distinction in their empirical research, actions are as salient as symbols in definitions of ritual.[74] Ritual is a form of "patterned" and "formulaic" action that establishes order against the indeterminacy of random temporal and spatial organization.[75]

In their discussion of secular ritual, Sally Falk Moore and Barbara Meyerhoff argue that the formal properties of ritual, such as staging, repetition, action, and stylization, are intrinsic to its message. They conclude: "Ritual is in part a form, and a form which gives certain meanings to its contents. The work of ritual, then, is partly attributable to its morphological characteristics. Its medium is part of its message."[76] Kertzer takes a similar stance: "Ritual action has a formal quality to it. . . . Ritual action is repetitive and, therefore, often redundant, but these very factors serve as important means of channeling emotion, guiding cognition, and organizing social groups."[77]

This sample of definitions lends support to two propositions: first, ritual is a form of cultural action; and second, ritual derives its distinction as a cultural entity from its formal characteristics. These propositions have implications that support my contention and evoke Norton's point that meaning is embedded not in the representation of action but in the experience of continued exposure to ritual representations, or the repetition of ritual action.

[73] Durkheim, *Elementary Forms*, 51.

[74] For example, Robert Wuthnow, *Meaning and the Moral Order* (Berkeley: University of California Press, 1987), 109; Lukes, "Political Ritual," 290; Bell, *Ritual Theory*, 69–93. Goody, "Religion and Ritual," notes that ritual applies to the "action" rather than the "belief" component of magic and religious phenomena (147) and defines ritual as "a category of standardized behavior (custom) in which the relationship between means and ends is not 'intrinsic'" (159).

[75] Jack Goody, "Against 'Ritual': Loosely Structured Thoughts on a Loosely Defined Topic," in *Secular Ritual*, ed. Moore and Meyerhoff, 33; David Parkin, "Ritual as Spatial Direction and Bodily Division," in *Understanding Rituals*, ed. Daniel De Coppet (London: Routledge, 1992), 18.

[76] "Secular Ritual," 7–8.

[77] Kertzer, *Ritual, Politics, and Power*, 9.

By studying ritual as a type of cultural action, we can develop plausible narratives of how the citizens of fascist Italy received the regime's cultural messages. Reception includes assimilation, resistance, and in some instances reinvention. I argue that the form of ritual action is more important than the specific content, although my analysis does not ignore content. Form is what we recognize as implicit, whereas content is variable. Form is central to a politics of emotion that eschewed text.

Ritual action takes place in real time—it is diachronic as well as synchronic. By diachronic, I mean the repetition of ritual acts over days, months, years. Analysts tend to assume the synchronic nature of ritual time and focus on calendars and schedules and the breaking up of singular temporal units such as days or years.[78] Victor Turner's processual view of ritual incorporates time into the study of ritual and suggests that ritual meaning is located in the long, as well as short, ritual *durée*.[79] Turner argues that ritual activities are composed of social dramas that exist as single instances or sequential accumulations of events:

> Social dramas and social enterprises—as well as other kinds of processual units—represent sequences of social events, which, seen retrospectively by an observer, can be shown to have structure. Such "temporal" structure, unlike atemporal structure . . . is organized primarily through relations in time rather than in space, though, of course, cognitive schemes are themselves the result of a mental process and have processual qualities."[80]

Social drama as an analytic frame brings time and historicity to ritual theory. In later work, Turner explicitly links these features to ritual meaning. He argues that meaning is the end of process: "Meaning is apprehended by looking back over a process in time. We assess the meaning of every part of a process by its contribution to the total result. Meaning is connected with the consummation of a process—it is bound up with termination, in a sense, with death. The meaning of any given factor in a process cannot be assessed until the whole process is past."[81] Ritual action's formal characteristics, such as staging, permit us to identify its meaningful patterns.

Ritual patterns are powerful interpretive prisms and vehicles of political communication. First, they address the issue of regime intention, because they suggest that there was some deliberate political attempt to create the pattern; second, they address the question of citizen reception, because they

[78] See, for example, Ozouf, *Festivals*, 161–66.
[79] Victor Turner, "Social Dramas and Ritual Metaphors," in *Dramas, Fields, and Metaphors* (Ithaca: Cornell University Press, 1974), 23–59.
[80] Ibid., 35–36.
[81] Victor Turner, "The Anthropology of Performance," in *The Anthropology of Performance* (New York: PAJ, 1988), 97–98.

display formal properties that a body of citizens might recognize over time. Patterns take ritual form and time into account and allow us to separate analytically the observer from the participant. In short, they permit us to formulate plausible and nondistorting narratives of political meaning.

Identifying patterns of ritual action over time in a specific historical context, such as Italy during the fascist period, enables us to establish what was ordinary, customary, and recognizable in fascist political ritual. The mapping of the familiar has the added advantage of allowing us to construct a story of political meaning that, first, does not conflate the observer and the participant and, second, holds separate analytically, if not empirically, the subcategories of participation.

Intention and Reception

To capture the "meaning" of political ritual, in this case fascist ritual, we must distinguish two levels of meaning and sites of participation: the meaning of public spectacle to the regime—the creator of political ritual; and the meaning of spectacle to the citizens—the audience at whom these events were aimed. The first level of meaning involves questions of political intention.

Imputed intention does not imply that the regime could impose whatever meanings it chose. Fascist regimes, and the Italian fascist regime in particular, may be based on the politics of nonrationality, but they are not irrational. Political symbolism is useless if no one understands it. Although no regime can guarantee the effects of its aesthetic actions, some symbols are more likely to resonate with a public than others. How a regime goes about choosing symbolic actions that have a greater probability of resonance than others has to do with its ability to co-opt or create cultural practices that form recognizable or comprehensible genres.[82]

The problem as I am stating it may be recast in terms frequently applied to aesthetics, that is, as a problem of authorial intention and audience reception, or, in the language of ritual analysis, that of observer and participant. The case studies that follow explore the interaction between regime intention and citizen reception. I constructed them, to borrow the Comaroffs' metaphor, as a "conversation" between the colonizer and the colonized.[83] Ritual is a form of social action whose consequences may owe more to the cultural schema and resources, to invoke Sewell, that its designers have at

[82] For sociological accounts of the issue of recognition and resonance, see Wendy Griswold, "A Methodological Framework for the Sociology of Culture," *Sociological Methodology* 14 (1987), 17–20, and Michael Schudson, "How Culture Works: Perspectives from Media Studies on the Efficacy of Symbols," *Theory and Society* 18 (1989), 167–70.

[83] Jean Comaroff and John Comaroff, *Of Revelation and Revolution* (Chicago: University of Chicago Press, 1991), 199.

their disposal than to any political meaning it seeks to convey, and whose principal consequences may be as unintended as intended. My central analytic argument is that the fascist meaning or identity which was created, which was understood and internalized, lies in the space between intention and reception.

Period and genre as analytic frames provide a convenient shorthand that lends terminological consistency to the case studies and structures the narrative construction of the interaction between intention and reception. Period, historically plausible time segments within which events can be mapped, suggests regime intention if we can link ritual events to political events. Genre, standard ritual forms, suggests audience recognition if we can establish their repetition. Period and genre are the scaffolding for the empirical study of fascist ritual that follows. History, the careful analysis of content and context, is the basis for these classification schemes.

Period

Because the Italian fascist regime lasted twenty-one years, it affords a methodological opportunity to trace changes and variation in fascist ritual. The years between 1922 and 1943 fall into five historically sensible periods in which diverse political events affected patterns of ritual action.[84] The first of the five, the Matteotti period, begins on October 28, 1922, the day Mussolini marched on Rome and took over the Italian state, and ends with the murder of the socialist parliamentarian Giacomo Matteotti on June 10, 1924. This political murder, which scholars ascribe to the fascist regime, ended the period during which Mussolini attempted to govern with some semblance of a political coalition.

The second period begins after the Matteotti murder and ends on March 24, 1929, the day of the plebiscite when Mussolini received the highly orchestrated unanimous vote of confidence from the Italian electorate that consolidated his dictatorship.[85] The consolidation of fascist power characterizes this period. The regime focused on building a fascist infrastructure, consolidating its rule, and legitimating itself both nationally and internationally.

---

[84] The periodization follows standard historical works: Adrian Lyttelton, *The Seizure of Power : Fascism in Italy, 1919–1929* (rpt., Princeton: Princeton University Press, 1987), and Renzo De Felice, *Mussolini Il Duce: Gli anni del consenso, 1929–1936*, vol. 1 (Turin: Einaudi, 1974); and also fascist propaganda: *Il primo e secondo libro del fascista* (Rome: Partito Nazionale Fascista, 1941).

[85] The "plebiscite of 1929" was a highly rigged election in which Mussolini proposed a list of four hundred fascist names for parliament and the nation was asked to support them en bloc. Negative votes were discouraged with threats of violence and other less tangible forms of reciprocity. Denis Mack Smith reports that 98.4 percent of the Italian population voted yes, although many probably did not bother to vote at all. See *Mussolini* (London: Granada, 1981), 191–93.

The third period runs from the plebiscite to September 8, 1935, when Mussolini decided to invade Ethiopia. During this period of consensus, relative political and social stability prevailed within fascist Italy as the regime began to build the fascist state and develop fascist institutions.

The tranquility of the consensus period ended when Mussolini embarked on the building of a fascist colonial empire. The first step in this process was the Ethiopian campaign, and its culmination was Italian entry into World War II on the side of the Axis powers. This period of mobilization began in September 1935 and ended June 10, 1940, when Italy entered the war on the side of nazi Germany. The last period, the World War II years, is bounded by the end of the regime on July 25, 1943, when Mussolini was voted out of office at the Grand Council meeting. A puppet fascist government existed at Salo until the war ended in 1945, but the regime itself officially ended with Mussolini's fall.

Genre

The various forms of public political spectacle that proliferated in fascist Italy suggest discernible ritual genres. From among the numerous narratives and events I traced, I identified five genres: commemoration, celebration, demonstration, symposia, and inauguration. These genres were not pure types, and they frequently appear as a collage of various forms of ritual action. I use them not to reify ritual experience but to develop a classificatory vocabulary that suggests the aggregate characteristics of the multiple ceremonies and events that transformed the Italian physical and social landscape during the fascist period.

Commemorative events marked the anniversaries of significant events in Italian history, such as the Vittoria, which signaled the end of World War I, and in fascist history, such as the March on Rome. Public funerals for local fascist heroes or memorial services for national fascist figures also fell into the commemorative category.

The watermark of the commemorations was the past as embodied in dead events and dead persons. In contrast, celebrations reveled in the present and the future. They included visits of distinguished persons such as Mussolini, ongoing fascist events such as the *leva fascista* (the passage of fascist youth from one level of the party to the next), birthdays of living fascist heroes, as well as sporting and theatrical events. The visit of an emissary from Rome to Italian cities and towns was the principal symbolic vehicle that the regime and party used to draw the periphery to the center. Distinguished party members visited at both commemorations and celebrations.

In contrast to commemorations and celebrations, demonstrations were purely expressive events, usually rallies, held to display public emotion in support of fascism. As a genre of event, demonstrations were eclectic as to content. What set them apart as a distinct type was that they all claimed the appearance of spontaneous collective emotion and tended to be large rather than small events.

Symposia included national-level congresses and conventions as well as lectures and meetings at the Fascist Party headquarters. Inaugurations consisted of the initiations of public works, such as the opening of a new building or the laying of a plaque to honor a local hero. Symposia were bound to persons; inaugurations were bound to place, as they frequently entailed the dedication of new buildings.

Fascism, as political idea, is best understood as an ideology that fuses the public and private self. In the Italian fascist case, this fusion occurred de jure in the state and emotively in spectacles in the public piazza. The public ritual created a "community of feeling," a metaphorical phrase for the emotional fusing of the two dimensions of the self in public space.

Fascist political rituals did not necessarily represent fascist power, and the shape of ritual events must be addressed as an independent analytic category—the interplay of schematas and resources. We now turn to the historical context, or systems of cultural meanings, that provided the schematas and resources for fascist ritual production.

CHAPTER 2

Imagining a New Political Community:
The Landscape of Ritual Action

The Boundaries of Political Imaginings

Intellectuals imagine movements; people live regimes. As the nineteenth century turned into the twentieth, political imagining flowered. Intellectuals who had imagined nations in the nineteenth century imagined new citizens, new communities, and spectacle states in the twentieth. If the politics of prose embodied in the final carving up of Europe into bureaucratically organized nation-states characterized the nineteenth century, the politics of theater characterized the early twentieth century. Rationality and the "career open to talent" governed nineteenth-century politics; emotion and the "career open to art" governed early-twentieth-century political movements.

Artists as well as politicians and social philosophers became engaged in the political discourse of the early twentieth century. The intertwining of spectacle and politics was a routine component of the political practices of early-twentieth-century European utopian movements and fascist regimes.[1] George Mosse argues that drama represented "tangible expressions of a new political style," which "was based upon artistic presuppositions" and aimed "to transform political action into drama."[2] At first glance Italy appeared to exist at the forefront of the aestheticization of politics.

Italian futurists led by poet and playwright Filippo Tommaso Marinetti smashed bourgeois cultural ideals before fascists smashed socialist workers'

---

[1] See George L. Mosse, *The Nationalization of the Masses: Political Symbolism and Mass Movements in Germany from the Napoleonic Wars through the Third Reich* (rpt., Ithaca: Cornell University Press, 1991); for the Italian case, see Emilio Gentile, *Il culto del littorio* (Rome: Laterza, 1993).

[2] Mosse, *Nationalization*, 8.

organizations. In 1915, Marinetti wrote, "Everything of value is theatrical (Tutto e teatrale quando ha valore)," and staged futurist *serate*, anarchical theatrical evenings, in which he provoked his audience by putting glue on their chairs.[3] In 1919, he led a group of *arditi* as they burned the offices of *L'Avanti*, the socialist newspaper in Milan.[4] Gabriele D'Annunzio, the aging poet, novelist, and dramatist, mobilized the same *arditi* to storm Fiume, the city on the Italian Yugoslavian border which had been left in dispute at the end of the First World War.[5] The career of D'Annunzio fused art and life. As the warrior poet, he used the Fiume episode to synthesize action and expression in a political drama.[6]

But movements must turn into parties if political visions are to have constituencies; and parties into regimes if they are to have social and political consequences. The flamboyant actions and noisy proclamations of the aesthetic avant-garde drew international attention and captured the imagination of Italian university students.[7] This youthful constituency represented a small and elite group of Italians, however. In the main, the aesthetic avant-garde was far removed from the concerns of ordinary Italian men and women, and when it came to practical politics, they were hindrances rather than assets. When the Milanese Fascist Party with Mussolini at its head ran in the local elections in 1919, futurists including Marinetti were on the electoral list and the fascists suffered a crushing defeat. When Mussolini and the fascists ran again in 1921, the artists were gone from the slate and Mussolini won. During the years of the regime, Marinetti and D'Annunzio were re-

[3] F. T. Marinetti, "Il teatro futurista sintetico (1915)," in *Opere di F. T. Marinetti*, ed. Luciano De Maria, vol. 2, *Teoria e invenzione futurista* (Milan: Mondadori, 1968), 100. For a description of futurist *serate*, see Michael Kirby, *Futurist Performance* (New York: Dutton, 1971), 12–19. On the connection between futurism and fascism, see George L. Mosse, "The Political Culture of Italian Futurism: A General Perspective," *Journal of Contemporary History* 25 (1990), 253–68; on aesthetics and fascism, see Walter L. Adamson, *Avant-garde Florence: From Modernism to Fascism* (Cambridge: Harvard University Press, 1993).

[4] The *arditi*, "daring ones," were groups of students and war veterans drawn largely from the middle classes. Many, such as Giuseppe Bottai, later became prominent figures in the fascist regime. The *arditi* were heavily influenced by futurism and fancied themselves warrior/artists, thus resolving the split between thought and action which they saw as plaguing bourgeois liberalism. See Ferdinando Cordova, *Arditi e legionari dannunziani* (Padua: Marsilio, 1969). On the storming of the press offices, see Adrian Lyttelton, *The Seizure of Power: Fascism in Italy, 1919–1929* (rpt., Princeton: Princeton University Press, 1987), 52.

[5] Ernst Nolte (*Three Faces of Fascism*, trans. Leila Vannewitz [New York: New American Library, 1969], 242–52) provides a brief description of the Fiume episode that captures its spirit of drama and romantic adventurism. He describes Fiume as the "first successful bluff in postwar Europe" and claims that "never in the world's history has there been a more impressive farce or one with greater implications for the future" (243).

[6] See Michael A. Ledeen, *The First Duce: D'Annunzio at Fiume* (Baltimore: Johns Hopkins University Press, 1977).

[7] For a comparative analysis of the political affinities of educated European youth in the early twentieth century, see Robert Wohl, *The Generation of 1914* (Cambridge: Harvard University Press, 1979), esp. 160–202.

duced to ossified cultural icons to be pulled out of the closet when political exigencies demanded their presence.

From 1922, spectacle replaced aesthetics as a defining force within popular fascist cultural practice. Spectacles and public political rituals at the local and national level multiplied in fascist Italy. Experiential, emotional, and dramatic, spectacle entailed more than the simple gathering of masses in public spaces. While citizens participated in public spectacle, they were part of in a new political community that they would internalize when they left the piazza and stopped marching. The cultural resources of fascist Italy, such as a limited national linguistic capacity and urban cityscapes that provided natural stages, made spectacle a favored form of political communication. In the public piazza, the complexities of the Italian past played themselves out against the fascist agenda for the Italian future.

The fascist regime sought to penetrate the principal sources of the Italian self—religion and family—and to replace them with a fascist self based on a new conception of citizenship that fused the public and private self in the state. Religion and family provided cultural schemata, or rules, formal codes of behavior and symbols, which Italians implicitly understood and from which they fashioned their private understandings of themselves. Sewell has argued that "the real test of knowing a rule is to be able to apply it successfully in *unfamiliar* cases."[8] Transposability suggests cultural knowledge of schemas or rules. The fascist regime used the resources of the state—parties and laws—to "play" with the rules of Italian culture.

The power to transpose does not imply that new cultural knowledge will emerge. Culture, in the broad anthropological sense of that term, established the mental boundaries within which a new Italian fascist political community could be imagined. Preestablished and deeply held cultural norms and practices were resistant to political manipulation, and they limited the regime's capacity to imagine other foci for its cultural project. Just as the regime could not create political culture out of whole cloth, so too the citizens of Italy, whether or not they were supporters of fascism, were not blank slates on which the regime might fashion its ideological designs. Political, social, and cultural factors that even the creators of fascist culture could not escape leveled the terrain on which the fascist project was built.

The Dead Weight of the Risorgimento

The Italian nation-state project, the Risorgimento, was a font of cultural and political memory from which the fascist regime crafted its political narratives. *Risorgimento* meant "rebirth," and the term was, as historian Clara

---

[8] William H. Sewell, Jr., "A Theory of Structure: Duality, Agency, and Transformation," *American Journal of Sociology* 98 (July 1992), 18.

Lovett notes, carefully chosen, instead of "revolution," which the fascists favored, to suggest a pact between Italy's past and future.[9] But the future that the Risorgimento looked toward was hardly radiant, and the past was highly fragmented. Three features of the unification project are salient to the analysis here: (1) there was a relatively short time span between official unification in 1860 and the advent of the fascist regime in 1922; (2) the Italian nation-state came together relatively late in comparison with England, France, and Germany; and (3) possibly most important of all, unification was not popular.

In 1860, Giuseppe Garibaldi's band of "Thousand" (paramilitary volunteers) and King Vittorio Emanuele's troops met at Teano, a small city outside Naples.[10] The "handshake" exchanged between the king and Garibaldi fused the north and south of the Italian peninsula, and Italy was born. The meeting at Teano and the subsequent political unification of Italy (the first "Italian" parliament met in January 1861) was the result of years of political machinations on the part of Count Camillo Cavour, a Torinese aristocrat popularly viewed as the "father" of Italy. Cavour died just six months after the unification, and an assortment of liberals, monarchists, and nationalists was left to forge the new nation-state.

"Italy" had a weak hold on the imagination and consciousness of a people who were now forced to think of themselves as Italians. To say that Italy was culturally fragmented in 1860 is to attenuate the deeply felt regional identities and loyalties that divided the inhabitants of the new nation-state. Historians so frequently cite Massimo D'Azeglio's epigram on Italian culture, "Having made Italy, we must now make Italians," that they rarely reference it. Commenting on the condition of Italy in 1860, Christopher Seton-Watson has noted: "Parochialism and provincialism were deep-seated, reinforced by the still living traditions of the Renaissance Communes. Few outside the restricted educated class thought of themselves as primarily Italians. Among the people there was not even a common language. Piedmont and Lombardy were divided from Naples and Sicily not only by physical space but by the space of centuries."[11] In 1860, Italy had a mere 2,404 kilometers of railroad track, mostly in Piedmont; the Kingdom of Naples had fewer than 100 kilometers.[12] As late as 1900, Italy had fewer kilometers of track than

[9] Clara Lovett, *The Democratic Movement in Italy, 1830–1876* (Cambridge: Harvard University Press, 1982), 1.

[10] I rely on Christopher Duggan, *A Concise History of Modern Italy* (Cambridge: Cambridge University Press, 1994), 117–42, for my sketch of the events of unification.

[11] Christopher Seton-Watson, *Italy from Liberalism to Fascism, 1870–1925* (London: Methuen, 1967), 13.

[12] Duggan, *Concise History*, 127; Benedetto Croce, *A History of Italy, 1871–1915*, trans. Cecilia M. Ady (Oxford: Clarendon Press, 1929), 51.

either France or Germany.[13] Robert Putnam's recent study of democracy in contemporary Italy suggests that patterns of civic engagement developed in Renaissance Communes still determine Italian political practices.[14]

The concept of a unified, democratic, and liberal Italy had limited popular appeal. Democracy and liberalism in Italy meant little more than a united territory and a parliament. This conception of nonaristocratic government was thin by contemporary standards of democratization and even by nineteenth-century standards of bourgeois states, but it was nonetheless a considerable advance for an agricultural territory dominated by nobles, brigands, and bandits. In comparison with France in 1789 and Germany in 1850, Italy lacked a prominent commercial, let alone industrial, bourgeoisie. The principal partisans of the *Risorgimento* were a group of men belonging to the relatively small social category of what we would today describe as the educated middle classes, university graduates whose parents possessed neither land nor capital.[15] The French Revolution as a model for political practice did not extert a strong influence on the Italian popular mentality. Italy was physically isolated from the rest of Europe until 1871, when the Frejus Tunnel was built through the Alps. Intellectuals made the trek across the Alps to Paris, but the marauding armies of Napoleon also made the trip in the other direction.[16]

In Italy, the work of mass-producing the traditions that were the glue of French, German, and even British nineteenth-century nation-state projects was beset with obstacles.[17] Unification was as much a French as "Italian" invention. The monarchy, a fundamental guardian of national tradition, was neither popular nor indigenous in Italy. The House of Savoy was French, and many Italians viewed it as foreign. Cavour orchestrated the unification of Italy from Piedmont in the northern corner of the new Italy. Piedmont and its capital, Turin, where the first parliament met, were culturally French. Cavour's first language was French, and the father of Italy spoke Italian only when necessary and with difficulty. Even the territory was contested. Advocates of unification found it difficult to determine where Italy began and

---

[13] Italy had 16,429 kilometers of track in comparison with France's 38,109 and Germany's 51,678 (Duggan, *Concise History*, 127).

[14] Robert Putnam, *Making Democracy Work* (Princeton: Princeton University Press, 1993), esp. 121–62.

[15] Lovett, *Democratic Movement*, 68.

[16] On the influence of the French Revolution on Italian nationalist thinking, see Adrian Lyttelton, "The National Question in Italy," in *The National Question in Europe in Historical Context*, ed. Mikulas Teich and Roy Porter (New York: Cambridge University Press, 1993), 63–75.

[17] See Eric Hobsbawm, "Mass Producing Traditions: Europe, 1870–1914," in *The Invention of Tradition*, ed. Eric Hobsbawm and Terence Ranger (New York: Cambridge University Press, 1983), 263–307.

ended. Italy's northern borders were in continual dispute, in part because Austria and France had spent most of the eighteenth century and first half of the nineteenth invading.

Cultural dissonance was not the only legacy of the Risorgimento. It left an intellectual stamp in the figure of Giuseppe Mazzini. According to Benedetto Croce, Mazzini was a complicated figure who did not grasp the practical dimensions of political life and who "shut himself up in a kind of organized Utopia, derived from Saint-Simon, invoking with quasi-religious prayers and exhortations an imaginary being called the People." Mazzini was forsaken by an elite who thought him "vague" and by workers, "real" Italian people, who turned to socialism.[18] Written in 1929 during the period of fascist regime consolidation, Croce's analysis, which aimed to discredit a Risorgimento hero whom the fascists had resurrected, had more than a grain of truth.

In practice, Mazzini did little for Italian unification, but his view of politics that posited a direct link between God and the people resonated powerfully with certain strands of the anti-Catholic and anticlerical Italian intellectual classes. Mazzini was the "spiritual" voice of the new Italy and a quasi-mystical figure who, except for a brief time in Italy in 1849, spent the greater part of his adult life in London organizing conspiracies and patriotic movements in various parts of Europe.[19] In 1831 in Marseilles, he founded "Young Italy," a society of exiled Italian revolutionaries. Young Italy was a "faith and a mission" unmediated by the institutional shackles of the Catholic Church.[20]

In contrast to Cavour, who advocated a free church in a free state and championed the liberal separation of church and state, Mazzini espoused a new political religion based on the motto "God and People." The "nation" was the arena where the "people" realized their essential selves. Mazzini celebrated the cultural meaning of the Italian family. A fascist school textbook cited his slogan, "The family is the Fatherland of the heart," to underscore the fascist regime's appropriation of the family.[21] Mazzini was the voice of an "intransigent unitarianism" with a "Messianic streak" that seemed to speak to the 1840s.[22] He also spoke to the 1920s and 1930s. "God," "Nation," "Family," and "People" were the key words of Mazzini's political

[18] Croce, *History of Italy*, 73.
[19] See Denis Mack Smith, *Mazzini* (New Haven: Yale University Press, 1994).
[20] Lovett, *Democratic Movement*, 11–21.
[21] Vincenzo Biloni, *Cultura fascista: Secondo i programmi delle scuole secondarie d'avviamento professionale* (Brescia: Giulio Vannini, 1933), 143. School textbooks required the state's sanction before they could be employed, which made them official fascist documents (Herbert W. Schneider and Shephard B. Clough, *Making Fascists* [Chicago: University of Chicago Press, 1929], 98–99).
[22] Lyttelton, "National Question in Italy," 82–83.

religion that the fascist regime borrowed to legitimate its own cultural project.

A State without A Nation

In 1922, sixty years after unification, Italy remained a state without a nation. "Feeling" Italian was a tenuous emotion. Nationalism as ideology had as limited an appeal as unification. The Italian Nationalist Association, founded in 1910 by Enrico Corradini, was principally a literary organization. The crisis over whether to intervene in World War I and the subsequent loss of Italian territory in the war provided the opportunity for nationalism to emerge as a mass political force. But fascism easily and expeditiously co-opted nationalism. Mussolini viewed nationalism's emergence as a popular ideology, as evidenced by the development of nationalist syndical organizations, or labor unions, as an opportunity to expand the base of his fascist movement. Between 1919 and 1922, he harnessed the rhetoric of nationalism to the organizational forces of fascism. The Fascist Party and the Nationalist Association merged in 1923 after fascism came to power.[23]

The standard institutional buttresses—education, common language, and print culture—of the nation side of the nation-state dyad were weak and ineffective. Scholars have frequently noted the widespread theatricality and emotionality of Italy and its citizens. This was not simply a biological or cultural trait. Italians could not speak to one another very easily. Lexicographers had been lobbying since the eighteenth century to promulgate the Tuscan dialect as the official language of Italy. They were joined by literary figures in the early nineteenth century.[24] Yet Italians by and large communicated in their local dialects. At the time of unification, only 2.5 percent of the population spoke Italian.[25] The standardization of the legal system with the passage of the civil code in 1865 and the penal code in 1889 forced members of the state bureaucracy to have a working knowledge of Italian.

The education system did little to diffuse the language. As Bolton King and Thomas Okey, two early-twentieth-century British social observers, noted: "Education is the gloomiest chapter in Italian social history. . . . There have been thirty-three Education Ministers since 1860, each eager to distinguish himself by upsetting his predecessor's work. Money has been stinted, and State and communes, lavish in all else, have economized in the

[23] Mabel Berezin, "Created Constituencies: Fascism and the Italian Middle Classes," in *Splintered Classes: Politics and the Lower Middle Classes in Interwar Europe*, ed. Rudy Koshar (New York: Holmes and Meier, 1990), 149.
[24] Bruno Migliorini and T. Gwynfor Griffith, *The Italian Language* (London: Faber and Faber, 1984), 310–11; Lyttelton, "National Question in Italy," 72–73.
[25] Hobsbawm, *Nations and Nationalism*, 38.

most fruitful of national investments."[26] King and Okey painted a portrait of schools in disrepair, schoolteachers on charity, and a general indifference to education among a poor and, for the most part, illiterate population chained to local dialect. In the late nineteenth century, theater schools, a middle-class phenomenon, did as much as the education system to promulgate spoken Italian.[27]

The problem with language made the Italian public sphere, the hallmark of political modernity, comparatively weak.[28] The normal channels of liberal political discourse—newspapers and literary circles—existed, although they were inaccessible to many Italians. As late as 1921, Italy reported illiteracy rates ranging from a high of over 50 percent in the south to 25 percent in the center. Rates were in the single digits in the industrialized north.[29] Antonio Gramsci recounted that while he was in prison in Milan, newspapers were available but the prisoners, including political dissidents, chose to read the *Sports Gazette* —if they read at all. According to Gramsci, Italy lacked a culture of print: "Even today, spoken communication is a means of ideological diffusion which has a rapidity, a field of action, and an emotional simultaneity far greater than written communication (theatre, cinema and radio, with loudspeakers in public squares, beat all forms of written communication, including books, magazines, newspapers and newspapers on walls)—but superficially, not in depth."[30]

Public spectacle was a convenient and rational mode of political communication in a culture that rejected text in favor of gesture and performance. Italy had a ritual tradition of public festival dating back to the Renaissance.[31] Public festival took the form of commemoration of local saints, Catholic holy days, and local festivals celebrating the harvesting of grapes and other commerce-oriented events. Until the advent of fascism, the state viewed national festivals—the grist of European tradition mills—somewhat skeptically. In an only slightly veiled criticism of the fascist spectacle state, Croce re-

[26] Bolton King and Thomas Okey, *Italy To-Day* (London: James Nisbet, 1904), 233.

[27] Migliorini and Griffith, *Italian Language*, 404–5; Mabel Berezin, "Cultural Form and Political Meaning: State-Subsidized Theater, Ideology, and the Language of Style in Fascist Italy," *American Journal of Sociology* 99 (March 1994), 1256–59.

[28] Jürgen Habermas is the principal proponent of this argument. See *The Structural Transformation of the Public Sphere*, trans. Thomas Burger (Cambridge: MIT Press, 1989). For the research directions Habermas's argument has taken, see *Habermas and the Public Sphere*, ed. Craig Calhoun (Cambridge: MIT Press, 1993).

[29] See Gabriella Klein, *La politica linguistica del fascismo* (Bologna: Il Mulino, 1986), 34.

[30] Antonio Gramsci, "Oratory, Conversation, Culture," in *Antonio Gramsci: Selections from the Cultural Writings*, ed. David Forgacs and Geoffrey Nowell-Smith, trans. William Boelhower (Cambridge: Harvard University Press, 1985), 382.

[31] The historical literature on premodern festival in Italy is vast. For suggestive accounts, see essays in Peter Burke, *The Historical Anthropology of Early Modern Italy* (Cambridge: Cambridge University Press, 1987).

counted the national reluctance to commemorate the taking of Rome from the French in 1870. He noted that the *London Times* had derided the "Italian love of celebrations and festivities" and had referred to Italy as "the nation of carnivals." Invoking the *Times* article, Croce argued that "a free country should beware of following the customs of despotic governments, which must needs distract the minds of their subjects with festivities, in order to prevent them from dwelling on their own grievances, or bewailing their lost liberty."[32] The long-forgotten English criticism had little effect on the fascist ritual state; the post-unification state, however, with the exception of an annual pilgrimage to the tomb of Vittorio Emanuele, had avoided developing an extensive battery of national festivals.[33]

The Italian education system not only failed to disseminate the language and create the sense of patriotism that was the province of other European education systems but also exacerbated cultural tensions and class dissatisfaction. In 1922, Italy was a country with an urban industrial north, a vociferous working class, an illiterate and underdeveloped peasant south, and a quasi-educated and economically disadvantaged middle class.[34] Culture, and access to culture, was rigidly stratified. Italian high culture, from art to literature, and its political manifestations, from nationalism to avant-gardism, was the property of a small elite. The one apparently democratic door to culture and status, a professional degree, was for the most part a dead end. King and Okey describe the situation in 1902: "Men, who in England would go into business . . . and be trained for it, here [Italy] swell the ranks of the educated unemployed. . . . Every successful tradesmen hopes to see his son a lawyer or doctor or civil servant and spends L.300 to L. 500 in

[32] Croce, *History of Italy*, 82–83.

[33] See Bruno Tobia, *Una patria per gli italiani* (Rome: Laterza, 1991), esp. 100–113, for a discussion of the weak Italian foray into the invention of national traditions. In an impressionistic but still useful study, Herbert W. Schneider, *Making the Fascist State* (New York: Oxford University Press, 1928), supports this contention: "The Italian state is hopelessly bare and empty. Being of recent date, headed by a half French royal house and conducted by a very prosaic Parliament, having only occasional military celebrations and still more occasional visits of the King to make it impressive, represented continually by boyish policemen, petty officials and busy tax-collectors, it is comparatively quite remote and unattractive" (217).

[34] The social history of Italy has yet to be written, and scholars tend to rely on King and Okey, *Italy To-Day*. Work on the Italian middle classes is emerging; see, for example, Berezin, "Created Constituencies," 142–63; Jonathan Morris, *The Political Economy of Shopkeeping in Milan, 1886–1922* (New York: Cambridge University Press, 1993); and Mariuccia Salvati, *Il regime e gli impiegati: La nazionalizzazione piccolo-borghese nel ventennio fascista* (Rome: Laterza, 1992) and *L'inutile salotto: L'abitazione piccolo-borghese nell'Italia fascista* (Turin: Bollati Boringhieri, 1993). In general, historians have neglected this area but have freely made generalizations about Italian social life and culture with little that would pass for evidence in other contexts. In sum, the effect of social variables such as language, civic culture, and social practice is largely unexplored.

educating him for a useless life."[35] The crowding of the universities produced one of the largest groups of unemployed "intellectuals" in Europe,
which left the socially aspiring petite bourgeoisie with a deep sense of cultural inferiority.[36]

The popular Italian cultural idiom was a language of sentimentality and
emotion.[37] The love affair was the standard plot that enframed Italian social
imaginings. The characters in this Italian kitsch were frequently adulterous
wives or mothers who as deserted wives had to deal with the problem of
children. The Italian preoccupation with sentimentality went back to the
early nineteenth century. Mass circulation novels focused on the " 'irresistible' force of a blinding and compelling passion" and the " 'regeneration' of
[woman], fallen through the lure of the senses or through poverty, the 'regeneration' of [man] who has committed a crime, has been condemned by
the law and [has] made expiation."[38]

Juxtaposed against the language of sentimentality was the language of
melodrama. Italian opera is suggestive of the underside of Italian sentimentality with its frequent focus on unruly passions and uncontrolled emotion.
The Italian language of emotion became a part of the political vernacular of
a fascist regime that wished its citizens literally to fall in love with it.[39] The
language of sexuality and romance suffuses fascist prose. This language itself
is frequently viewed as fascist, but it was a cultural resource on which the
regime drew to construct its own political discourses. The language of sentiment and emotion spoke to the status-deprived petite bourgeoisie, which
craved the cultural outpourings of the new regime and was a major constituency of fascist cultural policy.[40]

Sources of the Italian Self: Transposing Schemata

The style in which Italian nineteenth-century nation-state builders imagined Italy sharply diverged from the style in which Italian citizens constructed their identities. Noncontingent Italian identities tended to be private and tied to family, local and tied to place, and religious and tied to the

[35] King and Okey, *Italy To-Day*, 249.

[36] Marzio Barbagli, *Educating for Unemployment* (New York: Columbia University Press,
1982), 119.

[37] See Gramsci's essays on Italian mass literary culture in *Selections from the Cultural Writings*, 342–86.

[38] Croce, *History of Italy*, 79.

[39] For the relation of gender, nationalism, and the language of sexuality, see Katherine
Verdery, "From Parent-State to Family Patriarchs: Gender and Nation in Contemporary
Eastern Europe," *East European Politics and Societies* 8 (Spring 1994), 225–55.

[40] See Victoria De Grazia, *The Culture of Consent: Mass Organization of Leisure in Fascist
Italy* (New York: Cambridge University Press, 1981), 127–50.

Catholic Church. The cultural communities of family, region, and religion provided the schemata that were the sources of the Italian self. The unification and the fascist project were attempts to supplant regional identities with national identities. Regionalism was, and is, a fact of Italian political and cultural life that no Italian regime has successfully overcome. The boundaries of family and religion were more permeable, more subject to transposition. The cultural architects of the fascist project, themselves bound to these schemata, played with them to transpose the rules of the Italian cultural game.

The Catholic Church as Institution

The neutralization of its principal competitor for the moral center of the Italian citizen—the Catholic Church—was a necessary first step to the realization of the fascist regime's social and political agenda. The Catholic Church did not accept Italian unification in 1861 and refused to recognize the new Italian state and its institutions.[41] In 1874, Pope Pius IX forbade Catholics to vote in national elections. The *non expedit*, as the pope's order became known, effectively barred Catholics from participation in Italian national civic life.[42] Although the rise of Catholic political parties at the turn of the nineteenth century suggests that Catholics did not observe the *non expedit*, it offered a powerful symbolic statement on the relations between church and state in Italy. The pope relaxed the *non expedit* in 1904 principally to encourage Catholics to vote against socialists.

The battle between church and state was also fought on a terrain that the average Italian could not ignore: the institution of marriage. The Italian state did not recognize religious marriage ceremonies; the church did not recognize civil marriage. Marriage was a Roman Catholic sacrament. If Italian Catholics married in a civil ceremony without benefit of a religious ceremony, the Catholic Church denied them access to its rites. Conversely, if they married in a religious ceremony without benefit of a civil ceremony, spouses had no reciprocal legal marital rights and children who were born of these marriages were considered illegitimate. The opposition between civil and religious matrimonial law left Italian Catholics who wished to marry in the awkward position of having to go through two ceremonies. The conflict over matrimony brought the fissure between the church and state into the

[41] On the origins of the conflict between church and state in Italy, see D[aniel] A. Binchy, *Church and State in Fascist Italy* (rpt., London: Oxford University Press, 1970), 3–29; A[rturo] C[arlo] Jemolo, *Church and State in Italy, 1850–1950*, trans. David Moore (rpt., Philadelphia: Dulfour, 1961), 53–83; and King and Okey, *Italy To-Day*, 29–60.

[42] Seton-Watson, *Italy from Liberalism to Fascism*, 59.

everyday lives of the majority of Italians whether they were politically engaged or spiritually devout.[43]

As early as 1925, the regime realized that if it was to have any authority in the "moral" sphere, it must resolve the "Roman question," the popular label for the Italian schism between church and state. On February 11, 1929, the regime and the Catholic Church signed the Lateran Pact. The church agreed to recognize the Italian fascist state as the legitimate political authority in Italy and not to ban Catholics from participation in the state; the regime agreed that Catholicism was the state religion of Italy. The "Conciliation," a political coup for the fascist regime, ended the seventy-year-old schism between church and state and paved the way for the Fascist Party to accelerate its infiltration of Catholic civic and voluntary organizations. Mussolini had succeeded with the Catholic Church where every other Italian statesman since Cavour had failed.[44]

Roman Catholicism as Popular Culture

In a frequently cited speech given in 1926, Mussolini described fascism as a new political religion. Noting that he had chosen the public piazza to articulate his ideas rather than the chambers of parliament, he proclaimed, "Fascism is not only a party, it is a regime, it is not only a regime, but a faith, it is not only a faith, but a religion that is conquering the laboring masses of the Italian people."[45] Scholars of the speech have tended to look for direct parallels between fascist and religious ritual practice, that is, to describe how fascism was similar to religion.[46] This, I argue, is a wrong turn, because it implies a static view of religion and fascism. Religion is not simply doctrine or rite: it is lived practice, and its symbols are reinforcing but not totalizing.

Roman Catholicism as a religion comprised doctrine and institutions. The doctrine was functionally irrelevant to the popular practice of Roman Catholicism in a semiliterate country such as early-twentieth-century Italy, where a battery of cyclical liturgical rituals obliterated whatever nuances of church doctrine seeped into popular consciousness. The popular practices of Roman Catholicism, engraved in the mental frames of even the fascists, provided an opportunity for cultural transposition. The central paradox in the

[43] See King and Okey, *Italy To-Day*, 257–58, and Binchy, *Church and State in Fascist Italy*, 388–406.

[44] On the negotiations surrounding the Conciliation, see Jemolo, *Church and State in Italy*, 225–39.

[45] Benito Mussolini, "Discorso di Pesaro," in *Dall'attentato Zaniboni al discorso dell'ascensione*, vol. 22 of *Opera omnia di Benito Mussolini*, ed. Edoardo Susmel and Duilio Susmel (rpt., Florence: La Fenice, 1956), 197. *Opera Omnia* is hereafter cited as *OO*.

[46] See, for example, Gentile, *Culto del littorio*, 3–38, 301–15.

relation between the Catholic Church and Italian politics in general is that, despite the church's obvious power, there is a high degree of anti-Catholicism and anticlericalism in Italy. Yet Roman Catholicism was a form of popular culture, that is, everyone participated in Catholic practices that were independent of doctrine or belief and shaped Italian fascist and public consciousness. What literature exists on the Italian practice of Roman Catholicism suggests that belief is low, more form than substance, but that its ritual practices are readily adopted to serve political ends.[47]

Although there was competition between the regime and the church, there was an affinity between fascism and Catholicism that the regime exploited. In contrast to Protestantism, Catholicism as religion does not acknowledge a private self. One is Catholic both inside and outside the church. Italian Catholics may not know or understand the theological reasoning behind the church's public positions, doctrinal decisions, or liturgy, but they understand that the Catholic Church does not recognize the separation of selves: to be Catholic is to be Catholic in the public and private sphere.

This fundamental "rule" of Catholicism was not lost on Italian fascist ideologues. In a 1925 speech entitled "What Is Fascism?" Giovanni Gentile presented "his" fascism and argued that fascism is a "faith" whose multiplicity and open-endedness could attract numerous followers of diverse positions.[48] Concluding on the note that "fascism is a religion," he draws an explicit connection between fascism and Catholicism as ethoses that do not separate the public and private self.

One cannot be a fascist in politics and not fascist. . . in school, not fascist in one's family, not fascist in one's work. Like a Catholic, if one is Catholic, one invests his whole life with religious sentiment . . . if one is truly Catholic, and has a religious sense, one remembers always in the highest part of one's mind, to work and think and pray and meditate and feel Catholic; so too a fascist, who goes to parliament, or to the fascist house, writes in the newspapers or reads them, follows his private life or converses with others, looks to his future or thinks of his past and the past of his people, ought always to think of himself as a fascist![49]

[47] Most work on the popular practice of religion in Italy focuses on the premodern period. See especially Carlo Ginzburg, *The Cheese and the Worms*, trans. John Tedeschi and Anne Tedeschi (London: Routledge, 1981). Scholars have noted the parallels between fascist and Christian symbolic practice, but there has been no sustained analysis of this interaction. On the Italian Communist Party's manipulation of Catholic practice, see David I. Kertzer, *Comrades and Christians* (New York: Cambridge University Press, 1980), esp. 130–68.
[48] "Che cosa è il fascismo?" in *Giovanni Gentile: Politica e cultura*, ed. Herve A. Cavallera, vol. 2 (Florence: Le Lettere, 1991), 86.
[49] Ibid., 36.

According to Gentile, the ethic of fascist religion was "hard work" and "sacrifice" with little time for "diversion," an ethic that was ideally suited to an economically underdeveloped country with a militant working class. This fascist transposition of the deep cultural ideal of Catholicism, the fusion of public and private self, would be recognizable to all Italians, whether they believed, practiced, or understood the text of Roman Catholicism.

An example of the fascist transposition of a tangible cultural object was the form of fascist propaganda books. Beginning in 1923, with the Gentile reform of education, it became mandatory to teach the Catholic religion in the schools. The Roman Catholic catechism, with its question-and-answer format to be learned by rote, was a standard feature of Italian education and Catholic socialization that was difficult to escape.[50] What follows is an excerpt from the official catechism in popular use at the turn of the century.

What is the Catholic Church?

The Catholic Church is the society of the baptized that believe and profess the doctrine and the laws of Jesus Christ, participate in the sacraments that He instituted, recognizing His Vicar on earth the Roman Pontiff and obey him and other legitimate Pastors.

Why is the Catholic Church the only true Church of Jesus Christ?

The Catholic Church is the only true Church of Jesus Christ, because it is the only one founded by Him and it is one, holy, catholic, and apostolic, which is as He wished.

How is the Church *one?*

The Church is *one,* because its members, in every time and in every place, have and had the same faith, the same sacraments and the same sacrifice, the same ties of charity and communion under the same visible head, the Roman Pontiff.[51]

The similarities between the form of the catechism and the form of a fascist propaganda tract are striking:

[50] On the history of the Italian catechism and its reform, see Luciano Nordera, *Il catechismo di Pio X: Per una storia della catechesi in Italia (1896–1916)* (Rome: LAS, 1988); on the Gentile reform of education, see Tracy H. Koon, *Believe, Obey, Fight: Political Socialization of Youth in Fascist Italy, 1922–1943* (Chapel Hill: University of North Carolina Press, 1985), 54–55.

[51] A copy of a page of the catechism of Pius X appears in Nordera, *Il catechismo di Pio X,* appendix 15.

What is the State?

The State is the political and juridical organization of the National Society, and it exists in a series of institutions of various orders.

But more precisely, according to Fascism, what is the State?

According to Fascism the State is the supreme Authority that subordinates the activity and interests of single citizens to the general interests of the Nation.[52]

Fascism and Catholicism were both in the business of indoctrination, and the form of the tracts would be recognizable to any Italian who had been to school, or before 1923, to church. As the regime did not aim to capture the minds of Italian peasants, the form of the tracts proved a more potent vehicle of cultural transposition than any discursive messages they might have conveyed.[53]

The Italian Family and the Cult of the Mother

Inability to transcend parochial notions of interest has shaped Italian politics. The cultural strength of the Italian family and the local identities this attachment engendered served as a barrier to disinterested democratic practice.[54] The fascist regime, like the regimes that preceded and succeeded it, needed to channel emotion away from this powerful source of the Italian private self and project it onto the nation. A school text reminds youth that according to Mazzini, "the first cell of the organism of the Patria is composed of the Family."[55] The fascist strategy to develop a cult of the mother that appropriated a visceral Italian feeling about the nature of motherhood did not need Mazzini for inspiration. Indeed, Mazzini's rhetoric and the regime's strategy sprang from the same cultural well. Motherhood has deep

[52] *La dottrina fascista*, with a preface by S. E. Turati (Rome: Libreria del Littorio, n.d.), 11, 39.

[53] The best portraits of the regime's relation to the Italian peasantry are fictional. See, for example, Ignazio Silone, *Bread and Wine*, and Carlo Levi, *Christ Stopped at Eboli*.

[54] The literature on the family has focused on the South. Edward C. Banfield, *The Moral Basis of a Backward Society* (New York: Free Press, 1958), generated a series of studies on this topic. In general, the effect of the family on Italian political practice has been neglected. Paul Ginsborg's recent work on postwar Italy seeks to reverse that trend (*A History of Contemporary Italy: Society and Politics, 1943–1988* [Harmondsworth, England: Penguin, 1990]).

[55] Biloni, *Cultura fascista*, 243.

cultural meaning in Italy, and the idea that motherhood is woman's most valuable role crosses class and educational boundaries.[56]

The argument for the cultural meaning of Italian motherhood can be made indirectly. David Kertzer's work on infant abandonment provides an inverse view of the meaning of motherhood.[57] Italy had one of the highest rates of infant abandonment in Latin Europe. Italy was an honor society, and honor is directly connected to the idea of shame. An Italian man's honor was tied to the sexual purity of his wife, sisters, and daughters. An unwed mother brought dishonor on the family. The legal system overlooked crimes in the name of family honor. The Rocco Code of penal law passed in 1930 continued the nineteenth-century tradition of defining murder in the service of family honor as an "extenuating circumstance" and extended the definition of "extenuating" to include "learning" of a family member's act of sexual impropriety. Previously, the dishonored person (a wife had rights here also) had to witness the "illicit relationship."[58]

Although a woman's father or brother could murder to restore family honor, women were not terribly well protected in the system. Rates of un-wed pregnancy in Italy were high. Unmarried pregnant women were regularly forcibly locked away to await the birth of their children and were frequently disowned. A woman had little recourse if the father of her unborn child was already married, as his family had to be protected at all costs. The church supported these practices in the eighteenth and part of the nineteenth century by running orphanages, foundling homes, and shelters for unwed mothers. In the late nineteenth century, as women entered the Italian labor force in great numbers, social reformers employed the "image of the evil mother" to legitimate their demands for protective labor legislation.[59]

Kertzer's story focuses on the nineteenth century but its cultural meaning held sway in the twentieth. In general, Italian culture viewed women's sexuality as dangerous, a potential source of dishonor, if not disciplined in the role of mother. According to a fascist school textbook, an Italian woman refused adornments that would court sexual attention: "The true Italian woman is not a slave to fashion, particularly beyond the Alps [a criticism of France]; she dresses modestly, refuses every affectation, and to conserve her

---

[56] The fact that no specific research supports my claim is perhaps sufficient evidence for making it. The importance of motherhood is such a taken-for-granted feature of Italian "local knowledge" that it has never occurred to anyone to study it.

[57] David I. Kertzer, *Sacrificed for Honor* (Boston: Beacon, 1993).

[58] The Rocco Code was in effect until 1981. On Italian law as it pertains to the concept of honor, see Eva Cantarella, "Homicides of Honor: The Development of Italian Adultery Law over Two Millennia," in *The Family in Italy from Antiquity to the Present*, ed. David I. Kertzer and Richard P. Saller (New Haven: Yale University Press, 1991), esp. 242–44.

[59] Kertzer, *Sacrificed for Honor*, 13, 26, 66, 174.

innate elegance knows 'to come from the mirror, without a painted face.' "[60] In the 1920s and 1930s, the height of fascist "modernization," a young couple engaged to be married was always chaperoned.[61] The cultural belief in a female sexuality in need of strict discipline manifested itself in the popular predilection for melodrama and sentiment and had social roots in the organization of the Italian family. Once a woman became a mother, she assumed absolute control over a family.

The pattern of female domestic authority was observable across class and region. Married couples frequently lived in extended households, where mothers-in-law made the decisions and allocated the family resources. According to survey data on women born between 1890 and 1910, mothers-in-law ran the house in the majority of worker and peasant households. Husbands and wives shared jointly in household decisions in the relatively small proportion of professional middle-class households. A similar pattern holds for the allocation of family resources.[62] These data, though limited, suggest that mothers had a form of cultural power that was far and above what one would expect—especially given the fact that in peasant and worker households the women often consumed their dinner in the kitchen while the men sat at the table.

The story of the "invisibility" of the dead spinster in Chapter 6 underscores the deeply held belief that women not only discipline their sexuality in motherhood but obtain their social visibility through this role. Mothers and motherhood became a linchpin of contradictory fascist social policies that directed women to be fertile and to reproduce as well as to be "modern" and to work. The fascists played out these contradictory ideas in public rituals where the living body of the mother served as cultural and political icon. Mothers of the war wounded and fascist dead were regularly paraded in public space and juxtaposed against the figures of the young girls and women who were part of fascist youth organizations and participated in sporting and gymnastic events. The strong future of the mother and the existing mothers were ritual emblems of the past and future production of Italian fascist bodies. Quoting Mazzini, a fascist text suggests the powerful influence of the sentimentalized mother:

The angel of the family is the Woman. Mother, wife, sister, the Woman is the caress of life. . . . They are in themselves treasures of sweet consolation

---

[60] Biloni, *Cultura fascista*, 246–47.

[61] Victoria De Grazia discusses courtship patterns and the control of women's sexual behavior as a struggle between "tradition" and the "lures" of commercial culture (*How Fascism Ruled Women: Italy, 1922–1945* [Berkeley: University of California Press, 1992], 128–40, 201–33).

[62] Marzio Barbagli, *Sotto lo stesso tetto* (Bologna: Il Mulino, 1984) 429, 430.

that numb every sorrow. And they introduce each one of us to the future. The first maternal kiss teaches the baby to love. The first holy kiss of friendship teaches man hope, faith in life: and love and faith create the desire to do better, the power to achieve step by step, the future of which the baby is the living symbol. . . . For her, the Family, with its divine mystery of reproduction, reaches toward eternity.[63]

Creating the Fascist Self: New Rules of the Cultural Game

Fascism did not simply attempt to transpose the readily available cultural schema. It also sought to create new rules of the cultural game, new forms of noncontingent identities. In this task, it was on much more slippery terrain. The regime wished to construct fascist identities based on new conceptions of citizenship, nation, and community. In contrast to church and family, the bedrock of noncontingent Italian identities, these abstract political concepts had little cultural resonance. Whereas the focus of transposing the traditional sources of Italian identity was on community, the cultural trigger for the new identity was the identification of enemies as embodied in liberalism and Marxism. Official fascist narratives defined fascism against "others"— enemies and emphasized an ethic of living rather than codified doctrine.

In attempting to codify fascist ideology, scholars have either criticized it for incoherence or focused on discursive elements of fascist argument.[64] But fascism had only a few central ideas that it repeated in mantra fashion in newspapers, school texts, propaganda tracts, and a scattering of official documents. And those key ideas related to how one should live a fascist life. Their specific content was highly contingent on external and internal political exigencies that occurred over the twenty-one-year period of the regime.

In short, fascism was about creating a new self in the state, and certain documents highlight its normative dimensions. Mussolini's essay *The Doctrine of Fascism*, written by Giovanni Gentile for the *Italian Encyclopedia*, is one such document. Gentile's speech "What Is Fascism?" as well as the 1927 Labor Charter and Mussolini's Ascension Day speech in the same year also articulate the dimensions of the new fascist self and argue for the merging of the public and private self in the state.[65]

[63] Biloni, *Cultura fascista*, 246.

[64] See, for example, Adrian Lyttelton, *Italian Fascism from Pareto to Gentile* (New York: Harper and Row, 1973), and Pier Giorgio Zunino, *L'ideologia del fascismo* (Bologna: Il Mulino, 1985).

[65] Corporativism, the policy outcome of the Labor Charter, is usually viewed as an economic policy; see Charles Maier, "The Economics of Fascism and Nazism," in *In Search of Stability* (Cambridge: Cambridge University Press, 1987), 70–120. I have argued in "Cre-

In 1925, Giovanni Gentile presented "his" fascism and argued that the "unity" of fascism resulted from the "multiplicity" of "psychologies and systems of culture and conceptions of life" it incorporated: "The force of fascism derives from these linked needs and spiritual energies. And fascism would desiccate and become arid in the mechanical monotony of empty formulas if they could define it and restrain it in articles of a determined creed."[66] Gentile rewrote Italian history to repudiate the aridity of the liberal era.

There were "two Italys": the Italy of the Renaissance, which Gentile identified as the seat of European modernity, and the Italy of the Roman Empire. Glory went to Rome; history belonged to the Renaissance. Gentile viewed the salience of the Renaissance in Western civilization as casting a long "shadow" over Italian political and cultural development. The importance of the Renaissance was a double-edged sword because it ushered in the "age of individualism" (foreshadowing Jacob Burckhardt), which led to "decadence," "frivolity," and a lack of interest in family and state. The Renaissance produced "culture," but it was "dead, infertile." The legacy of rampant individualism remained, and "even today there are too many people in Italy who believe in nothing, laugh at everything, and long for Arcadia and other academies; and become hostile toward anyone who might disturb their digestion."[67]

Skipping over the next two hundred years of history, Gentile locates the true spirit of the Italian nation in Giuseppe Mazzini's version of nationalism and suggests that the forces that created the Italian state in 1860 betrayed the spirit of nation to decadent liberalism. Bourgeois individualism is an illusion: "The particular individual is a product of imagination, mediated; each one of us is represented himself as one among many, in the crowd, circumscribed by the extreme limits of birth and death and in the brief confines of his physical person."[68] True liberty is located not in the individual but in the collectivity as represented by the state or the nation. Fascism made no distinction between the state and the nation, borrowing Mazzini's notion that the nation was an ever shifting "moral reality." Following Mazzini, Gentile argued that Young Italy is "fascism today": "The nation yes, truly, is not geography and is not history: it is program and mission."[69] Calling for a return to the Risorgimento of Mazzini, Gentile digressed on

---

ated Constituencies" and elsewhere that it is also a cultural policy. The centrality Zeev Sternhell (*The Birth of Fascist Ideology*, trans. David Maisel [Princeton: Princeton University Press, 1994]) ascribes to labor supports my contention.

[66] "Che cosa è il fascismo?" 8.

[67] Ibid., 14.

[68] Ibid., 23.

[69] Ibid., 25.

fascist violence, which he dismissed as an offshoot of the "revolutionary" character of fascism.

"What Is Fascism?" narrated Italian history in terms of a return to the religious character of Mazzini's nationalism. *The Doctrine of Fascism*, a directed critique of liberalism and Marxism, offered a clearer view of the new Italian community. Prepared for the 1932 edition of the *Enciclopedia italiana* and listed under the heading "Fascism," the *Doctrine* was ostensibly written by Mussolini. Actually, Mussolini wrote only the last half, and Gentile wrote the section entitled "Fundamental Ideas."[70] The work was a propagandist document published separately from the *Enciclopedia* and in foreign translation. It argued that fascism was a "general attitude toward life" founded on "spiritual" ideas. Fascism was an "ethic" and a "moral" system: "The Fascist conception of life is a religious one in which man is viewed in his permanent relation to a higher law, endowed with an objective will transcending the individual and raising him to conscious membership in a spiritual society."[71]

Fascism, following Mazzini, collapsed the nation and the state. Nation is a "quality," not a "quantity," which is displayed when disparate groups realize themselves as a "single conscience" and "single will." In contrast to liberal ideals that posit the nation and then the state, it is the "State which forms the Nation, by lending strength and power and real life to a people conscious of its own moral unity."[72] Because of its spiritual nature the fascist state could not respect the bounds of public and private:

The Fascist State, as a higher and more powerful expression of personality, is a force, but a spiritual one. It sums up all the manifestations in the intellectual and moral life of man. Its functions cannot therefore be limited to that of enforcing law and order, as the Liberal doctrine would have it. It is no mere mechanical device for defining the sphere within which the individual may duly exercise his supposed rights. The Fascist State is an inwardly accepted standard and a rule of conduct, a discipline of the whole person; it permeates the will no less than the intellect. It stands for a principle which becomes the central motive of man as a member of civilized society, sinking deep down into his personality: it dwells in the heart of the man of action and of the thinker, of the artist and of the man of science: soul of the soul.[73]

[70] A. James Gregor, *The Ideology of Fascism* (New York: Free Press, 1969), 206.
[71] Benito Mussolini, *The Doctrine of Fascism*, 4th ed. (Rome: Novissima, n.d.), 10–11, 13. The citations are from the English edition.
[72] Ibid., 16–17.
[73] Ibid., 19.

Liberalism, because of its commitment to individualism, destroyed rather than enhanced liberty:

> Liberalism denied the State in the name of the individual; Fascism reasserts the rights of the State as expressing the real essence of the individual. And if liberty is to be the attribute of living men and not that of abstract dummies invented by individualistic Liberalism, then Fascism stands for liberty and for the only liberty worth having, the liberty of the State and of the individual within the State.[74]

Liberalism bred democracy, which was a "kingless Regime infested by many kings who are sometimes more exclusive, tyrannical and destructive than a single one, even if he is a tyrant."[75] Liberalism was a political illusion of the early nineteenth century which was incapable of dealing with the political realities of the twentieth. The *Doctrine* argued that all the great political experiments of the twentieth century, including the fascist regime, were "anti-Liberal." In the twentieth century, the "collective century," the "century of the State," liberalism's commitment to individualism was outmoded. Despite its espousal of "collectivity," the *Doctrine* was as harsh in its assessment of Karl Marx, who "would explain the history of mankind in terms of the class struggle and of changes in the processes of production, to the exclusion of all else," as it was in its assessment of Adam Smith.[76]

Fascism redefined citizenship, the relationship between the individual and the nation, in terms of duties and not rights. The relations of production, central to Marxism, became central to the fascist conception of citizenship and belonging; but whereas in Marxism relations of production were an arena of struggle, in fascism they were loci of cohesion. Work, usually regulated by the private sphere of the market, under fascism destroyed the boundary between the public and private as workers submerged themselves in the national collectivity. The Labor Charter (Carta del lavoro), a thirty-point document written in a series of aphorisms by Giuseppe Bottai and Augusto Turati, defined the proper relation between the individual and the state and was a central statement of the fascist conception of the self that made explicit the contrast between fascism and socialism.[77] The Labor Charter was also a fascist co-optation of the church's official position on labor. On March 15, 1891, Pope Leo XIII issued an encyclical entitled "The Con-

[74] Ibid., 15.
[75] Ibid., 31.
[76] Ibid.
[77] The text of the charter is found in Giuseppe Bottai and Augusto Turati, *La carta del lavoro* (Rome: Diritto del Lavoro, 1929).

dition of the Working Classes." *Rerum Novarum* argued that the state
should help workers as an antidote to socialism and condemned unbridled
capitalism. The encyclical was widely hailed as the Magna Carta of labour. It
called for Christian trade unions and mixed corporations of employers and
employees that foreshadowed the fascist corporative state.[78]

In his speech to the Fascist Grand Council on January 6, 1927, Giuseppe
Bottai introduced the Labor Charter as "more than a legislative document"
and a "new way for everyone to be part of the national society." The Labor
Charter was a declaration of "solidarity of all citizens before national interests."[79] It advocated "progressive" labor reforms and included stipulations
about holidays, limited work hours, benefits, sick days, and adjudication of
labor disputes. According to Bottai, the Labor Charter was a "document
without precedent in constitutional history," because it used the labor process to solidify the bonding between the worker and the state. Fascism was
superior to socialism because it included white-collar workers as well as industrial laborers: "The problems of the most humble workers, the interests
of the salaried clerks and of manual laborers, exist on the same plane as the
interests of business."[80] The Charter laid the ideological groundwork for the
corporative organizational structure that was not firmly in place until the
1930s.[81] Work was the productive and social activity that linked the individual to the state. In a direct borrowing from *Rerum Novarum*, corporations,
fascist unions that encompassed the entire workforce, were the organizational vehicles that concretized the state-individual relation.

The Charter began with a biological metaphor asserting that the state was
a social body: "The Italian Nation is an organism having ends, life, superior
methods of power and endurance than those of the divided and regrouped
individuals which compose it. It is a moral, political, and economic unity
which realizes itself integrally in the fascist State." The Charter's second
proposition followed logically from the idea that the nation was a moral
collectivity. Economic production was national or "unitary," and all labor,
including intellectual labor, was a "social duty."[82] If one accepted the unifying nature of the state, then conflicts of interest between employers and
employees were not possible. In a single rhetorical stroke, the Charter declared that socialism and its principal premise of "class conflict" was irrelevant. Class collaboration was the premise of fascism, and corporativism the

[78] Seton-Watson, *Italy from Liberalism to Fascism*, 230, and Gene Burns, *The Frontiers of Catholicism* (Berkeley: University of California Press, 1992), 40–42, make the point that *Rerum Novarum*'s proposed reforms were based on neofeudalism.
[79] Bottai and Turati, *La carta*, 26, 27.
[80] Ibid., 31.
[81] On fascist union structure, see Domenico Preti, *Economia e istituzioni nello stato fascista* (Rome: Riuniti, 1980), 261–386.
[82] Bottai and Turati, *La carta*, 35.

ideological label attached to the principles the Charter espoused. Fascist syndicates replaced socialist unions.[83] All citizens, including employers, intellectuals, and professionals, were organized in "free" unions to which the state gave legal recognition.[84] The new fascist collective labor contract was the "concrete expression of solidarity among the various factors of production."[85]

The theory of fascist collectivity did not repudiate free markets. Proposition 7 declared: "The corporative State considers private initiative in the field of production the most effective and useful instrument in the interest of the Nation." This aspect of the Charter speaks to Sternhell's point that markets were compatible with fascism. Proposition 9 which asserted: "State intervention in economic production takes place only when private initiative is lacking or insufficient or whenever the political interests of the State are involved. Such intervention can assume the form of control, encouragement, and direct management," evoking John Maynard Keynes in black shirt.[86]

A month after the Labor Charter was introduced, Mussolini delivered a speech to the Chamber of Deputies in Rome which outlined the fascist conception of the polity and the role of the individual within it. Never bypassing a symbolic opportunity, particularly one that undercut the ritual space of the Catholic Church, Mussolini delivered "The Speech of the Ascension" on May 26, 1927—the Catholic feast day of the Ascension.[87] According to Roman Catholic liturgy, Christ ascended into heaven and completed the mission of establishing his kingdom on earth forty days after Easter. Mussolini's speech, a major policy address on the state of the Italian nation, celebrated the Ascension of the fascist regime; its temporal location on a significant Catholic feast day invoked, co-opted, and secularized resurrection imagery.

The Speech of the Ascension focused on another dimension of the Italian private self: the family and its relationship with the state. The speech had three parts: the first addressed the demographic situation of the country, the second was a meditation on the use of violence and surveillance, and the last was an attempt to set fascism apart from other political ideologies. Mussolini argued that in a "well-ordered State" the "physical health of the people should take first place."[88] This emphasis on the health of the nation turned into a discourse on the declining Italian birth rate and an argument for a

[83] Socialist unions were not outlawed but were left with no power. See Lyttelton, *Seizure of Power*, chap. 12, esp. 319, 322–24.

[84] On the relationship between the individual and the labor contract, see Preti, *Economia e istituzioni*, 125–78.

[85] Bottai and Turati, *La carta*, 36.

[86] Ibid., 37, 38.

[87] Benito Mussolini, "Il discorso dell'ascensione," in *Dall'attentato Zaniboni al discorso dell'ascensione*, vol. 22, *OO*, 360–90.

[88] Ibid., 361.

demographic policy that encouraged fertility and supported families.[89] As a policy remedy, Mussolini announced the foundation of the National Organization for the Protection of Mothers and Infants (Opera Nazionale per la Protezione della Maternita e dell'Infanzia).

Turning from maternity to the issue of consent to the regime, Mussolini argued that the fascist state of the future would not need to resort to violence, police, or censorship to establish political commitment. The moral dimension of the new fascist state obviated the necessity of institutional agents of social control. Mussolini exhorted the Chamber:

> We ought to preoccupy ourselves with the moral order, not the public order, because in the public order, in the sense of policing words, we have sufficient forces; we ought instead to preoccupy ourselves in the moral order and we ought to wish, working to the utmost, that the connection between the masses and the regime will be always wide reaching, always more attached, always more conscious. (*Applause*)

As an ideology, fascism was "anti-democratic, anti-liberal, anti-socialist, and anti-Masonic. (*Applause*)"[90] It rejected the principal premise of liberal democracy—the popular franchise. Mussolini argued that the majority of citizens in liberal democracies did not exercise their right to vote and that voting actually militated against creating an involved citizenry. Voting gave an illusion of participation that fostered indifference.

Corporative organization, groups of citizens that originated in their productive activity with the state at the apex, was an alternative to democratic participation and to socialist communalism that included all citizens in the polity. Thus, the fascist state was a social, not a political, entity.

> I do not think anyone in the twentieth century is able to live outside the State, if they are not a barbarian state, or savage state.
>
> It is only the State that gives people a consciousness of itself. If the people are not organized, if the people are not a State, they are simply a population that will be at the mercy of the first group of internal adventurers or external invaders. Because, oh gentlemen, only the State with its juridical organization, with its military force, always prepared, can defend the national collectivity; but if the human collectivity is fractionated and reduced

---

[89] On family policy under the regime, see De Grazia, *How Fascism Ruled Women*, 41–59; on the problems of Italian fertility and fear of population decline, see David G. Horn, "Constructing the Sterile City: Pronatalism and Social Sciences in Inter-War Italy," *American Ethnologist* 18 (August 1991), 581–601.

[90] Mussolini, "Discorso dell'ascensione," 382, 386.

to only the nuclear family, a few Normans will be enough to conquer Apulia. (*Applause*)[91]

Rituals and Resources

A central paradox of Italian political and cultural development was that the strength of the state was inversely proportional to the weakness of Italian national identity. Italy spent the post-unification period building the state, and by 1922, a labyrinthine structure of bureaucratic offices was in place. The fascist regime, the group of political actors who commanded the state and determined Italian political context until 1943, inherited an unwieldy and slow-moving public bureaucracy.[92] The reconstruction of the Italian state, a major portion of the fascist political project and one that lasted well after the fall of the regime, was an ongoing task.[93] The Italian state was a source of social mobility for large segments of the overeducated and under-employed Italian population.[94] This cadre of potential state employees provided the fascist regime with a human resource it could mobilize to coordinate its ever-expanding propaganda activities, from ritual to art.[95]

The state as a formal bureaucratic mechanism orchestrated the fascist cultural project, including the production of public spectacle. The state was enlisted by the regime to rewrite the rules of the cultural game. The principal institutional resources the regime brought to bear on the creation of public spectacle were the legal system and the institutionalization of the Fascist Party. Law regulated public holidays, and the regime redesigned the legal holiday calendar literally to make time for fascist spectacle. Diverse government ministries were responsible for public events. The regime had the police, the Ministry of the Interior, the army, and the National Treasury

[91] Ibid., 389.

[92] I draw a distinction between the terms "state" and "regime." Scholars debate as to whether one can speak of a fascist regime before the 1930s. From March 1929, the year of the plebiscite, Mussolini and the Fascist Party were in complete control of the Italian state. This was a formal event, however, and Mussolini and the party were de facto in control of the state from 1922. Adrian Lyttelton marks the beginning of the dictatorship, or "second wave" of fascism, as coincident with the speech Mussolini gave on January 3, 1925, in which he responded to the murder of socialist deputy Matteotti. See "Fascism in Italy: The Second Wave," *Journal of Contemporary History* 1 (1966), 75–100.

[93] See Alberto Aquarone, *L'organizzazione dello stato totalitario* (rpt., Turin: Einaudi, 1974), and Renzo De Felice, *Mussolini il Duce: Gli anni del consenso, 1929–1936*, vol. 1 (Turin: Einaudi, 1974), 127–322.

[94] The farther south one went in Italy, the more citizens distrusted the state and the more they depended on it for career advancement. See Berezin, "Created Constituencies," 157–58.

[95] See Mabel Berezin, "Organization of Political Ideology: Culture, State, and Theater in Fascist Italy," *American Sociological Review* 56 (1991), 643, 647.

(public spectacle was expensive) under its jurisdiction and could commandeer public space whenever it chose. Public spectacle was a primary concern of the Ministries of the Interior and Public Security because their respective purposes were to monitor subversive activity and maintain public order. The Ministry of War coordinated veterans' groups when spectacle required them. Frequently, Mussolini himself became involved in the planning of ritual events.

The Fascist Party mediated among the various state agencies and ministries that staged fascist spectacle and was in charge of the mundane aspects of coordination. Outside the Roman center, the organizational capacities of the local federal secretaries were crucial to the activities of fascist ritual. The production of ritual in fascist Italy ran in parallel with the development and ever expanding bureaucratic structure of the National Fascist Party. The party that developed in the years between 1922 and the late 1930s bore little resemblance to the rag-tag collection of artists, intellectuals, shopkeepers, and general ruffians who made up the early *squadristi* (squads) and *arditi*.[96] In the late 1920s, Mussolini declared that the party was an arm of the state at his disposal. The party was an organization that ran in parallel with the state, and competition emerged between national party leaders and high-ranking government ministers as to who was actually in control. Mussolini was technically head of both the party and the state. During the course of the regime, the party went through a number of reorganizations and its statute was revised several times.

In 1926, the National Fascist Party began to publish the *Folgio d'Ordini*, a news sheet that listed party events.[97] The party standardized the plans and schedules of ritual activities and published detailed reports that included the prescribed roster of activities in major cities, the names of party dignitaries who delivered Mussolini's message at various commemorations, detailed maps of parade routes, train schedules, and names and numbers of fascist squadrons imported for particular commemorations. In 1932, the *Foglio* began to publish a yearly calendar of party activities. For example, the 1935 calendar listed the inauguration of a new train station in Florence, the opening of the City University in Rome, the annual report of the prefects, and the opening of a fashion exhibit in Turin.[98]

Augusto Turati and Achille Starace were the national party secretaries who placed their stamp on this period. Turati was by all accounts somewhat

---

[96] There is no history to date of the Fascist Party in the post-1922 period. Emilio Gentile's *Storia del partito fascista* (Rome: Laterza, 1989) concludes in 1922. I rely on Aquarone, *L'organizzazione dello stato totalitario*, and what can be pieced together from the *Foglio d'Ordini*.

[97] A more elaborate version of this information is in the *Atti del Partito Nazionale Fascista*.

[98] PNF, *Foglio d'Ordini*, Rome #140, 22 August 1935.

dour and intensely serious.[99] Starace was an "intransigent" fascist who regretted the opening of the party to a broader membership in the 1930s. Scholars frequently attribute the increased militarization of the party and its emphasis on public ritual to Starace, who had the longest tenure as party head and who, as Mack Smith has noted, is commonly credited with putting all of Italy in uniform.[100] Starace assumed the role of national secretary of the Fascist Party in December 1931 and stepped down in October 1939. Looking to Nazi Germany as a model, he came up with some of the more flamboyant fascist symbolic actions, such as the Roman salute and the cult of the Duce. At some point in the 1930s even Mussolini complained that Starace's penchant for excessive "fascistifying" was making him appear foolish.[101] Giuseppe Bottai, coauthor of the Labor Charter, occupant of many posts within the upper echelons of the state ministries, and an architect of fascist cultural policy, noted in his diary that Starace was ultimately dismissed because he had permitted the party to become obsessed with style at the expense of a spirit of "dynamic association."[102]

But to ascribe the proliferation of fascist public spectacle to the fanaticism of Starace is to attenuate the extent to which it was part of the fabric of the fascist cultural project. Unlike Stalinist Russia and Nazi Germany, Italy had no single bureau of spectacle or government subcommittee of ritual events. Starace notwithstanding, fascist spectacle sprang from a general agreement among fascist elites, including Mussolini, that the state needed to theatricalize everyday life. Although patterns of ritual action clearly existed, much of the Italian spectacle was in a continual state of improvisation—commedia dell'arte as opposed to high theater. As in all improvisation, its content played with the available cultural schemata, but its timing frequently reacted to national policy priorities and international exigencies. The symbolic requisites of fascist youth organizations generated a portion of fascist public spectacles, principally sporting events; fascist appropriations of preexisting holidays engendered other spectacle events; and ritual surrounding the annual commemoration of the March on Rome was due to regime fabrication. Many public events were held in response to specific regime policy initiatives. Demographic policy elevated Mother's Day to an occasion of public ceremony, for example, and the war in Ethiopia and the journeys of Mussolini prompted a series of local and national public ritual events.

---

[99] The best available account of the career of Turati appears in Alice Kelikian, *Town and Country under Fascism: The Transformation of Brescia, 1915–1926* (New York: Oxford University Press, 1986), 127–206.

[100] Mack Smith, *Mussolini*, 203–5.

[101] On Starace and his propagandist activities, see Guido Nozzoli, *I ras del regime* (Milan: Bompiani, 1972), 85–102.

[102] *Vent'anni e un giorno* (Rome: Garzanti, 1949), 146.

The landscape of Italy provided a natural resource for Italian public ritual.[103] The Italian cityscape was a stage that served as a political resource for the regime. Every Italian city has a central piazza and a central road leading to it from the train station. Rome, with its residues of Italian history dating from antiquity, was replete with cultural monuments and public spaces that served as backdrops for fascist ritual events. The geographical size of Italy also aided the proliferation of fascist ritual. The trains did more than run on time—they carried the bodies, the ritual actors, from one part of Italy to another, from one event to another. Trains are as central to the story of fascist political ritual as ideology; they were a necessary infrastructure for Italian public spectacle. The small distances between Italian cities made it possible to import fascist bodies within hours.

The regime established "rules for ritual" that specified the order of parades, the protocols for wearing the fascist uniform, and the reception of Mussolini. These rules were variations of existing military and diplomatic protocols. An additional set of protocols developed around the ringing of bells, the illumination of public buildings, and the displaying of the flag.[104] In 1926, the regime began to develop a legal framework around public spectacle. Public manifestations were limited to "science, intellectualism, benevolence, sport, and commemorations of honor."[105] Religious functions and accidental gatherings of crowds were left under the Ministry of Public Security. All other events were relegated to the local prefects, who were to issue permits only for events that aggrandized the new Italian state. The Fascist Party exerted the greatest power on the local level, where it had a much more direct hand in the planning of ritual events. Prefects from every province in Italy were charged with establishing a local calendar of ritual activities and sending a monthly report to the president of the Council of Ministers. The December 1931 report from Bologna provides an example.[106] The prefect requested permission for eight events, including a soccer match, a visit of the bishop of the diocese, a convention of artisans, and an official funeral service in honor of Mussolini's brother Arnaldo.

The regime expended a great deal of effort in revivifying traditional holi-

---

[103] Scholars are beginning to turn their attention to the social and political uses of public space. See, for example, Henri Lefebvre, *The Production of Space*, trans. Donald Nicholson-Smith (London: Blackwell, 1984), and the essays in *The Power of Place: Bringing Together Geographical and Sociological Imaginations*, ed. John A. Agnew and James S. Duncan (Winchester, Mass.: Unwin Hyman, 1989), esp. Edward Muir and Ronald F. E. Weissman, "Social and Symbolic Places in Renaissance Venice and Florence," 81–103.

[104] See *Consuetudini di cerimoniale*, ed. F. C. (Rome: Tipografico Luigi Proja, 1936).

[105] Memo, 23 August 1926, Council of Ministers, "Disciplina e coordinamento delle pubbliche maanifestazioni," ACS, PCM 1926 1.3–5 (1.3.3. 1710).

[106] R. Prefettura della Provincia di Bologna, Prospetto delle pubbliche manifestazioni autorizzate dal Prefetto durante il mese di 31 dicembre 1931-X, ACS, PCM 1931-33, 339/348.

days and fairs and putting a fascist stamp on them. The cultural residue of centuries left three categories of holidays that the regime had to incorporate or abolish: national and religious holidays that Italians had celebrated for years, longstanding religious festivals, and occasional events such as public funerals. Emulating the French Revolution, the fascist regime began its history in 1922. Starting in 1926, the fascist year as well as the standard date—for example, 1930 A. VIII—appeared on all publications and official correspondence.[107]

The regime redesigned the official calendar of holidays four times between 1923 and 1940.[108] The struggle over the public holiday calendar predated fascism. From 1913, the central state actively sought to standardize secular and religious holidays. The debates over what was in and what was out culminated in April 1922—six months before Mussolini came to power—when the state officially sanctioned May 1, the socialist labor day. Three months after assuming power, the fascists outlawed the socialist holiday and replaced it with April 21, the date of the Birth of Rome and the new fascist labor day.[109] The conflict between giving official sanction to May 1 or April 21 as labor day was relatively easy. for the regime to resolve by fiat.

The regime was on much shakier terrain when it came into conflict with its principal competitor for ritual time, the Catholic Church. In theory, the holiday calendar could expand infinitely; the problem was that attendance at parades and ceremonies meant time off from work. The Catholic holidays also required time off from work to attend Mass. The issue of free time for public and religious celebration placed the regime in direct opposition to its own labor unions. It was difficult to justify paying workers to attend fascist rituals. Yet if workers were not paid, it was unlikely that they would be enthusiastic about fascist holidays that denied them income in economically harsh times.[110]

Time was not the only domain in which church and regime came into conflict over holiday space. The church was vociferously concerned with which holidays were celebrated and which were not. For example, beginning in 1925, the church began to lobby to include the feast of Saint Joseph in the official holiday calendar. The church argued that Saint Joseph, the carpenter and reputed stepfather of Christ, was a worker who could serve as a model for the new corporativist Italian worker. On a less spiritual note,

[107] Ezio Bonomi and Arnaldo Caro, *Celebrazioni patriottiche fasciste religiose* (Milan: Nuova Italia, n.d.).

[108] *ACS, PCM* 1937–39 3.3.3/f. 1558, sf. 8, "Pro-Memoria," summarizes the fascist legislation on holidays.

[109] See "Comunicato per Stafani e per la stampa," *ACS, PCM* 1923 2.4.1/f. 1123.

[110] These debates played themselves out differently in the public and private sector. Productivity was not an issue in the public sector of state bureaucracy.

Catholic Action's emissary reminded the regime that Catholics commanded votes and were "believing and practicing laborers" and that it might be useful to accommodate them. The church maintained that the civil and religious holiday calendar required coordination. The church won this round, as the 1929 Concordat included official state recognition of ten Catholic holidays, including the feast of Saint Joseph on March 19.[111]

The commemoration of the "Statuto," celebrated annually on September 20, was also of concern to the church. The Statuto, an Italian national holiday, commemorated the day that Italian troops liberated Rome from the French and celebrated the consolidation of Italy as a single geographical unit with Rome as its capital. The first "march on Rome" drove the pope into the Vatican and precipitated the "Roman question." In a letter dated August 28, 1930, written to Dino Grandi, the Minister of Foreign Affairs (the Concordat made the Vatican an independent political territory), the papal nuncio stated that the pope viewed "the celebration of the 20th of September as an offense to the Holy See and as a consequence to Catholics of Italy and the world, and a bowing to the few more or less veiled anticlericals who still exist in Italy."[112] The nuncio held that the continued celebration of the holiday gave "displeasure" and "offense" to the Holy See, which viewed the events of 1870 as a "violation" of its rights. By September 30, a note to Mussolini on stationery from the president of the Council of Ministers revealed that the regime was considering the nuncio's request to eliminate the holiday. The memorandum argued that the regime ought to give official sanction to holidays on a "case by case" basis and noted that the commemoration of the Founding of the Fascists might be a suitable replacement for the Statuto.

On December 10, 1930, a new law to regulate holidays was presented to the Chamber of Deputies. The law aimed "to standardize the celebration of dates that are already celebrated by tradition and custom, not only in the entire territory of the Kingdom, but everywhere groups of Italians wish to maintain living ties to the Patria and Fascism."[113] February 11, the official date of the Conciliation, replaced the celebration of the Statuto. The law articulated the new union of church and state to justify its elimination of the Statuto, which it described as "divisive." The Conciliation was a more

---

[111] I draw my narrative from a letter written in 1928 by the head of Italian Catholic Action to Mussolini and the Ministry of Corporations (ACS, PCM 1937–39 3.3.3/f. 1558, sf. 1-1), and the text of the Concordat, Gazzetta Ufficiale del Regno D'Italia- n. 130 (Straordinario) (ACS, PCM 1937–39 3.3.3/f. 1558, sf. 1-3).

[112] ACS, PCM 1937–39 3.3.3/f. 1558, sf. 1-1.

[113] Disegno di Legge, Modificazione dell'elenco delle feste nazionali, dei giorni festivi a tutti gli effetti civili e delle solennita civili, Presentata alla Presidenza il 10 dicembre 1930, Atti Parliamentari, Camera dei Deputati, N. 717-a., ACS, PCM 1937–39 3.3.3/f. 1558, sf. 1-1.

appropriate holiday, because it was a "work of the highest spiritual and political importance and everlasting glory of two great intellects, Benito Mussolini and Pius XI, which sanctions a united national territory and consecrates a spiritual and moral unity, worthy of elevation to civil celebration, full of happy recognition on the part of the Holy See that Rome is the capital of Italy!" The holiday calendar established in 1930 remained, for the most part, unchanged until 1941, when the war effort required a reduction in holidays. The thirteen officially acknowledged Catholic holidays, in addition to the recognition of every Sunday, suggested that the church had won. Closer inspection of the dates of civil and national holidays, however, reveals that many were chosen in close proximity to Catholic holidays, intensifying rather than resolving the conflict between church and state, Catholicism and fascism, for ritual space and the Italian private self.

Culture is context; history is trajectory. Italy in 1922 was a bloated bureaucracy with weak national traditions and an undereducated and quasi-literate population that defined its private self in terms of family, region, and a popular culture of Roman Catholicism. On this landscape, the regime embarked on a course of rewriting the rules of the cultural game. New corporativist men and women would define their fascist selves in labor—the labor of the market and the labor of biological reproduction—and submerge themselves in the state. Fascist public ritual dramatized in the public piazzas of Italy the new political community and new Italian self.

   In order to transcend mere rhetorical formulations, fascism needed to appropriate family and religion and reinvent them in the service of the regime. The regime engaged the resources of the state, created a fascist party, and mobilized public space and civil law to reinvent and renarrate the Italian past and create a fascist future. Public political ritual dramatized the tension between past and present, history and culture. We now turn to an analysis of those rituals to examine how they attempted to create a new fascist and Italian nation-state—a new identity.

CHAPTER 3

Convergence and Commemoration: Reenacting the March on Rome

The Iconography of Emotion

On the morning of October 29, 1923, the state suspended public and private enterprise in Bologna. Stores and businesses closed, public transportation stopped, and the ubiquitous, ever open Italian cafes did not serve customers. The "splendid" autumn sunlight merged with flags and banners that "throbbed" with excitement in the breeze. Commerce ceased in celebration of a new Italian public holiday, the first anniversary of the March on Rome.[1] A year or two earlier, violence and armed skirmishes had dominated the Bolognese landscape. The capital of Emilia-Romagna, a rich agricultural area in central Italy, Bologna was the seat of the oldest university in Europe and the strongest socialist movement in Italy. In Bologna, tradition and modernity met and engaged in bloody conflict.[2]

Architecturally dominated by red terra-cotta roofs and red brick, Bologna was figuratively red as well. The association of the physical image of the city with socialist political activities was not lost on the fascist regime and the planners of the first anniversary commemorations. An emerging fascist mythology reconstructed the events of October 1922 that brought Benito Mussolini to power as prime minister and made Italian fascism a legitimate party within the Italian state in terms of a revolutionary march on the Italian

---

[1] *Il Resto del Carlino* (Bologna), 24–30 October 1923.

[2] See Anthony L. Cardoza, *Agrarian Elites and Italian Fascism: The Province of Bologna, 1901–1926* (Princeton: Princeton University Press, 1982), and Adrian Lyttelton, *The Seizure of Power: Fascism in Italy, 1919–1929* (rpt., Princeton: Princeton University Press, 1987), 57–61; on the contingent nature of fascist violence, see Adrian Lyttelton, "Causa e caratteristiche della violenza fascista: Fattori costanti e fattori congiunturali," in *Bologna 1920: Le origini del fascismo*, ed. Luciano Casali (Bologna: Cappelli, 1982), 33–55.

capital. In 1922, the fascist squads bypassed Bologna on their route to Rome, yet in 1923, Bologna merited an entire day of celebratory activities owing to its role in fascism's overall march to power.

On October 28, the day before the celebrations, an editorial on the first page of *Il Resto del Carlino*, the Bolognese daily newspaper, noted, "It is not without clear significance that tomorrow the President will inaugurate the Bolognese Fascist House [Casa del Fascio]." Bolognese fascism had "struggl[ed]" against a "grotesque reformist subversion" that was "fatally romantic and voluntaristic" and had permeated "working class organization." With the fascist "conquest of power" and the emergence of the "new State," Bolognese fascists needed their own meeting place for "fraternization," "education," "conviviality," and "study." Fascists who were "first" in "action" would now "address their energies to tranquil works of reconstruction and above all to the education of the spirit."[3]

The Bologna celebrations dramatized that the fascists had taken over the city and were the first steps in the public "education of the spirit" that would create the new fascist political community. *Il Resto del Carlino*'s accounts of the spectacle, written in the charged and emotive style that dominated Italian melodramatic prose, anthropomorphized Bologna. The city as well as the crowds waited "expectantly" for Mussolini, who was scheduled to arrive at nine-thirty on the morning of the celebration. The wait was "fervid" and "wrenchingly full of jubilation and enthusiasm." "Vain words" were inadequate to convey the "heat and rhythm of the grand manifestation." Few times in its history had Bologna demonstrated such "a superb and fascinating spectacle of vitality." The "anxious" city "dressed" itself in anticipation of Mussolini's arrival. Every corner, piazza, and road prepared "feverishly." Festoons of greenery and Italian flags were hung from all the balconies of the city. Even the shops that were closed on the day of the event took the opportunity to redesign their windows to demonstrate to passing foreigners that Italy was the land of "good taste and riches." Bologna would welcome Mussolini as an "apostle and conqueror," and he would "feel" in the "delirious greeting of the multitude" the "throbbing" and "maternal passion" rising from the "earth of his Emilia . . . the profound heart of Italy."[4]

On the day of the ceremony, the local notables and throngs of fascist squads moved with "rigorous precision" to the train station to await Mus-

---

[3] "Domani," *Il Resto del Carlino*, 28 October 1923, 1. The Case del Fascio were direct appropriations of the socialists' Case del Lavoro, Labor Houses, which were voluntary associations of workers.

[4] "Il primo saluto di Bologna al Duce," *Il Resto del Carlino*, 30 October 1923, 1. Mussolini was born in the commune of Predappio in the region of Emilia-Romagna.

solini.[5] Citizens, watching from sidewalks, windows, and balconies, cheered as troops and flags passed. The "rigorous precision" was highly constructed given that the railroads carried fascist squads from other parts of Emilia to participate in the commemorative events and many had never been to Bologna. The main road to the train station, the Via Indipendenza, was not sufficiently large to hold the throngs, and the squads spilled over to neighboring streets. The citizenry strained to view the ceremonies from the sidelines of the parade route; the events themselves were restricted to ticket holders who usually were local fascists and their families.

The city "dressed" the train station for the occasion with an exterior mural of the March on Rome and decorated the piazza in front of the station with flags, disks with fascist iconography, ornamental plants, and laurel wreaths. At nine-twenty-five, the presidential train arrived; the band played "Giovinezza," the fascist anthem; a guard of honor presented arms; and Mussolini, with an entourage of fascist generals and high-ranking Fascist Party members, stepped off the train. Roman salutes and "resounding applause" greeted Mussolini, and a five-year-old girl presented him with a bouquet of flowers. Mussolini left the station and began the march down the Via Indipendenza, which was "swarming with an anxious crowd." The fascist spectacle of commemoration began: "The imposing line-up of the Militia and the Syndacates offered an unforgettable spectacle. From the balconies an uninterrupted storm of flowers brought the gentle homage of the women of Bologna to the Duce."[6]

Il Resto del Carlino's accounts used the language of feeling to create an iconography of emotion: vivid mental pictorial images drawn from the repertoire of Italian cultural schemata. The editorial writers of *Il Resto del Carlino*, a newspaper with distinctly fascist sympathies, wanted their readers to feel excitement and anticipation. Their purple prose evoked the charged language of standard Italian melodrama: the words "throbbing" and "delirious" appeared repeatedly. Antithetical images of women as mothers and mistresses dominated the text. The city assumed the feminine aspect of a woman waiting for a lover, a familiar and congenial image in Italian cultural discourse. The Emilian earth exuded "maternal passion." The language of sexuality evoked the dual and contradictory aspects of fascism and its cadres of supporters. The fascists were men of tradition who beat back the "subversive" socialists and defended the established order—they saved the mother and family; they were also virile, romantic men of action who conquered women and cities with the same élan.

If we rewrite the newspaper narrative in stark analytic prose, a different story emerges. Bologna shut down until three-thirty in the afternoon, and

---

[5] Ibid.
[6] "Il primo saluto di Bologna al Duce," 1.

the events were in the center. The organizers of the event denied the public access to all but the parade, limiting the viewing of the spectacle to residents of the apartments over the shops on the parade route. The majority of Bologna's citizens inhabited peripheral neighborhoods, and with public transportation halted, incentive would have been low to attend. In addition, the city was filled with troops that were imported from other parts of Italy for the occasion, and the normal response would have been to stay away. The women who participated were the mothers and widows of the "fallen for the revolution," and their appearances at these events were in exchange for their widows' and family pensions and not necessarily due to an outpouring of fascist emotion. Mistresses and lovers were kept out of sight.

Il Resto del Carlino's narrative style was as much Italian as it was fascist. The iconography of emotion that colored journalistic accounts suggests the disjuncture between the language of feeling and the emotions that the commemorative events generated. My "rewriting" points to the tension between reportage and experience, discourse and action, representations of power and realities of power that any study of politics and culture must address. *Il Resto del Carlino*'s narrative was as much a cultural fantasy as the March on Rome was a political fantasy. How likely was it that "delirious" crowds "palpitated" with emotion in anticipation of Mussolini's arrival and "breathlessly" participated in ritual events? The subtext beneath the charged prose is revealing. The choice of Bologna as a site sent a clear message to its citizens as to who had won and who had lost in the battles between socialists and fascists only three years earlier. Conversely, the socialists did not go away, and there must have been subversive elements lurking in Bologna on that sunny October day.

The first anniversary commemoration of the March on Rome was a starting point in the creation of the communities of feeling that aimed to generate solidarity with the regime. But in 1923, the fascist cultural project was in its infancy, and emotion, except among the most committed, was pure fabrication. The first anniversary events established the parameters of commemoration as a ritual genre. Focusing on the recent past, the re-creation of the March on Rome was among the first public and ritualized exercises in fascist history making. This chapter explores the design and performance of that commemoration and the repertoire of cultural practices and resources on which it drew.

The Myth of the Founding Event

Burckhardt described the Italian Renaissance state, the new modern state, as the "outcome of reflection and calculation, the State as work of art."[7] The nation-state that the fascist regime attempted to craft from the nineteenth-

---

[7] Jacob Burckhardt, *The Civilization of the Renaissance in Italy*, vol. 1 (New York: Harper, 1958), 22.

century Italian bourgeois state aimed at similar artistry. The changing social and ideological structures of fifteenth-century Italy provided the raw material of the Renaissance state, just as the Tuscan landscape provided the marble for Renaissance sculpture. But the fascist state had limited social material on which to draw, and it sought to capture the imagination of a population that in the main had no compelling economic or social reasons to acquiesce.

The first "work of art" the fascist regime created was the reinvention of the events of October 27 and 28, 1922, as the "March on Rome." The fiction of the March, like all political myth, represented the tension between revolutionary aspiration and political possibility which the fascist movement confronted as it took over the reins of government.[8] Fascism conceived of itself as revolutionary, yet the fascist takeover of the Italian state did not meet the minimum requirements of a coup d'état: a rapid seizure of the state by an outside group.[9] The king asked Benito Mussolini to become prime minister and to form a government. Technically, there was an orderly and legitimate transfer of power that Mussolini and his fascist squads embellished with the spectacle of the March. The single critical account of the first-anniversary commemorations in the major Italian newspapers came from La Stampa, the liberal Turinese paper, which framed its criticism in terms of the regime's confusion of myth and history.[10] La Stampa's critique centered on the fact that the regime constructed itself as having saved Italy from social "decomposition," a fascist code word for socialism. According to La Stampa, the threat of socialism ended in Italy in 1920, and what the fascists saved Italy from, if one could speak of salvation, was the chaos of the inefficient liberal regime. La Stampa argued, "To speak in 1921–22 of an Italy in decomposition, due to bolshevism, truly would suggest taking too much audacious license with history, or with one of its eyes, chronology."[11]

Popular culture reinforced the image of pre-fascist Italy as a cauldron of socialist violence and chaos. Mario Carli's 1930 propagandist novel Mus-

[8] For an anthropological discussion of the political meaning of the myth of a founding revolutionary event, see Victor Turner, "Hidalgo: History as Social Drama," in Dramas, Fields, and Metaphors (Ithaca: Cornell University Press, 1974), 98–155.
[9] Whether or not the fascist regime effected social change is a question historians are beginning to confront as they acknowledge the continuities between the fascist period and the democratic state that followed. For a slightly ironic account that glosses over the issue of violence in the fascist "revolution," see Curzio Malaparte, Coup d'Etat: The Technique of Revolution, trans. Sylvia Saunders (New York: Dutton, 1932), 175–220.
[10] "Mito e storia," La Stampa (Turin), 30 October 1923, 1. La Stampa's criticism of the regime was not surprising, as Turin was a center of Italian socialism. Il Duce's reception in Turin, the day before the first anniversary commemorations began, was so cold that Mussolini canceled his appearance in Cremona on October 27. For a description of Mussolini's visit to Turin on October 25, 1923 and its place in the historical memory of the city, see Luisa Passerini, Torino operaia e fascismo (Rome: Laterza, 1984), 228–33.
[11] "Mito e storia," 1.

solini's Italian (*L'italiano di Mussolini*) conjures up the image of Italy in chaos in its opening pages. Falco, the hero, welcomes his uncle back to Italy after an absence of several years. The uncle, who has been in America, muses that the Italy he left was a land of "strikes, disorder, acts of sabotage, crime."[12] Falco agrees and argues that pre-fascist Italy could be defined as a "cradle of anarchy," where

> the trains either did not part, or, if they parted, one did not know if and when they would arrive at their destination; public services in the most distressing disorder did not function; strikes, with related closing of stores, were improvised every day; industries shut down; vagabonds and panhandlers were the norm on the streets; the piazza ruled the palace with blackmail and usurpation; the governments permitted all criminal *experiments* from the occupation of the factories to the assault on shops; numbers surpassed reason, demonstrating in practice how a communist regime would have betrayed the moral and intellectual values of the nation; from the breast of heroes they tore away war decorations, stepping on them as though they were signs of ignominy; they hit the mutilated, they sneered at the wounded, they provoked patriots with political innuendo. In four years, the situation has reversed itself: order, labor, discipline, Patria, sacrifice, duty: these are the living formulas. The State dominates the parts. In the fields and in the offices they produce singing. The right to strike and the class struggle have been relegated to the formulas of utopia.[13]

Until 1914, Mussolini himself had been a socialist and was part of the depravity that fascism reputedly deplored. He was the editor of the socialist newspaper *L'Avanti* and supported its policy of neutrality in the war. In 1914, he suddenly changed his mind on the issue of intervention (a habit that characterized his political style), abruptly quit *L'Avanti*, and founded his own newspaper, *Il Popolo d'Italia*, financed by Milanese industrialists. Italy was torn by labor strife in the years following World War I, and there was a continuous turnover of prime ministers as different political factions attempted to rule the country.

In this climate of instability, numerous extraparliamentary groups emerged. Among them were the Fighting Fascists (Fasci di Combattimento), a group of nationalists, war veterans, futurists, and university students. Their desire to see Italy take its rightful place in the international order and a romantic

---

[12] Mario Carli, *L'Italiano di Mussolini* (Milan: Mondadori, 1930), 27. Carli was a futurist, *squadrista*, and regime publicist who wrote numerous works on the fascist ethos and style. See Vanna Gazzola Stacchini, "Mille eroi da leggenda," in *I best seller del Ventennio: Il regime e il libro di massa*, ed. Gigliola De Donato and Vanna Gazzola Stacchini (Rome: Riuniti, 1991), 461–77, 481–85, 675–77.

[13] *L'Italiano*, 29–30.

conception of action held this polyglot group together. The Fighting Fascists directed their public anger at the socialist policy of noninterventionism, to which they attributed the Italian defeat at the Battle of Caporetto.

Mussolini recognized this agglomeration of malcontents as a free-floating political force to which he could provide leadership and organization. In 1919, he founded the Fascist Party in Milan and assimilated the Fighting Fascists. Mussolini ran a Fascist Party slate for office in the same year, and it met a crushing defeat. He spent the years between 1919 and 1922 building his fledgling movement by encouraging its rowdier elements, the provincial war veterans, and waiting for the appropriate moment to acquire political power for himself. He used *Il Popolo d'Italia* as a forum to express his views on national and international events and to keep fascist "intellectuals" out of the electoral arena, where they had proved in the 1919 election to be of little use. By the summer and fall of 1922, labor unrest had come to a halt in Italy and the turnover of prime ministers was the most urgent national problem. Mussolini seized the moment to persuade the king to appoint him to the Council of Ministers and became part of the inner circle of rule. He began simultaneous negotiations with the king, the ousted liberal prime minister Giovanni Giolitti, and leaders of fascist squads. With the king and Giolitti, Mussolini discussed becoming part of the cabinet; with the fascist squad leaders, he discussed taking over the state.

Historical accounts are vague as to the details of what happened during the four days in 1922 between October 28 and October 31 that brought Mussolini and fascism to power.[14] Historians have described the March as a "colossal bluff" and a "campaign of psychological warfare."[15] The Italian government fell into crisis in October 1922, and it appeared that there would be no government at all. Mussolini began acting on both fronts. He negotiated with the king and told the fascist generals to prepare to march; he told neither side that he was negotiating with the other. On the morning of October 27, when Prime Minister Luigi Facta's coalition government fell apart, Mussolini gave the order to prepare for a state takeover. The fascists seized the post offices, telegraph lines, and all communication mechanisms in the key Italian cities of Milan, Florence, Perugia, and Rome. No news circulated except the news Mussolini released. Fascist forces were relatively small and no match for the Italian army or the police, both of which were

---

[14] Lyttelton, *Seizure of Power*, is the standard account in English; Renzo De Felice, *Mussolini il fascista: I. La conquista del potere, 1921–1925* (Turin: Einaudi, 1966), provides a dated but still useful history in Italian. Other accounts are Gaetano Salvemini, *The Origins of Fascism in Italy*, ed. Roberto Vivarelli (New York: Harper and Row, 1973), and Roberto Vivarelli, *Storia delle origini del fascismo: L'Italia dalla grande guerra alla marcia su Roma*, vol. 2 (Bologna: Il Mulino, 1991).

[15] Lyttelton, *Seizure of Power*, 85; Alexander DeGrand, *Italian Fascism: Its Origins and Developments* (Lincoln: University of Nebraska Press, 1989), 36.

loyal to the king. The fascists were in no position to seize much more than communication lines, but this proved sufficient. Mussolini announced, and it was reported in *Il Popolo d'Italia*, that he had three hundred thousand armed fascists at his command ready to march on Rome. In reality, there were fewer than thirty thousand.

Sometime during the night of October 28, the king asked Mussolini to form a government. Facta resigned. Mussolini accepted the king's offer and began to prepare for the March on Rome. Mussolini obtained more than he had originally asked for, and all historical accounts agree that it was the king's decision that finally brought Mussolini to power, although no account is quite certain as to why the king decided as he did. He too may have been persuaded of the existence of the three hundred thousand fascists ready to march. The March on Rome gave the fascist regime its first photo opportunity:

But the fascist leader [Mussolini] was not satisfied with something so unspectacular as a royal appointment. He needed to develop the myth of a march on Rome by 300,000 armed fascists to enforce an "ultimatum" he had given to the king. . . . His [Mussolini's] fascist squads did not arrive in Rome until twenty-four hours after he had been asked to form a government and only after General Pugliese had orders to let them through. But the photographers were waiting to picture their arrival and the myth was launched of fascism winning power by armed insurrection after a civil war and the loss of 3,000 men. These fictitious 3,000 "fascist martyrs" soon took their place in the government-sponsored history books.[16]

The mothers and the widows of the fictitious three thousand would be called on for the next twenty years to appear at the Tomb of the Unknown Soldier to commemorate the March. Mussolini took the night train from Milan to Rome and got off at a stop outside the city. He marched into Rome after a full night of sleep.

Fascist History Making

The story of the March became grist for fascist propaganda mills. Eager provincial publicists wrote tracts such as "The Two Marches on Rome: Julius Caesar and Benito Mussolini."[17] The National Fascist Party manual, advertising itself as "accessible to all and containing what is indispensable to

---

[16] Denis Mack Smith, *Mussolini* (London: Granada, 1981), 63–64.
[17] Tito Vezio, "Le due marce su Roma: Giulio Cesare e Benito Mussolini," *Mussolinia* 1 (1923): 5–14.

know about our Revolution, the Party, the Regime, [and] Mussolini's state," published in catechism style the following questions and answers on the March.

Question: How can one define the March on Rome?

Answer: The March on Rome was a political revolt against central government forces that were incapable, and that let the authority of the State decline and threatened to stop Italy on the road to its greatest development.

Question: What was the historical import of the fascist Revolution?

Answer: The historical import of the fascist Revolution was to renew the Italian people, making them united, harmonious, disciplined for the greatness and imperial potency of the Patria.[18]

In a pamphlet entitled *What Every Young Laborer Ought to Know: Answers to 74 Questions*, published by the Fascist Confederation of Industrial Laborers, workers learned that "socialism had become heedless of labor's interests" and that the "March on Rome" signaled the "conquest of power" when the king authorized Mussolini to "reconsecrate the victory" of World War I.[19]

In addition to the numerous propaganda works directed toward an Italian audience, the regime supported the production of literature meant for international consumption, such as Mussolini's *My Autobiography*; Margherita Sarfatti's *Dux*, a biography of Mussolini; and Luigi Villari's *The Awakening of Italy*, which Gaetano Salvemini described as a "Fascist 'Vulgate,'" referring to the fourth-century edition of the Bible, the Latin Vulgate, aimed at the popular classes.[20] In his autobiography, Mussolini described his ascent to

[18] PNF, *Il primo e secondo libro del fascista*, preface, 29.

[19] "Cio che il giovane lavoratore deve sapere," 6–7 in ACS, PNF, MRF, 89.151.3.

[20] According to Salvemini (*Origins of Fascism*), *The Awakening of Italy* reached a large international audience, in part because of the *Encyclopedia Britannica*'s role in its marketing. He notes: "To credit the Fascist regime with 'bringing order out of the Chaos,' all the journalists affiliated with Fascist propaganda described the postwar crisis in the most appalling colors. A book soon embodied the Fascist version, Signor Villari's *Awakening of Italy*. Signor Villari did not need to worry about, or waste time on, conscientious and tiresome research and documentation. He only needed as rapidly as possible to put on the market a book which might become a handy source of information for whoever wanted to form an idea of Italian affairs, and *Awakening of Italy*, published at the beginning of 1924, met such a need and constituted what might be called the Fascist 'Vulgate.' Then the publishers of the *Encyclopedia Britannica* put their concern at Mussolini's service, and Signor Villari rehashed his 'Vulgate' in the 1926 supplement (II, 558–71) and in the 1929 and 1938 editions of the

power as a world historical event that would forever change the course of Italian history. The autobiography repeatedly emphasized the revolutionary character of the new regime. In the chapter "Thus We Took Rome," Mussolini began, "And now we were on the eve of the historic march on the Eternal City."[21] Mussolini ran the March with the help of four paramilitary leaders—Emilio De Bono, Cesare Maria De Vecchi, Italo Balbo, and Michele Bianchi—who formed the National Directorate of the Fascist Party. Ever conscious of Roman imagery, Mussolini referred to this group as the "Quadrumvirate," and they were paraded out on celebratory occasions thereafter.

Mussolini invoked spatial images to describe the preparations for the march: "Trusted Fascist messengers wove webs like scurrying spiders." The image of spiderwebs expanding over the Italian peninsula suggests how space contributed to the March as bluff. Mussolini chose Perugia as fascist command headquarters because "many roads flow to [Perugia] from which it is easy to reach Rome."[22] The logistics of the March depended on the quartering of fascist troops to the north, south, and east of Rome, so that they could march into the capital from all directions.

Detachments of Fascisti were to march along the Tyrrhenian Sea, toward Rome, led by chiefs, all of them brave former officers. The same movement was to take place on the Adriatic side, from which direction was to be launched on Rome the strength of the low Romagna, March, and Abruzzi districts. . . . From middle Italy the squadrons already mobilized for the meeting at Naples were also to be directed upon Rome.[23]

Evolving narratives of the March suggested solid blocs of fascists converging from all points on the Roman center. In *The Awakening of Italy*, Luigi Villari followed Mussolini's lead and described the March as an appropriation of Italian space. In two pages, he minutely outlined the train stops along the way to Rome and specified which gates of the city the particular squadrons would enter—details of the landscape that would be familiar to some Roman natives and maybe a few members of the city planning commission. The image of fascist squads pouring into Rome through all its gates

---

Encyclopedia. Thus the Fascist version reached an immense public in all countries and became daily bread of any college professor who wanted, without any headaches, to become an 'expert' in Italian recent history" (44n).

[21] Benito Mussolini, *My Autobiography*, trans. Richard Washburn Child (New York: Scribner's, 1928), 173.

[22] Ibid., 175.

[23] Ibid., 174.

is the most salient descriptive feature of Villari's account.[24] The imagery of the spatial convergence is as much a part of the story as the March itself. Ten years afterward, a display prepared for the Exhibition of the Fascist Revolution (Mostra della Rivoluzione Fascista) prominently featured a map of the March with all the troops converging on Rome (see Figure 1).

Figure 1. Itinerary of the March on Rome. Mussolini's commemorative pilgrimage of 1923 is superimposed. Itinerario della Marcia su Roma, *ACS, PNF, MRF,* b. 89, f. 491.

[24] Luigi Villari, *The Awakening of Italy: The Fascist Regeneration* (New York: George H. Doran, n.d.), 179–81.

An essential component of the story of the fascist revolution was that in contrast to other revolutions, such as the French, it was bloodless. The Roman nationalist daily, *La Tribuna*, did not hesitate to make this comparison and attack liberalism in the process. A front-page article proclaimed that the fascist revolution represented a unity of doctrine and action which shaped the "force of its passion," whereas "the excesses of the French Revolution were the products of the contradictions between ideas and sentiments, between the methods and ends of the revolutionaries. The ideas were new but the sentiments were old. The ends were liberal but the methods were tyrannical." Fascism gave Italy a "government," and not a "Committee of Public Safety."[25] This fascist fiction belied the violence directed against socialists that occurred in the north in the years before October 1922. It also suggested that the fascists took liberties with the narrative of events when they continually referred to the "three thousand martyrs" for the revolution. October 30, 1922, yielded only skirmishes. The March was kept deliberately peaceful. Mussolini disbanded the fascist squads and ordered them to leave Rome soon after their imposing entrance. Before leaving, the squads participated in the first official ritual act of fascism.

> The immense cortege first went to pay its tribute to the tomb of the Unknown Soldier on the monument to Victor Emmanuele; it then marched up the Via Nazionale, and the Via 24 Maggio to the Quirinale to pay homage to the King. The beautiful piazza was thronged with people, and every window and roof black with spectators. The King appeared at the balcony. . . . Slowly the hundred thousand Black Shirts . . . marched past the King, whom they saluted in ancient Roman style, the right arm outstretched. . . . From the Quirinale, the Fascisti went to the Villa Borghese, where they were reviewed by Mussolini.[26]

The visit to the Tomb of the Unknown Soldier, the parade through the streets, the act of paying homage to the king set the pattern for action and reenactment that would dominate future commemorations of the March. It also suggested how future fascist spectacle would incorporate public space and social landscape.

Redesigning the March on Rome

The 1922 March was political fiction. Its reenactment in 1923 introduced the commemorative ritual genre to the Italian citizenry, a genre Italians

[25] Rastignac, "28 ottobre," *La Tribuna* (Rome), 28 October 1923, 1.
[26] Villari, *Awakening*, 182.

would experience repeatedly in the ensuing years. The first anniversary com-memoration, an instance of the numerous holidays and spectacles that would become part of daily life in fascist Italy, was a pastiche created from the cultural archives of Roman Catholic liturgy, military protocol, and the remnants of working-class organization.

Mussolini wanted fascism as ideology to transcend previously existing po-litical categories. In his *Autobiography*, he discussed, somewhat ingenuously, the problems he confronted as he tried to define the new fascist political community.

> It was necessary to imagine a wholly new political conception, adequate to the living reality of the twentieth century, overcoming at the same time the ideological worship of liberalism, the limited and finally the violently Uto-pian spirit of Bolshevism.
>
> In a word, I felt the deep necessity of an original conception capable of placing in a new period of history a more fruitful rhythm of human life. . . .
>
> . . . This was my problem—to find the way, to find the moment, to find the form.[27]

The Doctrine of Fascism articulated the solution to Mussolini's problem. The "form" Mussolini found was devoid of content. Fascism was a "general atti-tude towards life" based on a "spiritual" idea, a "creed."[28] Fascism as a style of behavior dominated official discussion of fascist public ritual.

A few days before the first anniversary commemorations began, Mar-gherita Sarfatti, Mussolini's biographer, paramour, and principal consultant on art, published a lengthy article in *Il Popolo d'Italia* on aesthetics and the new fascist regime.[29] Sarfatti wrote in the style of the educated upper middle class to which she belonged. Yet her prose was charged with the same sense of emotion that characterized the more mundane journalistic outpourings. Pointing to the ineffable quality of fascist public ritual, she began, "Where are certain artistic ideas born? Who can speak of their mysterious genesis?" She drew an explicit parallel between works of art and the regime as work of art: "But how were those events that are the true art of Fascism, the beauty of its exterior performances—I would dare to say, its rituals, part new and antique, part simple and solemn, stately and warlike—born?" She argued that fascism was mysterious and transcendent: "We ourselves, who assisted and participated in this birth, do not know." Gaining emotional fervor as

---

[27] Mussolini, *Autobiography*, 68.

[28] Benito Mussolini, *The Doctrine of Fascism*, 4th ed. (Rome: Novissima, n.d.), 10, 12, 24.

[29] On Margherita Sarfatti, see Philip Cannistraro and Brian Sullivan, *Il Duce's Other Woman* (New York: Morrow, 1993).

she proceeded, Sarfatti located the birth of fascist ritual in recent and distant Italian history, and most important, in the Italian soul.

> The aesthetic of Fascism was born from necessity, from labor and from war. What is the black shirt? A memory of Garibaldi transformed by the ardor of war; from blood red to the black of death: from the ringing romantic fanfare of '48 to the concentration of energetic realism. . . . But there is also in the black shirt the tradition of the labor and sweat of our workers, unskilled workers and provincial artisans who want to be able to work in their shops without dirtying themselves with dust and stains.
>
> . . . From where, if not from the atavistic memory—the rebirth of ancient religious spirits—through the sacrifice of war that takes sublime effort not to sink to the bestial—from where, if not from the dark whirlpools of the conscience of generations, the purist aesthetic that consecrates and celebrates these gestures of high and solemn life.[30]

The planning of the first-anniversary commemoration owed more to rationality and expedience than to spirituality. In 1923, the regime appointed a National Planning Commission for the "Celebration of the Anniversary of the March on Rome" and began the process of institutionalizing the commemoration of its founding nonevent. A National Fascist Party (Partito Nazionale Fascista, or PNF) press communiqué announced that after "hardworking meetings" the members of the committee had designed a program orchestrated to the "minutest particulars."[31] Il Popolo d'Italia reported the scheduled events in typical hyperbolic language as the "most grand program," and the newspaper spent the days before the ceremonies trying to generate a public enthusiasm that was commensurate with the energy of its rhetoric.[32]

The planning committee included members of the Fascist Party, the commissioner of Rome, Emilio De Bono and Michele Bianchi, and representatives from the National Association of Combatants and National Association of War Wounded. The central planning commission was located in Rome, but every city involved in the commemorations had local planning boards that kept the central committee informed of their activities. The local planning commissions consisted of the usual combination of fascists, military

[30] Margherita G. Sarfatti, "Nei dodici mesi dall'avvento: L'arte," Il Popolo d'Italia (Milan), 26 October 1923, 4.

[31] "Communiqué no. 1, n.d.," Press Office, National Fascist Party, ACS, PNF, MRF, b. 50, f. 121, sf. 3, 1.

[32] "Il grandioso programma della cerimonia commemorativa della Marcia su Roma," Il Popolo d'Italia, 2 October 1923, 1. There is no suitable English translation of the term "grandioso." I have used the words "most grand," but they only partially convey the extremes that the Italian word suggests.

persons, and notables. For example, Perugia's planning commission consisted of the mayor, a general, two lawyers, the secretary of the local Fascist Party, two representatives of war veterans' associations, and a countess who was the president of the National Association of War Mothers and Widows.[33]

The first anniversary commemoration centered on five sequential ceremonies that replicated the fascist march to power. The planning commission allocated the days between October 27 and October 31 for the ceremonies. During this period of official festivity, public, military, and private buildings throughout Italy displayed the national flag.[34] The five cities chosen as ceremonial sites were sacred to an emerging fascist history and geographically located on the route to Rome. Cremona had the largest number of fascist martyrs; Milan was the birthplace of the fascist movement; Bologna was the site of intense socialist agitation that fascism had subdued; Perugia was command headquarters for the March; and Rome was the home of the Tomb of the Unknown Soldier as well as the seat of national government.[35]

The final event was scheduled for Rome on the morning of October 31, when Mussolini would repeat his triumphal entry into the city. According to the exuberant planning commission, a large parade "in the august presence of the sovereigns and Princes and all the aristocracy of blood, of thought, of heroism, and of labor in the Nation, will ensure the importance of an austere and grand symbolic synthesis of a reunited Patria walking toward its most glorious destiny." The parade route retraced the walk from the Tomb of the Unknown Soldier to the Palazzo Quirinale which the Black Shirts had taken the previous year. In 1923, there would be banners representing every fascist group in Italy. In addition, a "colossal storm" of airplanes would fly over the "great procession," providing public security and a display of Italian air power.[36]

On Sunday, October 28, a Roman Catholic mass celebrated in the open air at nine in the morning in every city and small provincial center in Italy united all the commemorative events. The mass was offered to honor the "three thousand fascist martyrs" and every other fascist who had "fallen" for the revolution from 1919 to 1922. Provincial party secretaries were responsible for seeking the cooperation of local clergy to guarantee that the mass occurred. The mass as commemorative event aimed at merging Catholic and

[33] "Alla Commissione Centrale per la celebrazione dell'anniversario della Marcia su Roma," Comune di Perugia, 4 October 1923, ACS, PNF, MRF, b. 50, f. 121, sf. 3.

[34] "Communiqué no. 2, n.d.," Press Office, National Fascist Party, ACS, PNF, MRF, b. 50, f. 121, sf. 3, 1.

[35] "Il fascismo sara riconsacrato dalla prima celebrazione della Marcia su Roma," Il Popolo d'Italia, 18 October 1923, 1.

[36] "Communiqué no. 2, n.d.," 3. Airplanes were part of the cult of speed in pre-fascist Italy that the regime appropriated.

fascist identities and dramatized the struggle between church and state for the Italian self which would play itself out in diverse fascist events for the duration of the regime.

The official representation at the ceremonies consisted of the four members of the Quadrumvirato, all high-ranking Fascist Party officials, the commanders of Italian forces in the colonies, and various government ministers and undersecretaries of state. Crowds were made and not found in fascist Italy. The Italian railroads, the secret political actors in these events, transported from town to town the retinue of fascist bodies required to give the appearance of volume. Circumstantial evidence relating to lengthy discussions of train schedules and railway discounts suggests that a core body of veterans, fascists, mothers, and widows populated fascist ceremonies.

Mussolini participated in each of the ceremonies, and the trains that brought the "eager" participants also carried him to the various cities. If Mussolini was the star of these performances, the crucial supporting cast consisted of war veterans, particularly the wounded, and the mothers and widows of those who had given their lives both in the First World War and for the fascist revolution.[37] Wounded veterans would occupy "posts of honor in all military, civil, and religious ceremonies," and the mothers and widows would sit on the "Altar of the Patria," where the Italian Tomb of the Unknown Soldier was located, during the grand final ceremony in Rome.[38] The altar was on the steps of the monument to Vittorio Emanuele that sits in front of Piazza Venezia in the center of Rome. Built in a fervor of post-unification construction, the monument resembles an oversized wedding cake rather than a tribute to Italian nation building.[39]

The 1923 commemoration was replete with national and commercial iconography. A "Commemorative Medal" decorated with Roman imagery was issued and awarded to all persons who "participated in the Black Shirt Revolution." The medal had "ribbons with the colors of Rome" and an "artistic label carrying the signatures of the Duce and the Quadrumvirato." It carried the words "March on Rome," gave the dates of the revolution as "27 October to 1 November 1922," and left "free space" to inscribe the name of the recipient. One can easily imagine a black market in this piece of memorabilia. For those who were not so fortunate as to be awarded a medal, Italian entrepreneurship stepped in with various commercial ventures. For

---

[37] Italy was not unique in the commemoration of the war dead; see George L. Mosse, *Fallen Soldiers: Reshaping the Memory of the World Wars* (New York: Oxford University Press, 1990), 93–97.

[38] "Communiqué no. 1, n.d.," 1.

[39] On the monument, see Francesco Sapori, *Il Vittoriano* (Rome: Libreria dello Stato, 1946), 144–49.

example, on October 28 *Il Popolo d'Italia* prominently displayed an advertisement for Fascio, "a perfume of ardor and irresistible youth."[40]

Order and publicity were the principal nonspiritual concerns of the regime. The chief of police in Rome issued a fifteen-page memorandum two
days before the events in the capital on the subject of order.[41] The parade
route was divided into sixteen police zones, and twenty-four hundred police
were pressed into service. Although the official ceremonies were limited to
the central parts of the city, the police were concerned that "subversive"
groups from other parts of Italy might create "disorder." The police were
instructed to pay particular attention to neighborhoods where "popular elements" lived. The "inevitable disruption of persons" that the parade would
cause in pedestrian areas in the business districts troubled the Roman police
chief and would become more troubling as the number of parades and public spectacles increased.

The most firmly delineated audience for these events were the sixty foreign journalists who received special invitations and were taken on tours of
Milan and the Fiat plant in Turin. The purpose was to put foreign journalists
in touch with "eminent personalities from politics, finance, and commerce
who were 'securely' devoted to the fascist idea and the National Government." In prior years, foreign journalists had toured the remains of Italy's
"glorious past"; now they would visit an Italy "that produces, that fills itself
with the prodigious Italian productive activity that the fascist order favors,
that creates in the fields and offices—the fascist Government has brought
back the discipline and love of labor with the satisfaction of the same workers that ask only to be able to work and produce with serenity and peace."
This dose of fascist industrial reality was tempered with the showing of a
film over dinner that depicted the "marvelous" Italian combatants and their
victories in the war. The visitors ate and the fascists paraded around the
remains of the "glorious past."[42]

The spectacle of the first anniversary commemorations resembled a three-
act play. The central action of the first act was the open-air mass that
blended the sacred and the secular; the sequential city commemorations designed around Mussolini's exits and entrances made up the second act and
focused on the new orderly Italian nation; and the final act, the commemorations in Rome, centered on the war dead and the redemption of the legacy
of the First World War.

[40] "Communiqué no. 1, n.d.," 4. Advertisement, *Il Popolo d'Italia*, 28 October 1923, 5.
[41] "1 anniversario della Marcia su Roma," R. Questura di Roma Gabinetto, Ordinanza di
Servizio N 11075 B Roma, 29 October 1923, *ACS, PCM* 1923 2.4–1/ f. 2680.
[42] "Celebrazione della Marcia su Roma servizio della stampa estera," Rapporto a S.E. il
Presidente del Consiglio, *ACS, PNF, MRF,* b. 50, f. 121, sf. 3, 2.

Performing the Commemoration

The Mass of the Martyrs

The open-air mass in honor of the "three thousand fascist martyrs" represented the political union of church and state that the regime hoped to
negotiate. Its occurrence at exactly the same time in every part of Italy was a
symbolic enactment of the new national unity of fascism. The mass was also
a concrete attempt to combine the familiar liturgy of Catholicism with the
emerging ritual forms of fascism. In Rome the mass was celebrated in Piazza
Siena, located in the Borghese gardens, a large park in the center of the city.[43]
The account of the mass in *La Tribuna* displayed the tension between representation and reenactment, image and action, that one has to pick apart to
understand the political meaning of spectacle.

La Tribuna described the event as an "austere and moving rite" that was
"worthy of Rome." Sixty thousand persons attended. The size of the crowds
for all these events was always imprecise and somewhat suspect, and the
numbers reported were invariably in the thousands. Members of the Roman
Fascio, the militia, unions, fascist youth organizations, and the wounded war
veterans met in Piazza del Popolo and marched four abreast with flags and
standards waving to Piazza Siena. This march did not go directly through
the center of the city, as would the October 31 parade, but instead wound
through a more residential area. The parade entered the park to the tunes of
the "March Royal," a standard military march, and proceeded to Piazza
Siena, where a special altar had been constructed. The mothers and widows
of the fascist martyrs sat directly in front of the altar, which was decorated
with Italian flags instead of the more traditional religious icons. A military
chaplain assisted by three other priests recited the mass.

The "spectacle" of Piazza Siena was "grand beyond comparison," and the
"innumerable crowd . . . in its animation and its enthusiasm revealed that it
was not only a curious spectator, but an intense participant in the solemnity
of the rite that was performed." The rite, which exerted a "mystical fascination" on the crowd, was an intricate blending of Catholic and fascist practice. The use of the term "rite" instead of "liturgy," the more appropriate
term for variations on the staging of a Roman Catholic Mass, is itself a clue
to the subtle shifts in consciousness that the newspaper representation was
trying to encourage for those who could not attend.[44]

The elevation of the Eucharist, at which point the priest recites the words

---

[43] I draw my account from "La messa al campo Piazza di Siena," *La Tribuna*, 30 October
1923, 4.
[44] On the development of Catholic liturgy in Italy, see Gregory Dix, *The Shape of the
Liturgy* (Glasgow: University Press, 1946), 563–75.

that, according to Roman Catholic doctrine, change ordinary bread and wine into the body and blood of Christ, is the center of the Catholic Mass, and it would be a rare Italian Catholic who did not understand its significance.[45] The Mass for the Martyrs inserted fascist ritual practice into the most sacred part of the liturgy. At the moment the priest raised the Eucharist and turned to the audience, a trombone sounded, the troops presented arms, and the fascists raised their arms in a Roman salute. As the priest consecrated the Eucharist, the fascists consecrated themselves and blurred the distinction between what was sacred and what was secular—what was church and what was state.[46]

Fascist imposition on Catholic liturgy suggested that one could be fascist and Catholic. This is an important point, because the Socialist Party was not the only threat to fascist domination. The Popular Party, an essentially Catholic party, was competing for the same constituents as the fascists in 1923.[47] Although it was clear that one could not be socialist and Catholic, it was not so clear that one could not be fascist and Catholic. Of course, the Eucharistic transformation is also a miracle that one has to believe. The bread remains bread, and everyone knows that it is not the body of Christ. So too the fascist "revolution" was in 1923 more an object of felt belief than of experience.

The Local Commemorations

If the open-air mass suggested that one could be Catholic and fascist, the five sequential commemorations indicated that one could be disciplined and

---

[45] Liturgy in general warrants an entire sociological study. For a first attempt, see Kiernan Flanagan, *Sociology and Liturgy: Re-Presentations of the Holy* (New York: St. Martin's Press, 1991): "In Catholicism, the truth claims of this ritual transaction are enormous. It is believed that Christ is present under the appearance of bread and wine; that the word of God is spoken to those with a capacity to hear its truth; and that the rite represents an instance in a sacred calendar, a moment of immediacy in a timeless order. The mass contains many meanings. It can be conceived as a sacred drama. Like a great work of art, it bears endless representation without its meaning being any way exhausted. As a ritual, the mass is a condensed expression of a highly complex theology, that regulates and shapes the social contours of what is available for sociological understandings. Liturgical orders operate with a surplus of meanings greatly in excess of what appears in and through their social means of enactment" (112). On the significance of the Eucharist to Catholic liturgy, see P. J. Fitzpatrick, *In Breaking of Bread: The Eucharist and Ritual* (Cambridge: Cambridge University Press, 1993).
[46] There is a general recognition that fascism borrowed religious rites (see, for example, Emilio Gentile, *Il culto del littorio* [Rome: Laterza, 1993]) but no in-depth study that explores how the regime took over Catholic symbolism. On the contemporary period, see David. I. Kertzer, *Comrades and Christians* (New York: Cambridge University Press, 1980).
[47] On the struggle between popolari and fascists in the political arena, see Gabriele De Rosa, *Il Partito Popolare Italiano* (Bari: Laterza, 1966), 277–418.

fascist. Order and punctuality dominated the events, which were structured around Mussolini's arrival and departure from the train stations.[48] The events, including parades, building dedications, public visits, sports competitions, concerts, and military reviews, began at nine in the morning and lasted until five or six in the evening.[49]

The first ceremony was in Cremona, the fiefdom of Roberto Farinacci, a fascist noted for his propensity for violence and his purist commitment to the fascist revolution.[50] Farinacci led a band of Black Shirts in 1922 and portrayed himself as responsible for the fascist revolution's first victory in Cremona.[51] Farinacci owned a publishing house, Cremona Nuova, and the local newspaper and was a fervent chronicler of fascism. He wrote three histories of fascism and a play, *Redenzione* (Redemption), depicting the March on Rome which had little success when it was staged in 1927.[52]

Although Mussolini did not show up (he claimed to be resting after his enthusiastic reception in Turin), all other fascist notables did. Farinacci was able to command a great deal of local support for the parade and military review that formed the central part of the commemoration. Citizens made their private automobiles available to authorities, and local businesses as well as individuals contributed money. Donations ranged from five to fifty lire, and the Bank of Rome gave a thousand lire to the event. Thirty thousand lire in all was collected.[53]

Mussolini made his first appearance of the commemorations in Milan on October 28. He attended the mass for the "martyrs" in Milan's central park and then proceeded on horseback to the Piazza Belgioioso. A parade of fascists led by his wife and the mothers of the fascist dead followed him on foot. Mussolini reviewed the militia and gave a speech, the highlight of the commemoration, from the balcony of the palace in the piazza.

The Piazza Belgioioso had played a role in early fascist history. In 1919, Mussolini met with a small band of *arditi* in the piazza to encourage fascist mobilization. At that time, fascists were few and under siege as they fought

---

[48] On the small industry that developed around the image of Mussolini, see Luisa Passerini, *Mussolini immaginario: Storia di una biografia, 1915–1939* (Rome: Laterza, 1991), and Dino Biondi, *La fabbrica del Duce* (Florence: Vallecchi, 1967).

[49] I draw the timetable and schedule of events from "Communiqué no. 1, n.d.," Press Office, National Fascist Party, *ACS, PNF, MRF*, b. 50, f. 121, sf. 3, 1.

[50] Farinacci was committed to the regime until its demise, and he was executed with Mussolini in 1945. He was a constant thorn in the side of the regime, and Mussolini was afraid he might try to stage a personal coup. During the 1930s, Farinacci was firmly opposed to the development of the fascist technocratic state, which he viewed as changing the original goals of the revolution. See Mack Smith, *Mussolini*, 102–21, 372.

[51] See Lyttelton, *Seizure of Power*, 89.

[52] See "Dramma *Redenzione* : Anni 1927–1932," *ACS, SPDCR*, b. 42, sf. 22, "Farinacci Avv. Roberto."

[53] *Cremona Nuova* (Cremona), 26 October 1923, 2.

the socialists in Milan, carrying pistols for defense. In 1923, the fascists were more numerous and the pistols were for display. Mussolini began his speech by comparing the piazza of 1919 with the piazza of 1923: "We were small bands, today we are legions; we were then very few, today we are a boundless multitude."[54] The *Popolo d'Italia* reiterated the point in its coverage.[55]

Mussolini's speech lasted "exactly forty minutes." It was structured rhetorically to incorporate all the themes of the new fascist history and built to an emotional conclusion. The reactions of the crowd—cries of "yes, yes," notes of applause—punctuated the transcript of the speech.[56] Assuring the assembled militia that the revolution would continue, Mussolini pointed to the monarchy as the "sacred symbol" of the country that the regime had fortified and to the church as the "other pillar of national society." He asserted: "Religion, which is the sacred patrimony of the people, has not been touched or diminished by us. We have augmented its prestige. We have ensured the major respect and a more profound devotion for the Army: also today the Army of the Vittorio Veneto occupies a post of honor in the spirit of all Italians devoted to the fatherland." (*Applause*)[57] The Vittorio Veneto was the scene of the Italian victory in World War I. The speech blurred the boundary between church and nation by linking the church to the army, a rhetorical strategy that replicated the melding of fascist and religious practice at the mass in Piazza Siena.

Mussolini next targeted the socialist enemy when he spoke of the "tranquil rhythm" of labor that fascism had restored. Fascism gave Italy a "magnificent spectacle of discipline" in the factory and in the piazza and conquered the "false shepherds of the working masses." Building to the climax of the speech, he proclaimed that fascism's twelve months of life would become "twelve years multiplied by five," a modest vision in comparison with Hitler's thousand-year Reich. As Mussolini approached the conclusion of the speech, his arguments became metaphysical:

It [fascism] will endure, black shirts. It will endure because we, negators of the doctrine of materialism, we have not driven the will out of human history; it will endure because we want it to endure; it will endure because we will make everything possible; it will endure because it will systematically disperse our enemies; it will endure because it is not only the triumph of a party and of a crisis of ministers: it is something more, much more, infi-

[54] Benito Mussolini, "Il primo anniversario della marcia su Roma," in *Dal viaggio negli Abruzzi al delitto Matteotti*, vol. 20, *OO*, 61.

[55] "La Rivoluzione delle invitte Camicie Nere celebrata solennemente in tutta Italia," *Il Popolo d'Italia*, 30 October 1923, 1.

[56] Mussolini, "Il primo anniversario," 61.

[57] Ibid., 62.

nitely more. It is the springtime, and the resurrection of the race, and the people that becomes the nation, the nation that becomes the State, that seeks in the world the lines of its expansion. (*Prolonged applause*)[58]

He concluded with the slogans that would dominate successive addresses and were emblematic of the chanting in fascist public speech:

To whom Rome? (*And a shout responds: "To us!"*)

To whom Italy? (*"To us!"*)

To whom the victory? (*"To us!"*)[59]

In addition to articulating the themes that dominated the first anniversary commemoration, Mussolini's speech was remarkable because it introduced imperial aspirations that scholars tend to credit to a later phase in the regime. The remaining events in Milan concretized the thematic content of the speech. Mussolini dedicated a statue of an athlete in the Law Courts (Palazzo della Ragione). A parade to the new Milanese Fascist House (Casa del Fascio) followed where there was a ceremony to pay homage to the mothers of the fascist martyrs. The inauguration of a fascist cultural organization named after a fascist who died in a street battle with socialists in 1920 was the next stop. The day concluded with a torchlight parade and concert.

The commemorations in Bologna, Florence, and Perugia were variations of the Milan events with the exception that there were elaborate ceremonies to welcome Mussolini at the train station in each of these cities. I began this chapter with a description of the Bologna commemoration, in which Mussolini paraded down the Via d'Indipendenza to the central piazza. He entered a theater where Giacomo Acerbo, undersecretary of state, delivered the principal speech of the day, which went over much of the same territory as the speech Mussolini had given in Milan. What was different provides a political context for the prominence of the mothers in the ceremonies. Acerbo proclaimed that fascism was in the process of developing social reforms around the family and the church.[60] The required teaching of religion in the public schools, the Gentile reform, would link family values, church, and state.

Acerbo argued that the connection between the "crucifix and the flag" differentiated fascism from the liberal regime, which presumably under-

---

[58] Ibid., 64–65.
[59] Ibid., 65.
[60] "Il primo anno di governo fascista nel poderoso discorso dell'on Acerbo a Bologna," *Il Messaggero* (Rome), 30 October 1923, 1.

valued religion—or at least its institutional center, the Catholic Church. Acerbo's speech emphasized the importance of Bologna as a socialist strong-hold, and this historical detail shaped many of the actions that followed. Mussolini spent his time in Bologna visiting locations that were associated with the socialist-fascist violence, such as the Casa del Fascio, the war vet-erans' association, and the Federation of Agricultural Fascists. At the Pa-lazzo D'Accursio, where a particularly bloody riot had taken place between socialists and fascists in 1919, Mussolini was made an honorary citizen. He then presented a ten-thousand-lire check to the widow of a war hero who had received posthumously the Italian silver medal of honor.[61]

Mussolini spent a mere two hours in Florence on the evening of the Bo-logna commemoration—enough time to attend the parade, review the troops, and make a ceremonial entrance and exit.[62] On the morning of Oc-tober 30, he arrived in Perugia, the last city before the final commemoration in Rome. Perugia had been the headquarters of the Quadrumvirato, the four paramilitary leaders who commanded the March on Rome, making it a cru-cial city in the commemoration.[63] Perugia, a relatively small medieval city on a hill, is noted primarily for its university and for the manufacture of small chocolate candies called *Baci* (Kisses). The newspapers reported that over one hundred thousand people crammed into the city to participate in the commemoration. Perugia is also the capital of Umbria, dotted with many medieval towns such as Assisi and Gubbio that even in 1923 were more noted for past glories than for contemporary political relevance.

The journalist reporting on the commemoration in *L'Assalto* (The as-sault), the local fascist daily, drew on the historical meaning of the region to emphasize the significance of Mussolini's visit and his place in world history. Mussolini would charm the crowds as Saint Francis of Assisi charmed the birds and the animals.[64] Thomas Carlyle said that it would take "ten centu-ries" to make a great man of history, but Mussolini appeared a mere fifty years after Cavour. Mussolini combined the best qualities of the heroes of the Italian Risorgimento. He had "the passion of Mazzini, the cold audacity

---

[61] For Mussolini's description of the riot of 1919, see *Autobiography*, 117–19. For a more balanced historical account, see Cardoza, *Agrarian Elites*, 306–15, and Nazario Sauro On-ofri, *La strage di palazzo d'Accursio: Origine e nascita del fascismo bolognese, 1919–1920* (Milan: Feltrinelli, 1980), esp. 252–89.

[62] Florence was the scene of a Fascist Party congress in 1919 but was not a particularly strategic locale with regard to the March; see Lyttelton, *Seizure of Power*, 45.

[63] I draw the Perugia account from "Communiqué" no. 1, n.d.," Press Office, National Fascist Party, *ACS, PNF, MRF,* b. 50, f. 121, sf. 3; Benito Mussolini, "Celebrazione Perugina della marcia su Roma," in *Dal viaggio negli Abruzzi al delitto Matteotti,* vol. 20, *OO,* 70–74; *Il Messaggero,* 31 October 1923, 1; and *L'Assalto* (Perugia), a local fascist daily news circular.

[64] On the fascist appropriation of Saint Francis, see Herbert W. Schneider, *Making the Fascist State* (New York: Oxford University Press, 1928), 224–25.

of Cavour, the impetuosity of Garibaldi."[65] If there was any doubt left in the reader's mind as to Mussolini's importance, the journalist attempted to eradicate it with his closing statement, in which he declared Mussolini to be the "greatest statesman ever—better than Lloyd George, Asquith, Baldwin, Poincaré, Clemenceau."[66]

The train station in Perugia was located outside the city, which made the official procession into the center of the city extraordinarily long. Crowds began forming at seven in the morning to await Mussolini's arrival at nine. The workers from the Perugina chocolate factory gave Mussolini a particularly enthusiastic welcome, and showered his car with "flowers and laurel." Mussolini responded to their fervor by stopping the motorcade and promising to visit their factory in the afternoon. The ceremonial activities in Perugia followed the same general pattern established in Milan and Bologna.

The mayor received Mussolini in the Prefettura, a state government building, and a military review was staged in the central piazza of the city. Mussolini next proceeded to a hotel to dedicate a commemorative plaque of the March on Rome which had been engraved on the front of the building. From the hotel balcony, Michele Bianchi, a member of the Quadrumvirate, gave a speech that marked fascism as the start of a new civilization. He used the same choral form Mussolini had employed to engage the crowd in Milan, proclaiming: "Citizens, Fascism is not only a phenomenon that portends national rebirth; Fascism is also a sign of a new civilization that experiments with history. The after-war period has given two initiatives to civilization: Moscow and Rome. The world has to decide for one or for the other!" The stage directions that follow say, "*(Mussolini interrupts shouting: For Rome! the crowd shouts Rome, Rome!)*."[67]

Given the stark choice between Moscow and Rome, communism and fascism, and the constant assertion that Italian workers had firmly chosen fascism, it is somewhat ironic that the center of the Perugia commemorations was Mussolini's visit to the Perugina chocolate factory. The regime could hardly have chosen a more peripheral industry with which to demonstrate the new loyalty of labor. Of course, this was precisely the point, as it would have been difficult to find a factory in Milan or Bologna that was amenable to the regime. Although the chocolate factory was a major industry in Perugia, it was not typical of Italian industry. A week earlier, Mussolini had received a decidedly chillier reception at the Fiat automobile factory in Turin.

The director of Perugina displayed the factory as the "most modern of its kind" and asserted that Mussolini's visit would "signify a memorable date in

[65] "Le sacre giornate," *L'Assalto*, 27 October 1923, 1.
[66] "Salutiamo nel Duce l'Italia nuova che passa," *L'Assalto*, 29 October 1923, 1.
[67] "Un saluto dell'Umbria fascista," *L'Assalto*, 31 October 1923, 1.

the story of our young industry." With the same propensity to break into oration that seemed to afflict everyone involved in the commemorations, the director welcomed Mussolini, saying, "I am happy to tell Your Excellency that the great majority of laborers have finally understood the possibility and utility of class collaboration and the inexorable necessity of loving, serving, and laboring for Italy," concluding with the exclamation, "A Fascist Perugina for the Duce of Fascism, eja, eja, eja, alala!"[68] Mussolini congratulated the director and the workers and reminded them that "the welfare of labor cannot exist without the welfare of the collectivity that is called the Nation." The director gave Mussolini a leather box filled with chocolates, which Mussolini appropriated literally and figuratively in the name of the regime. Tasting one of them, he said, "And now Signor Director I tell you and *I authorize you* [emphasis added] to repeat it that your chocolate is truly exquisite!" With chocolates in hand, Mussolini spent the remainder of the day in the usual round of building dedications, memorial services for the dead, and a sporting event.

Reconverging on the Center: Rome

In Milan, Bologna, Florence, and Perugia, actions revolved around Mussolini's appearance at specific locations. The spaces and the act of Mussolini's visiting them carried the fascist message. The social space of Rome, scene of the old empire and the new revolutionary regime, was the central actor in the final day of ceremonies. Rome contained the architectural residues of Italian history and provided a natural stage for ceremonies that linked the Unknown Soldier and the memory of World War I, the king and the stability of the new regime with the Roman Empire.[69] The headlines on the day after the event drew the connections explicitly: "The Entire Italian People Rally around the Duce and Exalt in Eternal Rome the Grand Fascist Revolution."[70] The ceremonies in Rome lasted the entire day. All businesses were closed, and no civil aviation was permitted over the city. In addition to the public ceremonies, there was a banquet for visiting dignitaries and a public concert in the Piazza Colonna outside the Italian parliament. The concert program consisted of suitably militaristic arias from Giuseppe Verdi and Vincenzo Bellini and concluded with Giovacchino Rossini's *William Tell* Overture.

The two focal activities were the commemoration of the Unknown Sol-

---

[68] Ibid. The end of the exclamation is the fascist rallying cry; the words have no discursive meaning.

[69] On Rome as stage during the fascist period, see Pierre Milza, "La mise en scène du consensus," in *Rome, 1920–1945: Le modèle fasciste, son Duce, sa mythologie,* ed. Françoise Liffran (Paris: Editions Autrement, 1991), 19–25, and other essays in that collection.

[70] *Il Popolo d'Italia,* 1 November 1923, 1.

dier and the homage to Julius Caesar in the Roman Forum. Events began with a parade that went from the Piazza del Popolo down the Corso Umberto to Piazza Venezia. The Piazza del Popolo is a large piazza in central Rome capable of holding at least one hundred thousand persons. The planning commission for the ceremony imported such a large number of fascist squads for the event that, assembling for the parade, they spilled into the residential neighborhood beyond the piazza. The Corso Umberto, which connects the two piazzas, is a central commercial street that passes the Italian parliament. Observing the traditional military ceremonial to honor the dead, Mussolini marched beside a riderless horse that led the parade. Groups followed in an order that mirrored fascist hierarchy: the four members of the Quadrumvirato, the national directorate of the Fascist Party, members of the troops that marched on Rome in 1922, wounded soldiers who had received the Italian medal of honor, government officials, unaligned militia, the railroad militia, representatives of the Fascist Party from all of Italy, the railroad fascist organization, and the entire fascist organization from Lazio and Rome. The various groups carried their appropriate banners and were separated at intervals by military bands. The last group was made up of fascist confederations and union organizations followed by patriotic associations, and if there was space available, "the people." The bells of the Capitoline Hill tolled for the half hour that it took to march down the one-mile Corso.

At the Piazza Venezia, the mothers and widows of the war dead as well as members of various veterans' associations sat before the steps of the monument to Vittorio Emanuele, where the Altar of the Patria housed the Tomb of the Unknown Soldier.[71] By custom, speeches are not permitted at the ceremony for the Unknown Soldier.[72] Instead, the groups that had formed the parade filed in front of the altar for two hours of visual commemoration. While the groups were marching, a squadron of airplanes flew in formation over the piazza, introducing a note of future militarism. The groups then left the piazza and paraded through another central commercial district to the Palazzo Quirinale to pay homage to the king. Up to this point, the parade replicated the route the fascists had taken the year before when they "captured" the city. After the visit to the king, the parade marched down the Via Nazionale and ended in the Piazza Esedra, near the central train station. Here, the crowds rushed the ropes that held them back and tried to grab at Mussolini. The police quickly carried him away.

The last official ceremony was at the Roman Forum, behind the monu-

---

[71] On the cult of war that had developed among Italian intellectuals in the pre-fascist period, see Mario Isnenghi, *Il mito della grande guerra*, 1970 (rpt., Bologna: Il Mulino, 1989), esp. 169–304.

[72] *Consuetudini di cerimoniale*, 222.

ment to Vittorio Emanuele. The Roman fascist organization placed a laurel wreath and a fascist plaque on the Altar of Julius Caesar. A university professor lectured on the Sixth Canto of Dante's *Paradiso*, which deals with the Roman Empire, and reminded the audience that Charles V had marched through the Roman Forum on his way to Saint Peter's Basilica, where the pope crowned him emperor.[73]

Four days after the commemorations in Rome, on November 4, Italians celebrated Veterans Day in association with the commemoration of the Vittorio Veneto. The *Popolo d'Italia* announced that the war was the first victory and the fascist revolution the "second victory."[74] With the two state holidays linked both temporally and ideologically, Italians, whether they celebrated and marched or not, had two holidays in close proximity, October 28 and November 4, from 1923 until the fall of the regime—a small irony given that it was not until November 7, 1923, that the *Popolo d'Italia* proclaimed, "Work! After the fervor of commemorations the fervor of works."[75] The first anniversary commemoration had absorbed at least five work days, and it was the beginning of a regime policy of settling labor unrest by sending workers on holiday.[76]

Narrating Commemoration

Journalists were central to the regime's national and international self-representation.[77] Mussolini addressed a professional meeting of journalists held in Milan a day before the official celebrations began and stated that journalism was his "passion." He argued that journalists were different from mere publicists, "because journalism is above all an instinct . . . one is born a journalist; it is difficult to become a journalist. . . . Journalism is a burning passion and something that takes over one's entire spirit: one lives of news-

[73] "L'austera cerimonia al Foro Romano," *Il Messaggero*, 1 November 1923, 1.

[74] "La seconda Vittoria," *Il Popolo d'Italia*, 3 November 1923, 1.

[75] *Il Popolo d'Italia*, 7 November 1923, 1.

[76] By 1930, twenty-nine official state holidays potentially kept persons away from work. This number excluded various local celebratory dates. The large number, due in part to the fact that Catholic holidays were considered state holidays in Italy, was a constant source of discord between the regime and Italian industry (*ACS, PCM* 1937–39 3.3.3/f. 1558, sf. 8).

[77] Schneider, *Making the Fascist State*, points to the flourishing of fascist journalism: "The flood of fascist journalism is the most conspicuous witness to this fact. The regime is a regime founded by a journalist, carried on by journalists, to the undoing of journalism. Every ambitious young fascist thinks it his duty to have his own journal; and as a matter of fact, the government fills a large percentage of its jobs with journalists who have succeeded in making a loud and loyal noise. There is a saying that the first principle of fascist philosophy is not *cogito ergo sum*, but *faccio rumore quindi sono* [I make noise, therefore I am]" (237).

papers, in newspapers, for newspapers."[78] Mussolini described the profession of journalism with the same language of mystery and instinct Sarfatti used to evoke the ineffable quality of fascist spectacle. Under the spirituality lies the same instrumentality; noting that he was an avid daily reader of hundreds of newspapers, Mussolini added, "A newspaper article puts the Government in contact with the aspirations, the unsatisfied needs of the largest classes of the Italian people."[79] Mussolini's affirmation of the peculiar insights of the true journalist served to legitimate the vast outpouring of reportage that came from fascist Italy, at the same time providing incentives to journalists to reproduce the emotions the regime wished to convey.

Newspaper representations of the first anniversary commemorations are important vehicles of information, if we keep in mind that they are exactly that—representations, a window into the intentions of the regime. The newspapers must be read as text and subtext: the reports that were sympathetic to fascism were artifice; the events were actions. The links between the language that journalists used to describe events and the actual events and ceremonies were tenuous.

The newspapers with distinctly fascist sympathies provided detailed descriptions for persons who could not witness the spectacles. One must keep in mind that space was limited and public order a central concern. The accounts were tedious in detail, lavish in prose, and surprisingly similar, probably because they relied heavily on official regime and party press communiqués for their information. Given the limited public sphere in Italy, the newspapers preached to the converted; the nonconverted probably passed over the wordy descriptions. Newspapers that were not supportive of the regime provided strikingly different coverage: the *Corriere della Sera* reported in two columns events that the other papers such as *Cremona Nuova* and *Il Popolo d'Italia* treated in five pages.

The newspapers were fictional narratives of the narrow range of enthusiastic emotions that the events were intended to generate. The real events were messier. The description of the events must be kept analytically and empirically separate from the events themselves. Failure to make this distinction leads to a fascist reading of the events: by simply analyzing the rhetorical constructions of these events, we accept the regime's propaganda. If we keep this caveat in mind, the newspapers provide the script for the public performance and suggest the salient themes that the events enacted.

The stylistic vehicle of the popular language of emotion was the anthropomorphic descriptions of the cities where the ritual events took place. As Bologna "throbbed" with expectation, Milan "made herself up" for the cer-

---

[78] Benito Mussolini, "All'associazione Lombarda dei giornalisti," in *Dal viaggio negli Abruzzi al delitto Matteotti*, vol. 20, *OO*, 60.
[79] Ibid.

emonies and prepared to "relive the days of passion and battle."[80] The accounts blended sacred and secular imagery and melded the language of religion and the language of fascism. Headlines read, "Fascism Will Be Reconsecrated by the First Anniversary Celebration of the March on Rome"; "The Consecration of the Revolution and Fascism: We Affirm with Firm Hearts: Life Will Not Be Destroyed"; "Cremona Celebrates with Profound Italian Soul, the Commemorative Rite of Revolution and Liberation"; "From Rome, Italy Has Reconsecrated Yesterday Its New Luminous Era."[81] The dominant themes were the return to order after the conquering of the socialist enemy, the new prestige of the nation, the emergence of new national spirit of discipline, and an affirmation of Catholicism.

The redemption of the memory of the Unknown Soldier was the emblem organizing the rhetoric of national prestige. Enrico Corradini, a prominent Italian nationalist, in an article entitled "The Solemnity of the Fatherland," argued, "Fascism seeks to save the work of sacrifice and heroism of the Unknown Soldier and to reconquer those ends that make the greatness of the nation." According to Corradini, a "religious cult" around the idea of the Unknown Soldier is the "unbreakable chain" that links the glories of the war to the "living spirit of the Nation."[82] In an editorial in the Roman daily *Il Messaggero*, the writer announced that the "rebirth of the prestige and fortunes of our Country" elicited "emotional fervor" in the hearts of all Italians. Fascism, and particularly the state, equaled moral regeneration:

> The restoration of national moral values that consolidates the authority of the State and reinvigorates the national conscience remains today as a rigorous and knowing impression of the work completed in twelve months by Benito Mussolini's government. And the new tonality in which the life of the nations evolves represents the certain guarantee that the work initiated will be carried out to a world mission.[83]

Il Popolo d'Italia summarized the meaning of the commemoration in an editorial entitled "After the Grand Parade." According to the newspaper, Italy was finally a governable country because the fascists had conquered "subversive ideas" that were debilitating its youth and causing general "indiscipline." Fascism made "a tranquil, compact, diligent Nation, full of love

[80] "La Rivoluzione delle invitte Camicie Nere celebrata solennemente in tutta Italia," *Il Popolo d'Italia*, 30 October 1923, 1; *Il Messaggero*, 28 October 1923, 1.

[81] *Il Popolo d'Italia*, 18 October 1923, 1, and 27 October 1923, 1; *Cremona Nuova*, 28 October 1923, 1; *Il Messaggero*, 1 November 1923, 1.

[82] *Il Popolo d'Italia*, 27 October 1923, 1.

[83] "Esultante e disciplinata l'Italia festeggia la sua rinascita nel primo anniversario della Rivoluzione," *Il Messaggero*, 28 October 1923.

of Country, pride in the victory of the Vittorio Veneto, jealous of its dead and its combatants." As the "legitimate heirs of the period of Italian unification," the fascists demonstrated that they were an "indestructible force."[84] On the level of organization, the article concluded that the Fascist Party was now firmly entrenched within the state, that Mussolini's militia, created as his personal foot soldiers, proved capable of orderly behavior, and that labor organizations by their participation in the various parades would now march with the regime.

The public events surrounding the first anniversary of the March on Rome established a ritual genre of commemoration that would be repeated yearly until the regime fell in 1943. The 1923 commemorations were a first step on the road to creating a new national history that was both fascist and Italian. The events dramatized in public space what the regime hoped would be meaningful in its new political community. Narrative construction in national newspapers that employed the familiar Italian idiom of emotion and propaganda documents provided a fascist reading of ritual action.

The overall image of the March was that of spatial convergence. The pilgrimage of the leader outward to the local events and then inward to the Roman center and the physical movement of fascist bodies across space and time set a pattern that was recognizable to the general public and difficult to ignore. Fascism used readily available cultural schemata to create a community of feeling around the memory of the March. The actions in public space—the carefully ordered parades and the appropriation of the public piazza—visibly proclaimed that a new social order was established.

In the accounts of the first anniversary commemorations, five core themes emerged: (1) the myth of the founding event, (2) the identification of enemies, (3) the appropriation of the commonplace, (4) the merging of the sacred and secular, and (5) the body as cultural icon. The March as founding event proclaimed that a new fascist nation-state project was under way. The constant reference to socialist violence, the choice of locations such as Bologna, and the emphasis on a new working Italy pointed to the socialists as enemies that had been overcome. Visits to everyday venues such as the Perugina factory suggested that the fascist values would inform ordinary life. The appropriation of the Roman Catholic Mass drew on the popular cultural knowledge of Roman Catholicism to link religious identity to fascist identity. The movement and massing of bodies provided tangible symbols of the new political community. The Unknown Soldier was the Italian nation; the sheer mass of bodies dramatized solidarity; and the omnipresence of the mothers' bodies tied the nation as family to the Italian family. During the

---

[84] *Il Popolo d'Italia*, 2 November 1923, 1.

first anniversary commemoration, clearly articulated rhetorics and actions embodied these ideas. The symbols and ritual actions changed as the regime evolved, developed, and responded to different national and international political exigencies. The genre of commemoration evolved and a repertoire of genres emerged, each contributing to the overall political task of creating citizens who would fuse their public and private selves in the nation.

CHAPTER 4

The Evolution of Ritual
Genres: The March Continues

Institutionalizing Memory

The first anniversary commemoration of the March on Rome established a repertoire of ritual actions around political themes that the regime would draw on in the ensuing twenty years. These actions included parades through the center of the city, homages to dead fascist heroes, and public display of fascist bodies, particularly mothers and soldiers. Neither the themes nor the actions stayed precisely the same: what remained constant and what changed provide a clue to explaining and interpreting political spectacle.

Commemoration as genre codifies the rituals surrounding the anniversary of the March on Rome as annual event. As I discussed previously, genre provides a classificatory vocabulary which permits parsimonious description of publicly recognizable ritual forms. As well as focusing on the past, the annual commemoration of the March was a public opportunity to reinvent and renarrate the founding event. It was a yearly public assessment of where the regime had been and where it was going. Genres are never pure types. As the years went by, the anniversary of the March on Rome encompassed the entire range of ritual genres—celebration, demonstration, symposia, and inauguration. Collage, not portraiture, was the dominant image.

Between 1923 and 1938, the memory of the March was institutionalized. The first anniversary commemoration was an artisan activity; subsequent commemorations owed more to techniques of mass production. Evolving from the basic pattern established at the first anniversary, the commemoration of the march articulated fascist history in accord with changing national and international circumstances. Nineteen thirty-eight marked a turning point: it was the twentieth anniversary of Italy's victory over the Austrians in the Veneto region, a victory that fanned the flames of Italian nationalists, who believed they were the legitimate victors in World War I and entitled to the spoils of war. It was also the year Mussolini's diplomatic moves brought the country irrevocably into the German camp. After 1938, Italy was no longer truly at peace. Commemoration of the March continued, but it was aimed at the war effort and lost its peculiarly fascist character.

Between 1923 and 1927, the process of commemoration was rationalized. The regime declared the anniversary of the March on Rome a legal holiday in 1926 and specified October 28 as the day of commemoration.[1] Centralization and coordination marked the succeeding commemorations, and in contrast to the first anniversary commemoration, which can be reconstructed only from newspaper accounts, subsequent commemorations could be read from official state documents.

Pilgrimage as ritual device structured the first commemoration.[2] Mussolini traveled to the sacred sites of the revolution to rearticulate and commemorate events of fascist history. After 1923, the regime used the leader's pilgrimage selectively. The crowds came or, more accurately, were transported to Rome. The dates Mussolini left Rome and where he went acquired political meaning. Rome as the principal site of commemoration articulated its centrality, as well as Mussolini's, in the new fascist state. Yet the regime did not choose to abandon the local character of this national commemoration. Mussolini's surrogates arrived at local commemorations with a copy of his annual message in hand and read it to the assembled crowds. It was not until 1935 that the regime began to broadcast Mussolini's annual message on the radio. The carefully constructed reports from the provinces to the Ministry of Interior, as well as accounts from the Stefani News Agency, are repetitive in their discussion of similar events. Both organizations regularly reported the presence of enthusiastic crowds at public meetings that were invariably described as enormous.

The March through Time and Space

Consolidation and Celebration: "Work" and "Passion" (1927)

By 1927, the regime was oriented toward the future, and the fifth anniversary of the March took on a celebratory cast. The crisis generated by the assassination of the socialist parliamentary deputy, Giacomo Matteotti, had

---

[1] Regio Decreto-Legge 21 ottobre 1926 n. 1779, *ACS, PCM* 1926 2.4–1/f. 3904.

[2] On the use of pilgrimage as a ritual device, see Ian Reader, introduction to *Pilgrimage in Popular Culture*, ed. Ian Reader and Tony Walter (London: Macmillan, 1993), 1–25. For Italian popular iterations of this device, see Annabella Rossi, *Le feste dei poveri* (Palermo: Sellerio, 1986), 85–115.

been overcome, and the tone of commemoration was optimistic. This was the height of the regime's consolidation period, and popular consent and social tranquility dominated the narrative construction of celebratory events. It was the year the regime introduced the Labor Charter and Mussolini gave his Speech of the Ascension. These core ideological statements articulated the regime's official position on the relation between the public and private sphere, self and society, work and state.

Fascism's social mission and sense of its public history dominated the celebrations. By 1927, the regime began to think of itself as having a past and accomplishments that could be summarized. A central feature was the defeat of the socialist enemy and the construction of the new corporativist state. Issues of labor and nation building permeated the celebratory events. Stability was a key theme. The headlines of *Il Popolo d'Italia* emphasized continuity and read, "Celebrating the works that signal a profound and indestructible mark on the history of the Patria."[3] The newspaper featured a front-page picture of Mussolini in civilian dress in a reflective pose, his head tilted downward, with the caption, "Continuing."

In honor of the event, Mussolini wrote an article for *Gerarchia*, the fascist review, entitled "Prelude to the March on Rome," in which he renarrated the events of 1922 as a national rebirth. Beginning with a litany of the fascist enemies that the regime had vanquished, he repeated the story of an Italy in chaos and disarray as a result of "Bolshevik" forces. The "period of the revolution" followed an "insurrectionary period" that characterized the months of August, September, and October 1922. Mussolini described the five years between 1922 and 1927 as extraordinary:

No one dares to doubt that a profound revolution has occurred. Substitution of men, transformation and creation of institutes, change of the spirit and moral climate of the people, works and laws. It is a fact that all the old parties—no one excluded: from liberalism to anarchy—whether they are anti-fascists and form a counterrevolution, [no one] can censure the powerful innovations that fascism has brought to Italian life.[4]

The old Italy was gone, and not even fascism's enemies wished to return to the "antique regime that fascism forever has thrown into a ditch."[5] Mussolini described fascism as an exercise in modern state building and underscored the centrality of corporativism to his new political idea. Invoking the language of the Labor Charter, he argued that

[3] *Il Popolo d'Italia* (Milan), 30 October 1927, 1.
[4] Benito Mussolini, "Preludi della marcia su Roma," in *Dal discorso dell'ascensione agli accordi del laterano*, vol. 23, *OO*, 52–53.
[5] Ibid, 53.

fascism has confronted the problem of the modern State, its character and its functions. In this creation of a new State, that is authoritarian but not absolutist, hierarchical and organic—that is open to people of all classes, categories, and interests—is the great revolutionary originality of fascism, and it provides a lesson, perhaps, for the entire modern world, that oscillates between the authority of the State and the excessive power of the individual; between State and anti-state.[6]

Mussolini's rhetoric elevated fascism above liberalism and socialism, the twin enemies of fascist political community.

"Work" and "passion" were the key words of the fifth anniversary commemoration. Mussolini's annual message emphasized political consensus and the building of a material and spiritual fascist infrastructure, proclaiming, "Not words, but works to celebrate [the Fifth Anniversary]! "New and grander works" were "expected" of a regime that did not "bow down" before "obstacles." The message listed "railroads, streets, aqueducts, public edifices, charitable institutions, houses" as "testimony to the world on how Fascism is transforming Italy and increasing its potency in all areas." Written as a three-part chorus, the message is rhapsodic, emphasizing the fascist future. The concluding chorus began:

Black Shirts!

As in the past "to endure" is our motto for the future.

To endure with perfect discipline, with absolute dedication.

To perfect the instruments of the Revolution, to multiply our forces, to toughen our spirits for all battles.

This is still and always the duty of Leaders and followers.

Black Shirts of all the vigils, anxious youth. . . .

The shout of our Faith and of our conquest, passing over the horizons today, will be heard near and far.

For all the ends that we will achieve with the firm step of our immutable certainty, fascists of all Italy:

TO US![7]

[6] Ibid., 53.
[7] Benito Mussolini, "Nel V. annual della Rivoluzione," PNF, *Foglio d'ordini*, 28 October 1927, #39, 1.

The emphasis on building a national infrastructure brought inauguration to the fore as a ritual genre. A building was never merely a building in fascist Italy. Inaugural ceremonies that launched the new headquarters of the Ministry of Corporations and the National Institute of Insurance offered opportunities to link the building of edifices with the new fascist nation as edifice. The Ministry of Corporations provided the bureaucratic apparatus within which the requirements of the Labor Charter were enacted, and thus the new headquarters was the physical space—the laboratory—of the fascist experiment with work and the state. Mussolini's speech on this occasion was brief and to the point:

I have three things to tell you:

First: this date is prophetic

Second: these headquarters are worthy

Third: your labor will be fertile for the regime and for Italy.[8]

Giuseppe Belluzzo the national minister of education, substituted for Mussolini at the opening of the social insurance building. Belluzzo's speech was far more verbose than Mussolini's. The social insurance building was the tangible embodiment of the regime's social welfare policies; its architectural features replicated the glory of the regime. The building derived its principal symbolic virtue from its speedy construction, a point Belluzzo underscored as a sign of fascist efficiency and discipline. The frequent reporting of the amount of time that actions took was a constant public reminder of the efficiency of the new regime. Belluzzo spoke of the grandeur of the building and the fascist "renovation of national life." He echoed Mussolini's phrase "not words but deeds" and rhapsodized:

In the sought-after field of insurance, social security finds its glorification in this imposing building, inaugurated today, a building worthy of the new Rome, erected by the National Institute as its headquarters, like a sign of grand conquest and power. A testimony to this power has already been marked and cited in very eloquent figures that turn to honor the rulers and their collaborators. We will not stop at their example: fascism does not pass its time contemplating that which was done; we search, instead, the

[8] Benito Mussolini, "Per l'inaugurazione della nuova sede del ministero del corporazioni," in *Dal discorso dell'ascensione agli accordi del laterano*, vol. 23, *OO*, 48.

many things in many areas that are yet to do, we clutch the threads, we elevate our devoted and grateful thoughts to the artifice of the new Italian dawn, and we continue our march with the same resolutions, with the same faith.[9]

Belluzzo's panegyric typified the speeches that were heard at fascist inaugurals for the duration of the regime.

In 1927, the parade in Rome was slightly less central than it had been in 1923 and would be in succeeding years. Newspapers provided the standard coverage.[10] In contrast to earlier years, the militia published a pamphlet with detailed directions for the staging of the parade.[11] The militia's instructions included printed train schedules, and it is clear that fascist bodies were imported from all of Italy. The event took place in the Viale Parioli outside the center of Rome, because the area around the Coliseum was undergoing renovation and redesign.[12] Fifty thousand troops, consisting of representatives from numerous fascist paramilitary organizations and the obligatory contingent of war wounded, were present for the occasion. Tickets were printed for spectators, and passes were issued to the press.

In contrast to the militaristic ceremony in Rome, the ceremony in Milan evoked the social dimensions of the fascist project. Dino Grandi, undersecretary of the Ministry of Foreign Affairs, inaugurated numerous public works in ceremonies that displayed the "greatest enthusiasm" of the public. He spoke in Piazza del Duomo before a crowd that exhibited "magnificent discipline." His brief address was typical of the speeches of Mussolini's emissaries. Grandi invoked Milan's contributions to the revolution and fascist history: "In the Fifth Annual [commemoration] of the March on Rome the firstborn Fascio [Milan was the home of the movement] powerfully lined up in your marvelous neighborhood groups, faithful to the wing of Italy that knew the heroism of Baracca and the crown of glory De Pinedo, the word of faith, and of love and of dedication to the Patria and the Duce that in this equinox of the sixth year of the fascist revolution, is a

[9] Report of the Agenzia Stefani, 30 October 1927, nos. 40, 41, 42, ACS, PCM 1927 2.4–1/f. 4060.

[10] I take my description of the celebration from reports of the Agenzia Stefani, 30 October 1927, nos. 8, 10, 11, 12, 13, 23, 29, 40, 41, 42, ACS, PCM 1927 2.4–1/f. 4060.

[11] Milizia Voluntaria per La Sicrezza Nazionale, *Disposizioni per la rivista del 30 ottobre 1927 in occassione della "Marcia su Roma"* (Rome: Colombo, 1927), ACS, PCM 1927 2.4–1/f. 4060.

[12] I could find no direct archival evidence to support my assertion that the parts of the city near the Piazza Venezia where the first anniversary and subsequent events had taken place were under construction between 1926 and 1929; see Antonio Cederna, *Mussolini urbanista* (Rome: Laterza, 1980), 58–59.

sacred pledge of discipline for immortal Italy. For Il Duce, Eja, Eja, alala! Giampoli."[13]

Children, the core of the Italian family, figured prominently in Milan. Mussolini's family took his place in the Milan ceremonies. His two youngest sons, Bruno and Vittorio, led a parade of Balilla, a fascist organization of boys between the ages of eight and thirteen. The Stefani News Agency reported that Bruno and Vittorio shouted the loudest "alala" and with their "little hands" gave a "Roman Salute." Aside from the obvious sentimentality in Stefani's report, the message was fairly straightforward: children were the future of fascism, particularly Il Duce's children. Although Mussolini's May 1927 Speech of the Ascension had emphasized the need to produce more fascist bodies, the regime's demographic policies were not in full force until the 1930s. The first step in demographic control was the "tax on bachelors," passed into law on December 19, 1926, which levied a "punitive tax on male celibacy." In the interim, Mussolini united theory and practice, and his wife gave birth to their fourth child, Romano, on September 26, 1927, just a little more than a month before the fifth anniversary of the March.[14]

"Passion" was the underpinning of the "work" of regime reproduction and, presumably, of biological reproduction. Arnaldo Mussolini, Mussolini's brother and editor of *Il Popolo d'Italia*, narrated the popular passion for the regime and for the work of revolution that the spectacles of commemoration displayed: "We affirm that the fascist demonstrations of this fifth anniversary of the March on Rome have shown clearly that the spirit that animates our faith has maintained itself intact with its original freshness. If in the past, it was the passion of tumult, today it is the same passion in a more serene, more solid, stronger ambience forged by time." Realizing that the regime had kept its promises, the Italian people were willing to go forward. Describing Mussolini's speech as "unforgettable," Arnaldo, concluded, "It is right that Rome has put on this superb spectacle of force. The capital is the brain, the pulse, and the measure."[15]

The fifth anniversary witnessed the beginning of a subtle shift in the language and style of public narrative. *Il Popolo d'Italia* began to describe the commemorations as "spectacles of force and faith." This language augured

---

[13] I take my description of the Milan celebration from reports of the Agenzia Stefani, 30 October 1927, nos. 33 and 34, and Ministero Dell'Interno, Telegramma n. 56487 and n. 56350, *ACS, PCM* 1927 2.4–1/f. 4060.

[14] Victoria De Grazia, *How Fascism Ruled Women: Italy, 1922–1945* (Berkeley: University of California Press, 1992), 43, 65. Mussolini had a wife, Rachele Guidi, to whom he was legally married and with whom he produced five children. This fact sometimes get lost in the stories of his more colorful paramours, such as Margherita Sarfatti, who figured prominently in the regime, and Clara Petacci, who chose to die beside him.

[15] Arnaldo Mussolini, "Passione," *Il Popolo d'Italia*, 1 November 1927, 1.

the beginning of a militarism that would become more pronounced as the years went by, culminating in 1935 with the fascist invasion of Ethiopia.

Inaugurating Itself: The Regime as Public Display (1932)

The commemorations between 1927 and 1932 repeated established patterns. The tenth anniversary occurred at the height of the consensus period (1929–35), a time of relative political and social stability and the midpoint of the regime, although no one knew that in 1932. After ten years in power, the regime was beginning to focus outward and to think of itself as an international political actor. The annual commemorations reflected this change.

The tenth anniversary commemoration, though it replayed many familiar themes, marked the end of commemorations that simply celebrated the regime—the revolution as new political institution. The 1932 commemoration was corporativist in that it drew in all state institutions and categories of persons while continuing to honor the soldiers and wounded that made up the original revolution. In contrast to the fifth anniversary commemoration, the tenth anniversary commemoration used history to legitimate future action rather than to celebrate present stability.

Public display of the regime at midlife was the hallmark of the tenth anniversary commemoration. The events included the ritual genres of symposia, commemorations, celebrations, and inaugurations. Among the celebrations were special performances at La Scala Opera House in Milan and the Royal Opera in Rome. The operas chosen, *I Puritani, Norma, Cenerentola*, were not notable in terms of political content although they were all part of the standard Italian national repertoire. A special choral symphony, *The March on Rome*, was composed for the occasion and broadcast on the radio, and the fascist educative cinema L.U.C.E. put out a propaganda book of photography, *Fascist Italy Walking Forward (L'Italia fascista in cammino)*.[16] Mussolini gave amnesty to those who had committed "moral crimes." Some of these crimes involved tax evasion, but others had to do with the moral policing of schoolteachers who had been suspended from work. For example, the National Ministry of Education petitioned the Duce for clemency for a woman schoolteacher who was suspended for six months as punishment for having "illicit relations with diverse persons" that compromised "her reputation and her morality."[17]

Rome as city and center of fascism was as much a focus of this commemoration as the numerous public events. The concentration on Rome, present

---

[16] Istituto Nazionale L.U.C.E, *L'Italia fascista in cammino* (Rome: L.U.C.E., 1932).

[17] For the law itself, see Relazione e R. Decreto 5 novembre 1932-XI, n. 1403, "Concessione di amnistia e indulto nella ricorrenza del I Decennale"; the petitions to il duce from the National Ministry of Education can be found in *ACS, PCM* 1931–33 3.3.3/f. 2754, sf. 19.

from the beginning of the regime, began to intensify in the 1930s and was coincident with the regime's growing emphasis on fascism as the seat of the "new" Roman empire.[18] The tenth anniversary commemorations lasted one month and colonized time and space in the name of fascism.[19] The first event was the autumn session of the Grand Council of Fascism, which met with more fanfare than usual. Next was a series of symposia. The National Assembly of Intellectuals convened on October 1, followed by the First Italian Legal Congress on October 5 and the Congress of the Italian Society for the Progress of Science on October 9. The National Council of Corporations had its annual meeting during this period.

On October 16, the regime staged a large public rally in Piazza Venezia to celebrate the Fascist Party and its organizations. The dates between October 23 and 26 were occupied with the inaugurations of several public works, including the Mussolini Forum in Rome and the reconstructed Roman monuments in the center of the city. On October 26, Mussolini made a pilgrimage to Milan to open the highway between Milan and Turin. He stopped in Turin, where he had considerably more success than in his 1923 visit.

The local inaugural event was the opening, on October 27, of the Mostra della Rivoluzione Fascista (Exhibit of the Fascist Revolution), a large exhibition in Rome that displayed in various forms the history of the fascist movement from 1914 to 1922. On the same day, a votive chapel in memory of the fascists who had "fallen for the revolution" was dedicated in the National Fascist Party headquarters. The final event was the "grand parade" of wounded militia men in Rome and the inauguration of the monument, in his home village, to Michele Bianchi, who in death entered an emerging pantheon of fascist heroes.

This catalog of public events fails to capture the deeper meaning of this collage of ritual genres. The various symposia became fascist rituals by virtue of the fact that they appropriated standard features of intellectual life, and intellectuals themselves, and wed them to the life of the regime and the nation. In 1932, the regime explicitly articulated the role it envisioned for intellectuals in the new fascist political community. Fascism redrew the terms of intellectual discourse and practice and suggested that there was no life of the mind, or work of the mind, outside the state.

Mussolini made these points in his address to the National Assembly of Intellectuals held at the beginning of the commemorative period. He said that he "despised" the term "intellectual" because it was a product of liber-

---

[18] On "Romanism," see Romke Visser, "Fascist Doctrine and the Cult of *Romanita*," *Journal of Contemporary History* 27 (1992), 5–22.
[19] The calendar of events is taken from *Foglio d'Ordini*, July 19, 1932; and *ACS, PCM* 1931–33 3.3.3/f. 2754, sf. 9.

alism. He preferred to concentrate on the "concrete activity of intelligence." Abandoning the term "intellectual," he viewed his audience as "representatives" of the individual intellectual activities of their respective corporativist organizations—architects, lawyers, writers, doctors, musicians, engineers. These corporative bodies would create a "personal act between fascism and culture." According to Mussolini, culture was not "cold erudition." Fascist culture creators had to disengage themselves from "ivory towers," which often masked "aridity of spirit." Mussolini exhorted intellectuals "to live life fully, to be men of your time, to avoid the isolation of sterile egocentrism. . . . With fascism for the first time in world history, professionals and artists would enter the State and come to be part of the State."[20]

Mussolini's message appears to have penetrated the consciousness of Guglielmo Marconi, an international star of Italian science. His entry in *The Working Nation* (*La nazione operante*), a biographical dictionary of all members of the regime, listed him as a senator for life, president of the Italian Academy, and a member of the Fascist Grand Council. He volunteered to fight in Ethiopia at the age of sixty-one, suggesting that his fervor for the regime was commensurate with his fervor for science.[21] In September 1932, he wrote a personal request to Mussolini for more money for scientific research. He asked that a "modest sum" be allocated for research laboratories and was careful to frame his request in the language of the regime.

Marconi compared the work of science to the work of fascism, arguing, "Scientific research is not made only by genius, it is made by order, tenacity, and great patience." He noted that the "titanic work" of the Duce which "saved" Italy might now be directed toward science. Marconi explicitly wed commemoration to scientific advance: "To remember the epic events that saved our country from catastrophe, and that we remember this year in the completed ten years, in the laborious harmony of a people who faithfully follow the way under a secure guide, a manner more noble, more useful that gives Italy the methods to valorize the hard work of its best men who dedicate their intellect and their life to science to make the Patria stronger, richer, and more respected."[22] Marconi's behavior was typical of Italian intellectuals, who during this period routinely used the language of fascism to court favor and money for their particular projects. The archives do not report whether his request for additional subsidy was granted.[23]

[20] "Il discorso del Duce," *Le Professioni e le Arti: Bollettino Mensile della Confederazione Nazionale*, 2 (October 1932), 2.

[21] Edoardo Savino, *La nazione operante*, 3d ed. (Novara: Istituto Geografico de Agostini, 1937), 213.

[22] "Pro-memoria per S.E. Il Capo del Governo," written by Guglielmo Marconi and dated 14 September 1932, *ACS, PCM* 1931–33 3.3.3/f. 2754, sf. 4.

[23] See Mabel Berezin, "Cultural Form and Political Meaning: State-Subsidized Theater,

Marconi's speech at the science symposium, which was broadcast on seventy-one European and one hundred American radio stations, was an encomium to the glories of the regime. The speech wed the Roman past to the fascist future and described the new fascist Rome as a home for artists and men of intellect. Marconi focused on the Italian Academy, which the regime founded in 1929 to mimic the French: "This Royal Academy is secure that invitations will be accepted from thinking men and artists from the whole world, with the same cordiality with which they are returned: they will be happy guests of the Italian people, among whom they will be able to feel above all the new spirit sustained by the impulse of an idea and the action of a Man."[24] Academy members, prominent Italian intellectuals such as Marconi, received a stipend of three thousand lire a month, three times the average shopkeeper's salary. In exchange for subsidy, the regime required members to appear at public ceremonies wearing ornate fascist uniforms.[25] Science may not have been adequately supported by the regime, but Marconi was.

The inauguration of the Mostra della Rivoluzione Fascista was the centerpiece of the tenth anniversary commemorations. The Mostra a museum of fascist memorabilia permitted the regime to display itself and the fascist intellectuals who had designed it.[26] The exhibition hall in the center of Rome was designed to resemble a modernist cathedral and functioned as a shrine to fascism. In contrast to other fascist cultural ventures, it was enormously popular with the public. Originally planned to last for six months, it remained open for two years and turned a profit. Its catalog pictured exhibit halls containing icons such as Mussolini's desk, a shrine to fascist martyrs, and numerous oversize posters and murals depicting images of Mussolini, fascist eagles, and swords.[27]

The Mostra staged a new Italian history that began in 1914 with the debate over entering World War I and ended in 1929, the period of fascist "regeneration." *Il Popolo d'Italia* summarized the Mostra's purpose in terms of "history" and "sensation":

Ideology, and the Language of Style in Fascist Italy," *American Journal of Sociology* 99 (March 1994), 1272–76.

[24] "Il vibrante messagio di Marconi agli uomini di pensiero ed agli artisti di tutto il mondo," *Il Popolo d'Italia*, 16 October 1932, 1.

[25] Edward R. Tannenbaum, *The Fascist Experience* (New York: Basic, 1972), 292–93.

[26] On the Mostra, see Marla Stone, "Staging Fascism: The Exhibition of the Fascist Revolution," *Journal of Contemporary History* 28 (1993), 215–43, and Jeffrey T. Schnapp, "Epic Demonstrations: Fascist Modernity and the 1932 Exhibition of the Fascist Revolution," in *Fascism, Aesthetics, and Culture*, ed. Richard J. Golsan (Hanover, N.H.: University Press of New England, 1992), 1–36.

[27] Partito Nazionale Fascista, *Mostra della Rivoluzione Fascista*, ed. Dino Alfieri and Luigi Freddi (Bergamo: Arti Grafiche, 1933).

Fascism is already History and it has not yet been chronicled.

It has already made a profound impression on the memory and thoughts of men and has already served as a point of reference and orientation in the history of the transformation, of the political, social, moral, and spiritual evolution of the people.

The Mostra of Fascism quickly gives this sensation and convinces immediately that the struggles and victories of the Fascists were not transient episodes localized in time, origins, and goals.[28]

The Mostra coupled public display and fascist community building. The exhibit consisted of "18,000 documents,"[29] whose collection involved the mobilization of the entire population as the Mostra's organizers instructed local prefects to gather artifacts from ordinary citizens. Contributing to the Mostra was a tangible method of participating in a community of fascist history makers. Viewing the Mostra was similar to attending rallies in public space, because both aimed to create a feeling of fascist history and recognition of national community.

The first event that combined commemoration and celebration—past and future—was the large public meeting in Rome on October 16 of twenty-five thousand top-ranking fascist dignitaries and representatives from the families of the "Fallen for the Revolution," as well as the wounded and incapacitated. The prominent presence of the battalions of fascist youth and university students signaled a public linking of fascist generations that was a harbinger of events to come. History and futurity dominated this ceremony, which brought large crowds of arguably fascism's most committed adherents into Piazza Venezia. In his speech Mussolini summarized the now familiar themes of fascist history. He observed that, with the exception of Michele Bianchi, the original founders of the revolution were still present. He ascribed the initial violence of the revolution to the "political and moral intransigence" required to found a new political project. In 1922, the political system was in "crisis" and what was needed was a "capitalism of the State."[30]

Directly addressing the youth in the crowd, Mussolini articulated the necessity of coming up with a new generation of fascists. With ten years behind it, the regime had to guarantee a replacement generation if the fascist project was to march into the future. Mussolini highlighted the "problem of youth" with a rhetorical retreat to the familiar image of the Unknown Sol-

[28] "La Mostra della Rivoluzione," *Il Popolo d'Italia*, 30 October 1932, 1.

[29] "La Mostra della Rivoluzione fascista sara inaugurata stamane," *Il Popolo d'Italia*, 29 October 1927, 2.

[30] Benito Mussolini, "Primo discorso per il Decennale," in *Dal dodicesimo anniversario della Fondazione dei Fasci al patto a quattro*, vol. 25, *OO*, 135, 136.

dier. His rhetoric wed the body of the soldier and the geographical image of the body of the nation to underscore futurity and mobilize youth.

> You are united here today in Rome, in this Rome from which we wish to generate the love and pride of Italians and the admiration of the world. You are united in this piazza that is in the heart of Rome and thus the heart of Italy (*extremely vibrant applause*), not only because it is the Palazzo Venezia, constructed as one of those cities that we may describe as imperial, such as Genoa, Pisa, Amalfi, Ravenna, and Florence, which diffuse the immortal imperialism of their genius.[31]

Mussolini added that Napoleon's mother died in the Palazzo Venezia, a fact that acquires importance not only because of the Italian cultural affinity for motherhood but also because Napoleon, according to Mussolini, was the catalyst of the Italian nation-building project. The most important feature of the building, however, is its location in front of the monument to Vittorio Emanuele, the home of the "altar of the Unknown Soldier" and the "altar of fallen fascists." Mussolini concluded: "The Unknown Soldier is the symbol of a united, victorious, fascist Italy, united from the Alps of a Roman Aosta to the seas of Trapani that saw the defeat of the Carthaginian ships. The Unknown Soldier is the supreme testimony to what was, the infallible certainty of what will be!"[32] *Il Popolo d'Italia* described the rally as a "national meeting without precedent in the history of Italy" and stated that the "25,000 members of the fascist hierarchy" who assembled in Piazza Venezia displayed an "indescribable manifestation of enthusiasm and devotion."[33]

Emotion governed the narrative representation of this event. At the first glimpse of Mussolini on the balcony, the crowd exploded with "passion": "The whole piazza is a fluttering of flags, a whirling of pennants. The whole crowd seems to vibrate with one soul to express with one outburst of passion its faith, its devotion, its admiration for Il Duce." When Mussolini finally appeared, "he is dressed in Black Shirt decorated solely with the Medal of the March on Rome. For a few minutes the manifestation [of the crowds] continues. These acclamations are the expression of the truest and most ardent sentiments, of an enthusiasm of incomparable force." According to *Il Popolo d'Italia*, the voice of the people blended with the roar of passing airplanes and linked the passion of the people to the strength of the regime. Mussolini began his speech with the dramatic proclamation, "I am your Leader!"[34]

---

[31] Ibid., 136.
[32] Ibid.
[33] *Il Popolo d'Italia*, 18 October 1932, 1.
[34] Ibid.

Mussolini's visit to Milan, undertaken a week after the October 16 rally, continued the narrative of the new fascist nation-state. The physical journey to Milan reenacted his journey to Milan in 1923 and gave a temporal and spatial dimension to fascist history. Speaking in Piazza del Duomo, he reminded the crowd of the speech he had made in Piazza Belgioiosi nine years earlier. Milan was the location of the first fascist cell, "Covo," and according to Mussolini, the past was "beautiful" but not more so than the present. Autonomy and consensus characterized the new Italy, and "the Italian people" were now the "protagonists of their own history."[35]

Mussolini's journey to Milan consciously invoked the past, but his speech was for the most part a celebration of the fascist future. He jubilantly noted, "We feel that destiny will be tomorrow, as today, in our hands and that it will be the result of our invincible will. (*Enthusiastic ovation*)." Eschewing conferences in favor of action, Mussolini recalled the ill-governed Italy of the pre-fascist period, and the crowd chanted "five for twelve," evoking the sixty-year reign Mussolini had promised in Milan in 1923. He responded to the chant: "Today, with full tranquility of conscience, I tell you, immense multitude, that the twentieth century will be the century of fascism (*applause*), it will be the century of Italian power (*applause*), it will be the century in which Italy will return for the third time as the director of civilized humanity (*grand ovation*)." How Italy assumed its role as director of civilized humanity would unfold in the next three years, but Mussolini's conclusion served as an intimation of what was to come: "In ten years Europe will be fascist or fascistified!"[36]

The concluding public ceremony on October 28 in Rome consisted of two rallies, one in Piazza Esedra and one in Piazza Venezia. They were united by the "walk" down the Via dell'Impero (Imperial Way).[37] To accommodate the walk from the Colosseum to the Piazza Venezia through the center of the city, whole portions of historic neighborhoods were gutted mindlessly, all in the space of one year so as to have the road ready for the ceremonies. (Figure 2).[38] The militia's detailed printed instructions read like stage directions for these ceremonial events. Maps demonstrated careful attention to spatial arrangement of fascist bodies and organizations. Security was tight and many streets were closed. Ceremonies began at ten in the morning in Piazza Esedra. Instructions included where troops would line up, who would line up, how they would enter the piazza, and what music

---

[35] Benito Mussolini, "Al popolo di Milano," in *Dal dodicesimo anniversario della fondazione dei Fasci al patto a quattro*, vol. 25, *OO*, 146.

[36] Ibid., 146, 147, 148.

[37] Milizia Voluntaria Sicrezza Nazionale, 20 October 1932, "Rivista per il Decennale della Rivoluzione," *ACS, PCM* 1931–33 3.3.3/f. 2754, sf. 9.

[38] Cederna, *Mussolini urbanista*, 167–75.

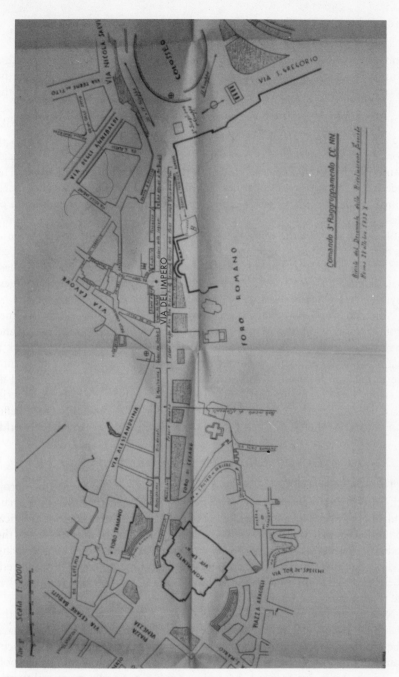

Figure 2. The Via del Impero. ACS, *PCM* 1931–33, 333/f. 2754, sf. 3.

would be played (Figure 3). At the end of the ceremony in Piazza Esedra, Mussolini led the way on horseback to the Via dell'Impero, where the troops followed him into Piazza Venezia for the ceremonies to honor the Unknown Soldier and the fallen fascists (Figure 4).

The walk down the Via dell'Impero required a literal and figurative breaking up of the Italian past. In the wake of the smashed neighborhoods of working-class apartments and ancient churches, the walk augured a fascist future in which building would not be restricted to mortar and stone. The speeches of October 28 addressed fascist history making and a calm, disciplined future. Yet there was a subtle change in the public representation of these events. An editorial cartoon from the first page of *Il Popolo d'Italia* spoke volumes: "In the mind of the Duce" (Figure 5). The word *fucina* is literally translated as "forge" or "mine". Colloquial English renders it best as "What's cooking?" The phrases on the more than vaguely phallic but less than artfully drawn symbols, "walk," "build," "fight," "conquer," suggest anything but a peaceful future.[39]

Nineteen thirty-two marked the end of the first phase of the regime. From that point on, the March commemorations focused on the future and served as vehicles of mobilization. The years 1934 through 1938 mark a sharp divide in commemorative activity as the consensus period moved into the mobilization period. Where the early commemorations were aimed at asserting that the regime had built itself and that new institutions were in place, the succeeding commemorations aimed at a considerably more bellicose future. As the fascists had taken Rome, they would now take the world.

Dead Bodies/Living Bodies: Crossing the Divide (1934)

The public display of bodies was a powerful force of the fascist ritual project. Fascist rhetoric describing ritual actions suggested that the sheer accumulation of bodies in public space created a feeling of emotion and political community. As the regime moved forward, its use of bodies, from the bodies of the mothers to the dead bodies of fascist heroes, to the living bodies that the trains carried to public events, became more pronounced. The Italian individual and collective body was a powerful ritual resource that the regime mobilized consistently.

Nineteen thirty-four was a turning point in the commemoration of the March on Rome and in the life of the regime. On the brink of what I have labeled the mobilization period, the regime was beginning to shift its focus from the building of national social and political institutions to foreign policy. From this point forward the regime took a decidedly more militaristic

[39] "L'Italia del sacrificio vittorioso ed inobliabile sfila davanti al Duce lungo la 'Via dell'Impero,'" *Il Popolo d'Italia*, 29 October 1932, 1.

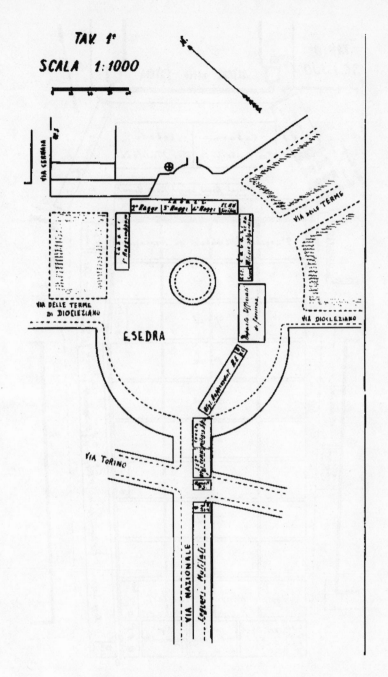

TAV. 1ª

SCALA 1:1000

VIA CERNAIA

2° Raggi   3° Raggi   4° Raggi   R. Gd
                                  Unità

VIA DELLE TERME

VIA DELLE TERME
DI DIOCLEZIANO

ESEDRA

VIA DIOCLEZIANO

VIA TORINO

VIA NAZIONALE

Figure 3. Piazza Esedra. *ACS, PCM* 1931–33, 333/f. 2754, sf. 3.

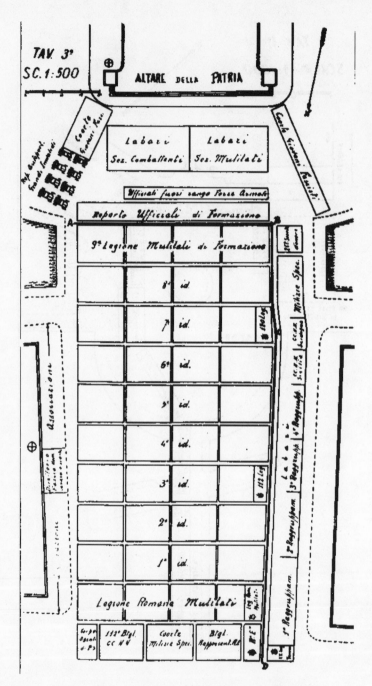

Figure 4. Altar of the Patria. *ACS, PCM* 1931–33, 333/f. 2754, sf. 3.

Figure 5. Newspaper propaganda cartoon. *Il Popolo d'Italia,* 29 October 1932, 1.

and aggressive cast and so did its public ceremonies. Two corporative physical bodies, the bodies of fascist martyrs and the bodies of fascist athletes—dead youth and living youth—carried the symbolic weight of the twelfth anniversary commemoration. The old and new generation of fascists, the past warriors and future fighters, were a harbinger of fascist aggression.

The reburying of thirty-seven fascist martyrs in the Cathedral of Santa Croce in Florence and the parading of the bodies of Italian athletes in the reconstructed Circus Maximus in Rome were the two ritual actions that dominated the twelfth anniversary commemoration.[40] The idea of Santa

[40] The idea of reburying is not particularly fascist and is a feature of political ritual worth pursuing; see Susan Gal, "Bartok's Funeral: Representations of Europe in Hungary," *American Ethnologist* 18 (1991), 440–58.

Croce as a national shrine for Italian heroes had originated in the Risorgimento period.[41] Mussolini and the entire hierarchy of the National Fascist Party attended the Florence ceremony, which was broadcast on radio. At eleven in the morning the coffins of the fascist martyrs were carried through the streets of Florence, arriving at the cathedral by noon. Each coffin was proceeded by a banner bearing the martyr's name with the phrase "Present!" written underneath. As the coffin reached the cathedral, the martyr's name was called out by members of the assembled fascist squads; then the coffin was passed from one group of fascists to another as it slowly descended into the crypt of Santa Croce.

La Nazione, the Florentine daily, reported on the reburying for three days and provided extensive photographic coverage. The first narrative, on October 26, began by situating the event in the context of fascist history and the "memory of the Italian people." The event signaled the end of regime "preparation" and the "opening of a period of constructive and creative activity."[42] Descriptions of the impending ceremony, which represented not only Florentine fascism but "Italian Fascism," melded the religious and the emotional:

> Feverish hours, hours of anxiety and tension: few hours separate us from a rite toward which the entire Italian soul prepares itself and stretches itself like a supreme and intimate source of religious energy without which life would be a colorless succession of useless days. . . . The civil liturgy of fascism testifies to the discipline of the masses and their great faith in the Leader.

The reburial would transform the history of Florence, which gave birth to Italian language, thought, and soul, from the "flower" of the "race" to the "flower of the new Italy" and location of the "eternal cult."[43]

Mussolini's speech, delivered in the sacristy of Santa Croce, is unambiguous as to the direction the regime was heading and the meaning of the bodies:

> Black Shirts of all Italy! I have come to Florence to the thirty-seven heroic
> Florentine Fallen Fascists to the Temple of Italian glories. The names and
> the memory of these Comrades of the vigil [of the revolution] are and

[41] The Italian romantic writer Ugo Foscolo was responsible for promoting Santa Croce as the location of a national shrine. See Adrian Lyttelton, "The National Question in Italy," in *The National Question in Europe in Historical Context*, ed. Mikulas Teich and Roy Porter, (New York: Cambridge University Press, 1993), 74–75.

[42] "I caduti fascisti fiorentini saranno accolti domani in Santa Croce," *La Nazione* (Florence), 26 October 1934, 1.

[43] "Firenze fascista consacra oggi il suo voto piu'alto," *La Nazione*, 27 October 1934, 1.

remain in our hearts. In difficult times, they had already adopted our pennant motto: Believe, Obey, Fight. They believed, they obeyed, and they consecrated in combat their supreme dedication to the cause. Their testimony is sacred, their warning is solemn and incontrovertible: Woe to the doubters, woe to the latecomers, woe to the cowards, and woe, above all, to the forgetful.

The Fallen of the Revolution have proceeded like a glorious avant-garde of the battles of yesterday. They proceed us in the battles of tomorrow, perhaps harder but always victorious. Black Shirts of all Italy! To whom does this century belong?[44]

The event was replicated the next day in Rome with a ceremony in the votive chapel at Fascist Party headquarters. The full-page photograph on the front of *Il Popolo d'Italia* on October 28 underscored the regime's intent: "DUX" in bold, oversized letters suggested a monument surrounded by waving pennants, hinting at guns as well as flags. The caption under the image read, "The potent and granite barrier of industrious fascist Italy"[45] (Figure 6).

On October 28, fifteen thousand fascist athletes from all of Italy paraded before Mussolini in the Circus Maximus. The road to the Circus was one of the new public works inaugurated in 1934. The Italian Olympic Committee assisted in the orchestration of this event, and the athletes paraded in the costume of their sports. For example, the golfers were required to wear gray pants, brown sweaters, and yellow shoes and were to carry sacks of golf clubs on their shoulders. Soccer players were to wear their local medallions, soccer shoes without cleats, and full uniforms. The parade into the Circus was to proceed at "132 steps per minute" with "nine men lined across." Fascism was not absent. Eighteen Olympic athletes carried a musket with the name of an athlete who had fallen in either the war or the revolution, and as a member of the Balilla called out the name of the fallen, an athlete stepped forward and the crowd responded, "Present."[46]

Expressing Fascism: The Mobilizations (1935–1937)

When taken as isolated events, fascist mobilizations of fascist bodies, living and dead, martyrs and athletes, seem to be pieces of a developing religious cult of fascism.[47] If we place them in the context of an emerging pattern of

[44] Printed in *La Nazione*, 28 October 1934, 1.

[45] *Il Popolo d'Italia*, 28 October 1934, 1.

[46] Partito Nazionale Fascista, "Celebrazione del XII annuale della Marcia su Roma, 28 ottobre XII, sfilata degli atleti sulla via del Circo Massimo," ACS, PCM 1934–36 3.3.3/f. 2344A.

[47] This is Gentile's argument in *Il culto del littorio* (Rome: Laterza, 1993), 168–95.

Figure 6. Newspaper display of fascist power. *Il Popolo d'Italia*, (Milan) 28 October 1934, 1.

ritual actions, however, they suggest other meanings. Nineteen thirty-five was the year the regime invaded Ethiopia. It was also the year of the first people's *adunate*. The *adunate* were huge rallies that brought masses of persons into public squares throughout Italy to demonstrate solidarity with the regime's colonialist and imperialist ventures. During this period, the commemorations of the March became distinctively more bellicose and took second place to the *adunate*.

Demonstrations as ritual genre, expressive events to generate emotion, were the purest type of community of feeling and had virtually no cognitive content. There were six national demonstrations in Rome between 1935 and 1937. Four of them focused on the war in Ethiopia and the founding of the fascist empire; Italian women were the centerpiece of the other two. As a state without a nation, Italy lacked a colonial empire. Its imperial ventures in Libya between 1911 and 1912 had met with dubious success, and its forays into the Balkans were equally qualified. Colonies would put Italy on the same footing as the liberal democratic regimes of England and France. The demonstrations that occurred between 1935 and 1937 fit popular conceptions of fascist ritual in that they were huge rallies held in Rome for purposes of emotional mobilization. They were purely expressive events that melded the social themes of the regime, as displayed in the women's mobilizations, with its imperial aspirations.

The *adunate* defy discursive description. They were spectacles of force that depended on the massing of bodies in the public piazza. They were also pure communities of feeling in which individual Italian bodies abandoned their sense of separate selves and fused with the regime. The pictures of these events in *Il Popolo d'Italia* are blurry and suggest a raw mass of living bodies giving consent to the regime. The headlines shout the imperial aspirations of a regime that was inventing colonies and imagining empire. There is an aesthetic sameness and shrillness to the representations of these events.

The war in Ethiopia was the focus of these mobilizations. The fascist colonial venture in Africa gave Italy a focus of political love and emotion. It also suggested that the fascist identity project was stumbling on rough national terrain as the economic hardships of the world depression took its toll on Italian life. The Ethiopian campaign was successful in garnering emotional solidarity with the regime, not because it was a civilizing mission to barbarian Africa, as the fascists claimed, but because it gave Italians an enemy against whom they could bond: the League of Nations and the liberal democratic regimes it represented.[48] The League of Nations, born of the Treaty of Versailles, was a reminder to Italians of their humiliating treatment at the

[48] Denis Mack Smith, *Mussolini* (London: Granada, 1981), discusses the support Il Duce was able to garner for this venture (228–35).

Peace Conference, a resentment that fueled the early fascist movement and was so deeply felt that it could be resurrected at will.

The first mobilization was on October 2, 1935, in response to the economic sanctions the League threatened against Italy if it pursued a course of gratuitous aggression in Africa. *Il Popolo d'Italia* reported the "fantastic spectacle of Piazza Venezia" and the "unprecedented demonstration in Milan." Mussolini declared, "I refuse to believe that the authentic British People, who have never had disputes with Italy, would be disposed to risk throwing Europe on the road to catastrophe, to defend an African country, universally marked as a country without a shadow of civility."[49] The League pursued its sanctions, and the aggression against Italy served to rouse Italian national sentiment. Seven months later, on May 5, 1936, Mussolini declared victory in Ethiopia. The headlines of *Il Popolo d'Italia* blared in bold letters, "THE DUCE TO ALL ITALY AND THE WORLD THAT VICTORIOUS TROOPS HAVE ENTERED ADDIS ABEBA, THAT THE WAR IS OVER AND PEACE RESTORED." These words surrounded a photograph of Mussolini in military uniform with his arms folded and the Latin word for leader, "DUX," printed under it.

To celebrate the "victory," Mussolini called another mobilization in Rome of five hundred thousand persons where he proclaimed in the language of colonial conquest, "Ethiopia is Italian: Italian in fact, because it is occupied by our victorious armies; Italian in law, because of the Roman gladiators and the civility that triumphs over barbarism, the justice that triumphs over arbitrary cruelty, the redemption of miseries that triumphs over a millennium of slavery."[50] The crowds gathered in all the piazzas of Italy, and bells pealed from the church towers and public buildings of the medieval landscape. The streets of central Rome from the Via dell'Impero to Corso Umberto were filled with cheering Italians. Three days later, on May 9, 1936, Mussolini declared Italy an "Empire." The king was now "King of Italy and Emperor of Ethiopia," and Mussolini was the "Founder of the Empire." The "Fascist Empire" was the end of "fourteen years of irrepressible energy and discipline of youth and the banners of generations of Italians."[51] Again the crowds were out in the piazza. The last grand mobilization was on December 11, 1937, when Mussolini announced that Italy was leaving the League of Nations as retaliation for its sanctions.

The *Rivista Illustrata del Popolo d'Italia*, the four-color photographic weekly appendage to *Il Popolo d'Italia*, prepared a special commemorative issue in honor of the new empire. A photo montage captured the multiple

[49] "Lo storico discorso del Duce alla Nazione ed al mondo," *Il Popolo d'Italia*, 3 October 1935, 1.

[50] *Il Popolo d'Italia*, 6 May 1936, 1.

[51] "Il Duce annunzia all'Italia ed al mondo la costituzione dell'impero fascista," *Il Popolo d'Italia*, 10 May 1936, 1.

cultural schemata on which the Italian fascist project drew as it attempted to create the fascist nation-state and new empire (Figure 7). At the forefront are Romulus and Remus nursing at the breast of the wolf (according to popular legend, Romulus and Remus founded Rome after the wolf saved them from starvation). The first backdrop features banners with fascist eagles waving, clearly an image from a rally. The background is a stone monument depicting a map of Mediterranean Europe, North Africa, and the Middle East. Italy and the colonies of the new fascist empire—Libya and Ethiopia— are in bold relief. This monument was, and is, on the Via dell'Impero, now renamed, but it is still visible in Rome, and tourists on the road to the Colosseum may stop to look at it. The words at the bottom of the photo montage read, "Rome ought to appear marvelous to all people of the world: vast, organized, powerful as it was in the time of the first emperor Augustus."[52] The image combines the myth of the founding of Rome with the emerging myth of empire. But the image is also one of maternity against the backdrop of empire. The mother's body, the second dominant image, taps into the Italian cultural idea of family.

In this period of increasing militarization, it would seem as though the image of maternity had disappeared. Yet women were to become more pronounced in fascist spectacle and narrative as the regime marched forward. Why the emphasis on women in a period of intense mobilization? The display of women and family in the service of fascism and the appropriation of marriage and motherhood were central to the regime's social and political mission. In a regime that expected to endure, women as producers of new fascist bodies were important. Despite the demographic campaign and the cultural importance of the family, the empirical evidence does not suggest that Italian women were all that enthusiastic about becoming mothers, and Italian fertility actually declined during the fascist period.[53]

The public display of women was the center of the other two mobilizations. The first, the "day of faith," occurred on December 18, 1935, and the second, the "woman's mobilization" in Rome, occurred on May 8, 1936, three days after Mussolini declared victory in Ethiopia and two days before the declaration of empire. The latter event simply featured the raw display of masses of women's bodies in the service of the regime; the "wedding ring campaign," as the former event was known, has greater salience for the arguments I am advancing. After three months of the Ethiopian campaign, the state coffers were emptying rapidly. The regime needed gold, and Mussolini asked Italian women to sacrifice their wedding rings to the glory of the

[52] *Italia imperiale*, ed. Giovanni Agnelli and Achille Starace (Milan: Manlio Morgagni, 1937).
[53] David G. Horn, *Social Bodies* (Princeton: Princeton University Press, 1994), discusses the failure of fascist demographic policies (123–26).

Figure 7. Photo-montage depicting regime's imperialist aspirations. *Italia Imperiale*, ed. Giovanni Agnelli and Achille Starace (Milan: Manlio Morgagni, 1937).

nation. There were ceremonies in all of Italy to donate wedding rings. The main ceremony occurred in Rome at the Altar of the Patria, where the queen of Italy led Italian mothers and wives in the donation of their rings. "Fourteen years of national education" mobilized Italian women to sacrifice their wedding rings to a cause "even more sacred than the family and the effects of the family." The Italian culture of the family was put on the line for the troops on the line, and *Il Popolo d'Italia* made explicit reference to the appropriation of the family: "This People, which has a cult of the family and its traditions, could not but fully and profoundly understand the significance of offering nuptial faith for a grander faith." The queen, who rarely spoke publicly in Italy, gave a brief oration at the foot of the monument to Vittorio Emanuele:

> In climbing the steps to the sanctuary of the Vittoriano, united, the proud mothers and wives of our dear Italy leave their wedding rings, symbol of our first joys and deepest renunciation on the altar of the Unknown Hero. In this purist offering of dedication to the Patria, bowing to the earth, almost merging our spirits with our glorious Fallen of the Great War. United, we invoke them, and to God, the "Vittoria."[54]

Commemoration and Mobilization: The Final March (1938)

The Meaning of the Vittoria

From October 1922, the March on Rome was wed to the commemoration of the Vittoria, the name given the Italian victory in the Veneto region during World War I. In his autobiography, Mussolini claimed to have rejected the Quadrumvirate's suggestion that the March on Rome occur on November 4, because "it would have spoiled a day of commemoration by introducing the element of revolutionary activity."[55] Mussolini timed the 1922 March so as not to conflict with the annual commemoration of the Vittoria. In 1938, the Vittoria's twentieth anniversary eclipsed the commemoration of the March. The "victory" in Ethiopia had fueled Mussolini's confidence in his capacities as an international political actor, and Il Duce turned his attention to giving Italy, and fascism, a larger role in foreign affairs. The shift in focus from the national to the international plunged Italy into its unfortunate alliance with Nazi Germany and ultimately brought down the regime.

Nineteen thirty-eight was a pivotal year for the Italian fascist regime and

---

[54] "La memorabile giornata a Roma," *Il Popolo d'Italia*, 19 December 1935, 1.

[55] Benito Mussolini, *My Autobiography*, trans. Richard Washburn Child (New York: Scribner's, 1928), 173.

for European political stability. After its exit from the League of Nations in December 1937, Italy entered into the Axis pact with Germany and Japan. This did not represent a firm commitment on the part of Mussolini, and he continued to deal with Britain. While Mussolini was playing Germany and Britain against each other, Hitler invaded Austria in March 1938 and the German *Anschluss* of Europe began. In April 1938, Mussolini signed a pact of friendship with Britain, which wished, along with other members of the League of Nations, to protect the territorial integrity of Yugoslavia and Czechoslovakia against German aggression. Mussolini continually vacillated and could not decide whether he wanted to move closer to war with or against Germany. In May 1939, he threw in his lot with Hitler and unwittingly committed Italy to an unpopular war.[56]

The ritual politics of 1938 foreshadowed the diplomatic events of 1939 that led to the final formation of the Axis. Nineteen thirty-eight was the twentieth anniversary of the "victory at Vittorio-Veneto"—the political phrase coupled the two battles that took place in June and November 1918 on the northern Italian river of the Piave and in the small town of Vittorio Veneto. The Vittoria loomed large in the consciousness of the Italian populace. Italian entry into World War I had been a source of national conflict. The socialists bitterly opposed "intervention"; Italian nationalists viewed it as an opportunity to annex the northern territories that the Austro-Hungarian empire had "usurped" and that rightly belonged to Italy.

Mussolini, as usual, had wavered on the question of intervention. As a socialist, he opposed Italian entry into the war. But by the time Italy decided to intervene on the side of the Allies in May 1915, he supported the war. The national conflict over Italian intervention led in the fall of 1917 to a series of strikes that preceded the Italian defeat of Caporetto at the hands of German-Austrian forces. The battle of Caporetto left three hundred thousand Italians prisoner and the Veneto in the hands of the Austrians.[57] Nationalists attributed the Italian defeat to the malaise that ambivalence toward the war produced. By June 1918, Italian forces had regrouped themselves and were able to defeat the Austrians on the River Piave and later in November in the town of Vittorio Veneto, two battles that firmly pushed back the Austrians. For Italian political elites, the Vittoria was a cause of national glory that quickly turned into international humiliation at the Versailles

[56] I draw this account from Mack Smith, *Mussolini*, 247–64, and Alexander DeGrand, *Italian Fascism: Its Origins and Developments* (Lincoln: University of Nebraska Press, 1989), 117–23. On Italian public opinion on military mobilization and the alliance with Germany, see Simona Colarizi, *L'opinione degli italiani sotto il regime, 1929–1943* (Rome: Laterza, 1991), 239–65.

[57] On Italian participation in World War I, see Adrian Lyttelton, *The Seizure of Power: Fascism in Italy, 1919–1929* (rpt., Princeton: Princeton University Press, 1987), 20–30.

peace talks, where Woodrow Wilson refused to recognize Italy's claims to the spoils of war and upheld the national integrity of border territory between Italy and Yugoslavia.

The combination of national glory and international humiliation made the Vittoria a rallying cry that echoed in Italian politics until the Second World War. The city of Fiume on the Italian-Yugoslavian border became such a cause célèbre that the flamboyant man of letters Gabriel D'Annunzio stormed it in an airplane and dramatically claimed it for Italy. Fascist propaganda fanned the flames of the Vittoria. The battle of Vittorio Veneto and the myth of Italian military victory was as essential a component of fascist catechisms and school textbooks as the March on Rome. Luigi Villari in *The Awakening of Italy* articulated, with some restraint, the Italian resentment of the League of Nations. Writing of Wilson's refusal to cede territory to Italy, he noted:

> There were no doubt reasons on both sides, and the Italian statesmen, people and Press were not blameless, but it cannot be gainsaid that while Britain and France obtained all that they wanted and annexed large and valuable provinces and colonies . . . Italy was accused of Imperialism merely for demanding a few small districts on her own borders containing highly civilized Italian communities; every Italian claim, however just, had to be fought for acrimoniously . . . before it obtained a grudging and incomplete recognition. There was, moreover, a tendency among the Allies to underestimate Italy's effort in the war, and its value for the common cause, to dispute the figures of her losses (which actually proved superior to the original estimates), and to attribute insufficient importance to the immense economic strain caused by war expenditure.[58]

Under its entry for the Vittoria, the *Dictionary of Fascist Doctrine* (a pastiche of excerpts from newspapers, journals, and speeches that defined central concepts and events of Italian fascism) printed the headlines of an article that had appeared anonymously in the Florentine nationalist newspaper *La Tribuna*. The excerpt proclaimed that Vittorio Veneto was a "military victory" because the defeat of the Austrian enemy made the German armistice necessary; a "political victory" because it led to the death of the Austro-Hungarian Empire and the "death" of a "type of State" that could no longer exist; and most important, "a spiritual and social victory. With it

---

[58] Figures on casualties are always subject to dispute. Luigi Villari (*The Awakening of Italy: The Fascist Regeneration* [New York: George H. Doran, n.d.], 45) estimates that, out of a population of 38 million, 600,000 Italians were killed and 1 million were wounded, with 220,000 permanently disabled. For a modern historical account that places Fiume in the context of postwar social unrest and the emergence of fascism, see Charles S. Maier, *Recasting Bourgeois Europe* (Princeton: Princeton University Press, 1975), 114–34.

interventionist, voluntary Italy, will make itself fascist and will give to Europe and to civilization a new type of Society and State."[59]

The commemoration of the Vittoria predated fascism. November 4, Armistice Day on the Italian front, became a legal holiday in October 1922.[60] The official day of commemoration a week after the March on Rome linked the two holidays temporally. The regime and the party linked them substantively. For example, a National Fascist Party communiqué written for the sixth anniversary commemoration of the Vittoria began, "Italians! The sixth anniversary of the 'Vittoria' can be today a commemoration of the People by virtue of Fascism, which freed the 'Vittoria' from the perdition of a betrayal that lasted four years."[61]

From its inception, the commemoration of the Vittoria was a holiday for soldiers. By 1926, the holiday was government business and the Military Command of Rome published official protocols. Among the Commemorative activities were a mass in the Santa Maria degli Angeli in central Rome with all members of the government, including Mussolini, present; a parade down the Via Nazionale to the Tomb of the Unknown Soldier; and mandatory commemoration in military barracks in the afternoon. Fifteen hundred tickets were printed for the mass and issued to various dignitaries, and five thousand tickets were available for the "general" populace.

As in the ceremonies that commemorated the March on Rome, the Fascist Party issued strict orders as to where troops and participants were to line up and how they were to enter the cathedral. The party mandated the participation of representatives of the Association of Mothers and Widows, the wounded, gold medal recipients, the navy, combatants, war volunteers, and *Arditi*. Each participant was required to dress in appropriate uniform. A military gun salute was provided as well as patriotic music. In the afternoon, the commemoration in the military barracks included music and cinema, a special distribution of wine, and free time until ten o'clock in the evening. At night, all military buildings were illuminated.[62]

The Vittoria was celebrated in every city in Italy. The reports that local prefects sent to the Ministry of Interior describing public order conveyed the flavor of local commemorations. For example, in Avellino, a town in the south of Italy which is not usually considered to have been an avid a participant in fascism, the prefect reported:

[59] Amerigo Montemaggiori, *Dizionario della dottrina fascista* (Rome: G.B. Paravia, 1934), 754.
[60] See "Pro-Memoria," *ACS, PCM* 1937–39 3.3.3/f. 1558, sf. 8.
[61] PNF, Sesto Anniversario della Vittoria, 29 October 1924, *ACS, PCM* 1924 2.4–1/f. 2709.
[62] Celebration dell'Anniversario della Vittoria, (4 November) 1926, "Comando della Divisione Militare di Roma (19), Ordine di Presidio N. 43, 2 novembre 1926," *ACS, PCM* 1926 2.4–1/f. 4021.

This morning associations of combatants followed the large imposing parade in which civil and military authority, invalids, spouses of the fallen, fascist and military organizations took part, and carried to the cemetery a crown of flowers for the tombs of the fallen. After the blessing given by the local clergy, and a letter written by the deceased Queen Margaret to the mothers of the fallen, the bulletin of the victory was read generating profound emotion among those present. The parade proceeded easily in perfect order.[63]

The report from the prefect of Rovigo, a Venetian city, was surprisingly similar with the exception that the prefect was slightly more verbose. He began, "The historic date 4 November was celebrated worthily with processions and other festive activities in all the principal provincial centers. In this provincial capital, the ceremony has assumed the solemn character of patriotic manifestations."[64] In addition to the usual round of visits to cemeteries and placing of commemorative plaques, the local bishop offered a funeral mass, which he interrupted before the consecration of the Eucharist to give thanks that the recent attempt to assassinate Mussolini had failed. The bishop expressed "joy" at the "salvation of the Duce that Divine Providence for the fourth time had preserved for the fortunes of Italy." The prefect concluded on the same note as his counterpart in Avellino: "Public order was absolutely perfect." The tenth anniversary commemoration merited a book, *Il Decennale*, describing the evolution of the holiday and how it was celebrated throughout Italy.[65]

The Joining of Generations

The regime convened a committee in December 1937 to plan the commemoration of the twentieth anniversary of the Vittoria. Mussolini gave specific orders concerning the design of the commemoration. The events were to focus on the military nature of the occasion and to be purely national in scope, eschewing the local commemorations that were typical of fascist holidays. Mussolini directed that the presence of war veterans and youth—Italy's past and future fighters—was to dominate the ceremonies. The 1938 commemoration of the Vittoria possessed a certain historical irony. The period from December 1937, when the planning began, to November 1938, when the last ceremony occurred, was replete with events that culminated in the downfall of the regime. In March 1938, Hitler marched into Austria and

---

[63] Celebration dell'Anniversario della Vittoria, (4 November) 1926, "Risposte dei Prefetti alla Circolare telegrafica 31 ottobre 26 n. 27097," ACS, PCM 1926 2.4–1/f. 4021.

[64] Ibid.

[65] *Il decennale: X anniversario della Vittoria, anno VII dell'era fascista*, ed. Associazione Nazionale Volontari di Guerra (Florence: Nuova Edizione, 1929).

virtually reversed the territorial gains of the Vittoria. The Italian-Austrian border was becoming insecure once more.

The plans for the twentieth anniversary commemoration revived the spatial and dramaturgical techniques that had been used in the commemorations of the first anniversary of the March on Rome, particularly the technique of pilgrimage. The commemoration ceremonies, which spread out over days and included ritual reenactment at the battle scenes, colonized time and space. There were two sets of events: in June, the victory of the Piave was commemorated with a restaging of the battle march with the appropriate actors present; in November, the battle of Vittorio Veneto was reenacted with a pilgrimage from the Veneto that ended in Rome with a ceremony to honor the war dead.[66]

The commemoration of the battle of the Piave lasted five days and consisted of ceremonies and speeches at all the major battle scenes. The ceremonies began on June 15 in the town of Nervesa with the dedication of a battlefield in memory of the war dead. On the banks of the Piave, a cohort of twenty-four hundred men who had been wounded in the war formed a guard of honor. On the next day, a military column departed for Monte Grappa where a mass was offered and a crown of laurel was left on the tomb of Maresciallo Giardino, commander of the troops at Grappa. The ceremonial troops proceeded to Redipuglia, where the duke of Aosta, the commander of the third Armata, was buried. The pilgrimage to this site included a ceremony organized around the leaving of laurel wreaths on the tombs of sixty thousand unknown soldiers.

As the commemorative week proceeded, the ceremonies became more elaborate. The third day began with a mass in the fields in honor of those who had died in the air strikes in the Veneto. The mass was celebrated at the monument to Francesco Baracca in Montello, and an air show took place over the fields. The commemorations moved on to Padua, where General Carlo Del Croix, president of the National Association of War Wounded and Incapacitated, inaugurated a "Pavilion of the Victory" with a speech that was broadcast on Italian radio. The events concluded with a spectacle of light against the dark—the "Sacred Night on the Piave." Floodlights and fireworks illuminated the low-lying mountains that formed the Italian border where the fighting took place. The grand finale began in Treviso with a "solemn full-dress parade" in which Fascist Party members, fascist youth groups, and combatant associations participated. Gabriele D'Annunzio gave

---

[66] I draw my accounts of the commemorations from "Verbali delle sedute 4/7/38" and "Verbali delle sedute 4/14/38," Ministera della Guerra, ACS, PCM 1937–39 14-2/f. 3546, sf. 2–3; Ministera della Guerra, *Ventennale della Vittoria: Battaglia del piave 15–23 Giugno* (Milan: Turati-Lombardi, 1938); and PNF, *Foglio d'Ordini*, Rome #212, 22 October 1938.

a speech at Treviso that evoked the memory of his storming of Fiume. The day concluded with a grand regatta in Venice in the presence of the king to commemorate the men who had died at sea.

The ceremonies of the Piave fused the nation and fascism. The prominence of the king coupled with the homage to the dead and the parading of the fascists, young and old, suggested a rapprochement between diverse factions. The masses once more imposed fascism on Roman Catholic liturgy. The diverse components of Italian culture and fascist culture were enlisted to suggest a national past, a fascist present, and a national/fascist future. Gabriel D'Annunzio's lyrical preface to the commemorative pamphlet describing the battle of the Piave captured the spirit of the occasion: D'Annunzio compared the river Piave to the "water of life" and ascribed to it the "regenerative" capacities of Catholic baptism. He concluded by referring to the initial Italian defeat at Caporetto: "And what was lost for days, will be reconquered for centuries. Long live Italy forever!"[67]

Pilgrimage as Public Ritual

The ceremonies of the Piave revived the technique of pilgrimage that had characterized the first anniversary of the March on Rome and had been eclipsed in succeeding celebrations. Pilgrimage was the leitmotif of the ritual events culminating in the commemoration in Rome on November 4. In the months between June and November, Hitler began to make aggressive moves into the rest of Europe while the Italians were busy fighting in Spain. By September 1938, Hitler was preparing to move into Czechoslovakia, and the vacillation of Mussolini between the liberal democratic regimes and the Axis powers placed him in the position of acting as mediator against Nazi aggression. In this role he traveled to Munich to negotiate on behalf of the Allies with Hitler over his prepared entry into the Balkans. Mussolini's trip to Munich was a pilgrimage with stops along the way in Padua and Vicenza and a grand celebratory event in Verona.

Mussolini's pilgrimage through the north used his physical presence to convey to the Italian people that Italy and fascism were on a journey of international recognition. The trip to Munich was a personal triumph in diplomatic terms although Mussolini gained little in political terms. For the country, it was a pivotal moment because Italy could indeed have gone either way.[68] But less than a week later, on October 6, 1938, it was clear in which direction Mussolini was heading when the Grand Council of Fascism introduced the racial laws.[69] A new enemy was created: the Italian Jewish

---

[67] Ministera della Guerra, *Ventennale della Vittoria*, 7.
[68] See Mack Smith, *Mussolini*, 258–64.
[69] PNF, *Foglio d'Ordini*, Rome #214, 26 October 1938.

population, which until that point had been one of the most highly assimilated Jewish populations in all of Europe and, in some quarters, avid supporters of the regime.[70]

By October 25, when the commemorations began for the sixteenth anniversary of the March on Rome and the twentieth anniversary of the Vittoria,
fascist public ritual was fully focused on mobilization for war. The Vittoria
commemorations highlighted every theme of the mobilizing regime and
summarized all that Mussolini was hoping to accomplish in terms of uniting
the old generation of 1918 to the new generation of fascist youth and
fighters. On October 28, members of the National Directorate of the Fascist
Party deposited a crown of laurel in the sacristy of the chapel for the fallen at
the Littorial Palace, party headquarters.[71] The *insigne* of the party was then
moved from the headquarters accompanied by a troop of the militia, to the
balcony of the palace in Piazza Venezia, where it would remain for the
duration of the March ceremonies.

After this ceremony, Achille Starace and the National Directorate accompanied a group of orphans of the fallen for the revolution to the palace to
give Mussolini his membership card in the party for year seventeen of the
regime. The duce's party card was marked number one. Next, the stone of
the Fascist Association of the Families of the Fallen, Mutilated, and
Wounded for the Revolution was taken to the Littorial Palace. *Il Popolo
d'Italia* was uncharacteristically restrained in its coverage and emphasized
the historical continuities rather than boldly proclaiming collective emotions.[72]

October 29 was devoted to the first anniversary of the founding of the
Gioventu Italiana del Littorio (GIL), an umbrella group for several fascist
youth organizations. Mussolini gave prizes in his office to the winners of the
"Scudo del Duce" (Shield of the Duce), and the guard at the Palazzo Venezia for that day was furnished by members of fascist youth organizations. In
the evening, a Balilla member spoke on the radio and the choir of the Littorio sang chants of the revolution and the war. *Il Popolo d'Italia* dramatically announced the "Feast of Italian Youth" and noted, "We will continue
to march with the same Inflexible Energy." By October 30, the headlines
were proclaiming that the first anniversary of the GIL was celebrated in
Rome with "imposing warlike rites," as its youth were mobilizing for the
coming war. On that symbolic day, too, the regime reaped some of the

[70] On the state of Jews in Italy, see Renzo De Felice, *Storia degli ebrei italiani sotto il
fascismo*, vol. 2 (Milan: Mondadori, 1972), 287–401, 426–52. Mussolini's paramour in the
1920s and cultural adviser, Margherita Sarfatti, was from a prominent Venetian Jewish family
and lost no time in leaving Italy after 1938.

[71] PNF, *Foglio d'Ordini*, Rome #212, 28 October 1938.

[72] *Il Popolo d'Italia*, 28 October 1938, 1.

benefits of its colonial and imperial aspirations when it sent eighteen hundred rural families from Genoa, Naples, and Siracuse to public housing villages it had created in Libya.[73]

The commemorations of 1938 reached a crescendo between November 1 and November 4 when the focus shifted to the Vittoria itself. The first event was the displaying of all the flags of the Vittoria in Vittorio Veneto. The organization of events was in the hands of the Ministry of War, although the Fascist Party provided bodies to participate in the ceremonies.[74] In the evening of the first day of commemoration, the hills around the city were illuminated and there was artillery fire. A military choir sang "songs of war" in the town. On the following day, there was a "grand ceremony" in honor of the "fallen." A mass in the fields was said and the flags were blessed. General Carlo Del Croix spoke again. In the afternoon, a "Museum of the Battle" was inaugurated. On the next day, a "special train" carried the flags back to Rome. The journey to Rome took an entire day, and the train stopped in Treviso, Padua, Ferrara, Bologna, and Florence. At each stop, "military honors [were] organized under the intervention of formations of the National Fascist Party, the Combatant Associations, and the GIL" to "render homage" to the "flags of the Vittoria."[75] On the morning of November 4, members of the National Directorate of the Fascist Party deposited a laurel wreath on the Tomb of the Unknown Soldier and then went to Rome's central station to welcome the train with the flags. One hundred thousand troops were on hand to greet the flags and to parade down the center of Rome to the monument to Vittorio Emanuele, where a religious ceremony was held at the Altar of the Patria.

Commemoration of the March on Rome continued until the regime fell in 1943. But in many ways, commemoration effectively ended in 1938 with the twentieth anniversary of the Vittoria. After 1938, the commemorations were warlike and curiously celebratory in that they focused on Italy's future as a world military power. The regime was in need of more solidarity to generate enthusiasm and commitment to fighting, but the emotion of the populace was waning. To rally popular enthusiasm, in 1938 Achille Starace introduced the "Reform of Custom," a decidedly perverse vehicle. Among Starace's "reforms" were, first, the replacement of the third-person "Lei" as the formal mode of address by the second-person plural "Voi"; the Roman salute to replace the traditional handshake; and the goose step at fascist parades, undoubtedly influenced by the growing presence of Nazi Germany.

---

[73] PNF, *Foglio d'Ordini*, Rome #212, 22 October 1938, and *Il Popolo d'Italia*, 30 October 1938, 1.
[74] "Programma delle cerimonie 10/10/38," ACS, PCM 1937–39 14-2/f. 3546, sf. 3/1a.
[75] Ibid.

There were also laws about female dress and a general injunction to get as many Italians into uniform as possible. But 1938 was Starace's last year as head of the National Fascist Party, and the reform may be viewed as a last-ditch effort to save a sinking ship.[76]

As the public communities of feeling were growing larger, they were losing whatever emotional appeal they had generated. Worsening economic conditions as evidenced by rising prices and declining wages throughout the 1930s generated a far greater sense of public urgency among Italian citizens than real or imagined enemies. In short, war was unpopular and the course Mussolini embarked on in 1938 required full national commitment. The support he had garnered in the sixteen years of the regime proved exceedingly tenuous as Italians were asked to sacrifice their bodies to a cause that appeared remote. The state without a nation ultimately proved rather ineffective when confronted with a constructed enemy, the plutocratic liberals of the Allied nations.

The March as Political Communication

When Italian troops marched on Rome in 1870, they seized it from the French and drove the pope behind the Vatican walls. The first march on Rome completed the Risorgimento project and made Rome the capital of the new Italy. In contrast, the march of Mussolini's Black Shirts began the fascist project. This particular evocation of the March would have been accessible to the majority of the minimally educated Italian citizenry. The liberal Italian state builders did not emphasize the 1870 march, and it became a schoolbook piece of dead history, a wasted cultural resource in the repertoire of possible symbolic actions on which the nation-state could project political love.

The fascists were not quite so wasteful with their symbolic resources; the regime did not leave its March on Rome to textbooks, even fascist textbooks. The annual commemoration became an ongoing vehicle of nation-state building, a primary feature of the fascist cultural project. By narrating and renarrating, acting and reenacting the founding event, the regime merged the fascist present with its past and laid the foundation for its future. The annual dramatic reenactment in public space imposed the memory of the March even on those who wished to avoid it. The March spun a web, to invoke Mussolini's image, over the Italian terrain. From the Roman center, simultaneous commemoration occurred throughout Italy. Pilgrimages,

[76] See Tannenbaum, *Fascist Experience*, 240–41, and DeGrazia, *How Fascism Ruled Women*, 224–25.

whether of Mussolini, his emissaries, or Italian soldiers reenacting battle scenes, covered the landscape.

During the 1920s and 1930s, *Il Popolo d'Italia*'s narratives provided a running chronicle of regime intention; the emerging patterns of ritual genres served as recognizable forms of public events that signaled, even to those Italian citizens who were less than enthusiastic supporters of fascism, the ever expanding regime. As the consolidation period moved into the mobilization period, commemoration turned into celebration: the past dissolved before the future. While the regime was focused on celebrating itself through the annual commemoration of the March, the present was slipping from its grasp. In the late 1930s, all the absurdities and cruelties that have contributed to the popular cultural images of Italian fascism came to the fore—Starace's Reform of Custom, laws against the Jews, increased surveillance of subversive activity. It was also a period when everyone was fascist and no one was fascist. The regime made membership in the Fascist Party a requirement for public and some private employment, and Italians rushed to join with minimal ideological commitment.[77] This was also the time Mussolini made the errors in foreign policy—most notably the alliance with Hitler—which brought Italy into an unpopular war that eventually destroyed fascism and unraveled whatever consensus the regime had enjoyed.

The five themes that emerged in the accounts of the first anniversary commemorations evolved over the years and structured succeeding anniversary commemorations. First, the myth of the founding event was transformed by fascist rhetoric from a myth of national revolution into a myth of a new Roman empire. Fascist history, as recorded in the public spectacle of the March commemorations, deepened with time. As the years passed, the differences between the soldiers who gave their lives in World War I and the "fascist martyrs" who gave their lives for the revolution blurred. The destruction of the boundary between these two groups, coupled with the incorporation of the new generation of Italian and fascist youth, identified fascism as the regime that redeemed the tainted victory of World War I and looked forward to new wars and new conquests. Empire completed the revolution. The proximity of the commemoration of the March to that of the Vittoria, the week between October 28 and November 4, provided an opportunity to create a space of temporal disruption that would implant the emerging narratives of the regime on the Italian people whether or not they joined in the spectacles of the piazza.

The Roman salute, Mussolini's transformation from "Duce" to "Dux," the parading around Roman ruins, and the centrality of Rome itself as ritual stage were attempts to reinvent the grandeur of ancient Rome in modern

---

[77] Tannenbaum, *Fascist Experience*, 68.

Rome. Colonialism and empire, war and Romanism never completely eclipsed revolution in the commemoration of the March. Beginning in the 1930s, with the imperialist aspirations of the regime on the rise, commemorations assumed a more militaristic hue. The mobilizations of the mid-1930s were devoid of cognitive content and were pure displays of emotion in the service of generating national solidarity.

Second, enemies and heroes evolved over time. Enemies create bonds of solidarity and intensify feelings of community.[78] In its early days, the regime clearly identified socialists as its enemy. The choice of ritual sites, such as Bologna, as well as official visits to and inaugurations of the Case del Fascio, which were in many cases old socialist union halls, suggested that the fascists had conquered the socialist enemy. As the regime became more entrenched, the socialists lost viability as an enemy. For example, "not words, but works," the slogan of the fifth anniversary commemoration, indicated that the only obstacle to work was the tendency toward lack of discipline among Italian workers.

Enemies shifted from internal enemies to external ones, from groups to nation-states and their leaders. By the 1930s, a new enemy emerged—the individualism touted by liberal capitalist regimes that threatened the fascist ideal of collectivity. Although anti-liberalism was salient in the Labor Charter and the *Doctrine of Fascism*, it was much more difficult to target as an enemy than socialists. In the years between the invasion of Ethiopia and Italian entry into World War II, national enemies multiplied and provided a focus for fascist emotional commitment. Anti-liberalism took the form of a generalized attack against liberal democratic regimes, which the fascists characterized as warmongers. In the 1930s, France, Britain, the United States, and the entire League of Nations, as well as Africans, Jews, and capitalists of all stripes, joined the amorphous communists, socialists, and liberals that had formed the early cadres of fascist enemies.

In addition to looking outward to international enemies, the regime sought to identify exemplary fascist heroes. Michele Bianchi, one of four apostles of the regime listed in *La nazione operante*, died in 1927 and was accorded a state funeral in Rome. Guglielmo Marconi, who figured prominently in the tenth anniversary commemorations, was an example of a new Italian fascist cultural hero.

Third, the regime continued to appropriate the commonplace. Mussolini's visit to the Perugina factory and his frequent attendance at sporting events and concerts suggested that fascism had placed its stamp on both work and leisure, both public and private time. The annual dedication of

---

[78] See Jeffrey C. Alexander and Philip Smith, "The Discourse of American Civil Society: A New Proposal for Cultural Studies," *Theory and Society* 22 (1993), 151–207.

public works that occurred on October 28 replaced the commonplace of factory visits. The regime celebrated its new infrastructure on the anniversary of the March on Rome, an infrastructure that included roads, schools, dams, post offices, and other public buildings Italians would see and use on a daily basis. The day of faith and the wedding ring campaign represented a shift in the familiar pattern of the regime's appropriation of the objects of everyday life from the somewhat public to the intensely private. The ritual appropriation of marriage's principal public symbol underscored the regime's continuing attempt to draw the family, a salient Italian private identity, into the community of the state.

Fourth, the regime persisted in its efforts to merge sacred and secular. The inclusion of the Catholic Church in fascist commemorative activity and the insertion of fascist ritual activity into Catholic liturgy was a fascist strategy to usurp a familiar Italian identity and ritual space which began in 1923 with the mass in Piazza Siena. The prominence of Santa Croce in the reburial of the fascist martyrs and the numerous masses celebrated during the commemoration of the Vittoria point to the ongoing attempts to convert religious community into fascist community.

The conflict between sacred and secular was frequently waged over the temporal position of holidays. By the 1930s, a struggle emerged over who was worthy of more public holidays—the church or the state. Since holidays required public ritual, who commanded more of these events was a powerful form of ammunition in the struggle for the Italian self. A note written in 1926 to Mussolini from an official of the Ministry of Corporations, the body that regulated labor relations in fascist Italy, suggested the multiple dimensions of the struggle. The note asked Mussolini how the General Confederation of Industry was to justify giving workers a day free from labor on October 28 and November 4, the respective dates of the March and the Vittoria, but force them to work on November 1, All Saints' Day, the "holiest Catholic holiday." In addition, the three holidays meant "inconvenience" to Italian industry.[79] The March and the Vittoria were not the only state holidays that trespassed on Catholic holiday terrain. For example, March 23, the date of the Founding of the Fascists, and April 21, the Birth of Rome, were positioned so that they would inevitably interfere with Easter celebrations, which always occurred between the end of March and the end of April.

Finally, the mobilization of bodies as cultural icons was expanded. From the first anniversary commemoration, the public display of mothers' bodies as living icons merged the public and private self and contrasted with the discourse of emotion and sexuality that permeated fascist political rhetoric.

---

[79] "Appunto per S.E. Il Capo del Governo," 22 October 1926, ACS, PCM 1926 2.4–1, f. 3904.

The presence of the mothers and the widows was a constant in the commemoration of the March in particular and fascist public ritual in general. The regime used the exhibition of mothers' bodies to appropriate the idea of motherhood, a powerful Italian cultural ideal, and to make it resonate with the ideal of the nurturing and stable fascist state.

In the ensuing years, the use of bodies as cultural icons became more complicated and articulated with an idea of a growing fascist public. Soldiers and fascists populated early commemorative events. But as the regime expanded its influence, it was able to mobilize more bodies, those of ordinary Italian men and women. As the Fascist Party grew to include youth and women's organizations, the boundaries of what would constitute a fascist public expanded. The mobilizations of the 1930s were the culmination of the massing of bodies in the service of public display and the purest type of community of feeling that the regime was able to create.

CHAPTER 5

Colonizing Time: Rhythms of Fascist Ritual in Verona

Ordinary and Extraordinary Events

Nineteen thirty-eight was the last year of peace in Europe before the onset of World War II. Verona, a city of 154,038 inhabitants nestled in the fertile agricultural region of the Veneto and on the train route through Brenner Pass into Germany, would play a pivotal role in Italian political and military affairs in the years between the German *Anschluss* and the Allies' liberation of Milan in 1945.[1] In the spring and summer of 1938, the political consequences of the German annexation of Austria were unclear, and fascist public life in Verona exhibited the slow and steady rhythm of previous years.

Events such as Achille Starace's visit to honor the Veronese war dead and inaugurate the new Fascist House (Casa del Fascio), which were part of the standard repertoire of fascist public political practice in Verona and other Italian cities, filled the spring and summer of 1938.[2] With public display, fascist Verona sent its youth to commemorative activities in other parts of Italy, celebrated its women, bade farewell to troops leaving for Africa, honored troops returning from Africa, and welcomed lower-ranking national fascist notables who were passing through on the inspection tours that were part of Fascist Party public ritual.[3] From the historical perspective of fifty

---

[1] Fernando Zappi, *Guida generale della citta e provincia di Verona* (Verona: Federazione Fascista Veronese dei Commercianti, 1936), 448.

[2] PNF, Federazione dei Fasci di Combattimento di Verona, "Documentario manifestazioni della Federazione Fascista dal 23 gennaio 1922 al 19 luglio 1942–xx" (typescript), 92–94, *ACS, PNF, MRF*, b. 12 (Verona).

[3] These activities were not unique to Verona. During the same period in 1938 in Frosinone, a small city in the center of Italy, there was a "Colonial Day," a ceremony to

years, these events appear transparent as military mobilizations and dress rehearsals for the coming war. In the spring and summer of 1938, they were simply features of the topography of ritual landscape, part of the quotidian experience of life in fascist Italy.

On September 26, 1938, Il Duce visited Verona. Mussolini had stopped at the train station a few times since he had come to power in 1922, most notably in September 1937 on his way to Berlin. But he had not made a formal visit to the city since 1921.[4] During the 1937 trip, Mussolini stopped in Verona on his return, and the crowds that greeted him displayed signs with "colossal" script that said, "DUCE! GRANT THE DESIRE OF THE BLACK SHIRTS OF VERONA THAT FOR 16 YEARS HAVE AWAITED YOU ON THEIR LAND" and "DUCE! FOR 16 YEARS WE HAVE WAITED FOR YOU ANXIOUSLY." The presence of Gabriele D'Annunzio during the 1937 stop at the train station evoked memories of the storming of Fiume and the early days of the fascist movement. Mussolini never left the train station during his 1937 visit but promised to return the following year and spend an entire day in Verona.[5]

Mussolini's return to Verona in September 1938 was part of his pilgrimage through the north linking the commemoration of the twentieth anniversary of the Vittoria to the consolidation of the Rome/Berlin axis. The visit preceded by a few days his trip to Munich to negotiate the partitioning of Czechoslovakia. Mussolini returned from the German trip to a hero's welcome in Italy and international diplomatic recognition. Retrospectively, his visit to Verona became a historical irony. Within months, his diplomatic coup had the unintended consequence of paving the way for Hitler's further aggression in the Balkans.[6]

On September 26 in Verona, the carnage and chaos of the Second World War was unimaginable. The spectacle of Mussolini's visit, its orchestration and its photographic representation in newspapers and propaganda booklets, evoked an exuberant potency, an iconography of power that made defeat unthinkable.[7] The publicity that remains from Mussolini's trip to Verona evokes the images of power that have typically become associated with fas-

---

award diplomas to young fascists and rural housewives, a "national gymnastic festival," and a visit from the duke of Bergamo to bestow a silver medal on a wounded soldier (R. Prefettura di Frosinone, "Avvenimenti e cerimonie autorizzate-Relazione Mensile," 13 June and 10 July 1938, "Cerimonie e manifestazioni," ACS, PCM 1937–39 3.3.9/f. 430).

[4] C[arlo] Manzini, *Il Duce e Verona (dal 1905 al 1938)* (Verona: C.E. Albarelli-Marchesetti, 1938), chronicles Mussolini's visits to Verona.

[5] Ibid., 64, 65.

[6] See Denis Mack Smith, *Mussolini* (London: Granada, 1981), 258–61, and C. J. Lowe and F. Marzari, *Italian Foreign Policy, 1870–1940* (London: Routledge and Kegan Paul, 1975), 315–23.

[7] On the power of images to generate emotion, see David Freedberg, *The Power of Images: Studies in the History and Theory of Response* (Chicago: University of Chicago Press, 1989), 1–26, 317–77. Though Freedberg writes about erotic emotion, the link between sexuality and politics, particularly in Italy, is evident.

cist public ritual in the popular imagination.[8] *Dux-Fascismo Veronese* romanticized Mussolini's relationship with Verona and began its history of Veronese fascism with a narrative of his "three encounters," his "dearest encounters," with the city before he came to power in 1922. Noting that "Mussolini has demonstrated in every time his predilection for Verona," *Dux* features a note from Mussolini to the head of the Veronese Fascist Party saying, "You know that I adore Verona."[9] On one visit he was greeted by a "shower of roses and carnations"; "subtle poetry" marked another visit; and on another "the personal fascination of the Man fatally attracted even preconceived enemies."[10]

Mussolini had received the news of his mother's death in Verona in 1905 when he was an infantryman in the Italian army. This crisis presumably engraved Verona in his memory as the public arena of his personal loss. In a 1905 letter to his commanding officer, written before fascism was even an idea, Mussolini articulated the themes blending private and public life, mother and Patria, that dominated the ideological discourse of the regime and the mental lives of its strongest adherents.[11] Thanking the officer for his expressions of sympathy, Mussolini wrote:

> Lengthy mourning and tears are suited to women—to strong men, to suffer and die—in silence—rather than to cry—to work and to act rightly—to honor domestic memories the most sacred of the Patria, not with sterile lamentations, but with worthy works.
>
> It is well to remember, to commemorate the heroes who with their blood cemented the unity of the Patria, but it is better yet to prepare ourselves in order to be stouthearted bulwarks, and not slothful descendants, against the Northern barbarians who would try to reduce Italy to a "geographic expression." These are my sentiments.[12]

Carlo Manzini, the Veronese Fascist Party secretary, prepared *Il Duce a Verona* (The Duce in Verona), a glossy commemorative booklet of photojournalism that elevated Mussolini's 1938 voyage of return to the status of myth. Pointing to the uncertainty of the precise date (a date that international events determined), the booklet's opening narrative conveyed the "anxiety," "desire," and "hope" engendered by the expectation of Mussolini's visit. The local party leaders realized that the "specter of war" could hang over the "huge march of the masses" they wished to stage. The date

---

[8] See, for example, *Dux-Fascismo veronese: Storia ed opere del fascismo scaligero* (n.d.) and Manzini, *Il Duce e Verona*.

[9] *Dux-Fascismo veronese*, 6. Despite Mussolini's adoration, sources document that il duce visited Verona only ten times between 1905 and 1938.

[10] Ibid., 6, 8, 7.

[11] Manzini, *Il Duce a Verona*, 11.

[12] Ibid., 12.

was finally set for September 26, and Mussolini arrived the night before with Achille Starace, the head of the National Fascist Party, and Dino Alfieri, the minister of popular culture. When this threesome emerged the following morning from the Palazzo del Governo in the "beautiful September sun," the narrator linked the fascist past to the present and noted with nostalgia, "Maybe, in that moment, He [Mussolini] remembered that faraway evening of May 13, 1921, in which, from the same piazza, at the same point, descending from a reserved car he spoke to the faithful of fascism 'terzogenito' and the adoring Veronese crowd."[13]

On the September morning in 1938, Mussolini rode down the central streets in a motorcade and reviewed battalions of fascist squads lined up between the Porta Palio and Porta Nuova, the two central gates of the city. At both gates, the city constructed enormous papier-mâché Roman eagles, symbols of fascist power (Figure 8). Mussolini ended the first part of his journey in the Piazza Bra, which was filled to its capacity of two hundred thousand persons (Figure 9). The federal secretary in Verona, Sandro Bona-mici, wanted to present Mussolini with a spectacle that superseded every other public performance he had experienced until that point. According to the account of journalist Cesco Tomaselli in the Milanese *Corriere della Sera*, Bonamici succeeded. Tomaselli described the scene: Mussolini was standing on a specially constructed podium.

The Founder of the Empire raises his arm saluting this army of the people, the horns intone *Giovinezza* [the fascist anthem], the crowd explodes in a loud and formidable ovation, that joins the powerful acclamation of the lined-up formations that, without breaking ranks, shout their enthusiasm and throw fez, caps in the air, and wave weapons and sparkling daggers. *In our voyages in the retinue of the Duce we never witnessed a similar scene.* When Mussolini left the podium to go into the Piazza Bra to speak to the multitudes, those that were rewarded by His very highest approval had a lump in their throat and were not able to say anything: they could only shout. *Fascist Verona has succeeded in presenting to the Duce a great and new thing*: it was not easy, if we think that eight city federals were in competition and all had sought to imitate each other in creativity as well as organization.[14]

Mussolini was "visibly struck" by the "spectacle" and the crowds. His visit reflected the form established during the annual commemorations of the March on Rome: he addressed the crowds; he paid his respects to the bishop, who was not a strong supporter of fascism; he met with fascist union

---

[13] Ibid., 70.
[14] Ibid., 77.

Figure 8. The fascist eagle. C[arlo] Manzini, *Il Duce e Verona (dal 1905 al 1938)* (Verona: C. E. Albarelli-Marchesetti, 1938).

leaders; he laid a laurel wreath at the monument to the fallen; he watched the "Roman step [*passo Romano*]" in the Piazza Dante (an Italian version of the German goose step that was not well received in Italy); he visited the local hospital and met with troops leaving for Libya.[15]

In the Roman amphitheater the Arena, Mussolini found a spectacle of

[15] "Documentario manifestazioni," 95–96, *ACS, PNF, MRF*, b. 12 (Verona).

200.000 persone acclamano il Duce in Piazza Bra.

Figure 9. Piazza Bra, Verona: Crowd awaiting Mussolini. C[arlo] Manzini, *Il Duce e Verona (dal 1905 al 1938)* (Verona: C. E. Albarelli-Marchesetti, 1938).

"36,000 souls" waiting for him—"8000 fascist women, 8000 rural house-wives and laborers, 20,000 members of the GIL [fascist youth groups]."[16] To begin the performance, the secretary of the party cried out to the crowd, presumably without sound amplification, "*Fascist women, housewives, workers, youth of the Littorio, salute the Duce the Founder of the Empire!*" Each group shouted the fascist chant "To us" as its name was called and then began a collective chorus of "Du-ce, Du-ce" that the singing of fascist anthems only briefly interrupted. Using the language of emotion that was now rote in all accounts of fascist spectacle, the narrative invoked the spell of the crowd as a blend of sexuality and romance.

> The Arena is throbbing totally with love and devotion toward Him, 36,000 hearts are offered to Him as one heart, because they are at His disposal, because He consumes them, burns them at the fire of His genius. And the Duce does not know how to resist: He feels all the regret that He would leave behind Him if He would not at least say some words to this crowd that cry out in the last spasm of love, and He shows himself yet another time, after having signaled yet another time to leave.[17]

The words Mussolini left behind were, "I want [*voglio*] to tell you only that I will never forget the spectacle of faith and joy that you have offered me in this grand and sacred vestige of Rome."[18] His choice of the word "voglio," the strongest expression of volition, reinforced the feeling of emotion and desire that the spectacle presumably invoked.

The magnitude of the crowds and their photographic representation in newspapers and propaganda suggest that Mussolini's visit to Verona was indeed extraordinary. The photographs in newspapers and commemorative booklets are pictures of power; they have become the standard fare of popular perceptions of fascism and the regime's favored self-representation. The photograph of the crowds in the Arena, reproduced in national newspapers, is particularly illustrative of fascist photojournalism (Figure 10).[19] The Arena, one of four remaining Roman amphitheaters in Italy, dominates the center of Verona. It served frequently as a stage for public political events during the fascist period. The city began staging operas there during the late nineteenth century, and when Mussolini arrived at the amphitheater, the mayor asked Il Duce to choose the opening operas for the coming theatrical year.

[16] Manzini, *Il Duce a Verona*, 86.
[17] Ibid.
[18] Ibid.
[19] See, for example, the front-page reproduction in *Il Popolo d'Italia* (Milan), 27 September 1938, 1.

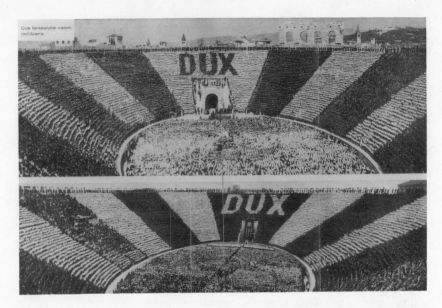

Figure 10. L'Arena, Verona, on the day of Mussolini's visit. C[arlo] Manzini, *Il Duce e Verona (dal 1905 al 1938)* (Verona: C. E. Albarelli-Marchesetti, 1938).

Mussolini named Verdi's *Tosca* and *Rigoletto*, displaying the traditionalism that characterized the regime's aesthetic preferences.[20]

The performance of the crowds in the Arena wed the spectacle of the fascist state to the memory of the Roman past and a popular theatrical form, the lyric opera. The photograph of the Arena, taken with a wide-angle lens, suggests raw mass. The black-and-white film reveals that the participants were seated according to the color of their uniforms to create a human halo effect and to form the word DUX in alternating colors. Individuals are invisible, and the image is one of pure force.

In this chapter, I refuse the seduction of the iconography of power and focus on the ordinary, the customary, and the habitual. In her essay *On Photography*, Susan Sontag argued, "The ethical content of photographs is fragile."[21] Sontag suggests that the moral content of a photograph diminishes as its audience becomes further removed from the event photographed. Time atrophies the emotional charge. Fascist propagandist photography reverses Sontag's proposition: the less likely a viewer is to have experienced a fascist event, the more powerful the fascist images appear.[22]

[20] Manzini, *Il Duce a Verona*, 86.
[21] Susan Sontag, *On Photography* (New York: Farrar, Straus and Giroux, 1978), 21.
[22] The classic essay on the relation between fascism and photography is Walter Benjamin,

The picture of the Arena was a depiction of fascist power that was not necessarily consonant with the regime's capacity to wield that power, a representation of power that did not necessarily equal a reality of power. The spectacle of fascist power in Verona that Mussolini's visit generated was not part of
the daily routine of ideological production in fascist Italy. As an extraordinary event, Mussolini's visit was a caesura that punctuated the rhythm of
fascist public life in Verona and placed in relief the day-to-day process of
fascist ideological production.

This chapter explicitly addresses my proposition that ritual is a form of
cultural action as it maps how fascist public rituals remade the patterns of
civic life and community in Verona. Studies of public political ritual tend to
assume what Clifford Geertz has described as the "myth of the exemplary
center" and fail to explore how cultural policies conceived and enacted at
the center are reenacted in the periphery.[23] Most Italians lived outside
Rome, and local studies have the advantage of considering the dissemination
of political meaning to the periphery. The ritual colonization of time in a
peripheral city such as Verona provides yet another window on the process
of fascist identity creation.[24]

"The Work of Art in the Age of Mechanical Reproduction," in *Illuminations* (New York:
Schocken, 1978), 217–51. According to Benjamin, art forms such as cinema and photography, which can be reproduced in multiples, lack "aura," the contextual immediacy of older
art forms. The absence of aura opens the door to polyvalence and permits art works to serve
as vehicles of political manipulation. Departing from Sontag, I argue that political art becomes more manipulative the more temporally distant it is from events.

[23] See Clifford Geertz, *Negara* (Princeton: Princeton University Press, 1980), 3–18. Edward Shils, "Center and Periphery," in *The Constitution of Society* (Chicago: University of
Chicago Press, 1982), 93–109, is social theory's preeminent formulation of the relation between center and periphery. Clifford Geertz, "Centers, Kings, and Charisma: Reflections on
the Symbolics of Power," in *Local Knowledge* (New York: Basic, 1983), 121–46, reformu-
lates Shils's concepts and applies them to issues of symbolic politics. Geertz's position is
diametrically opposite to the one espoused here: "The 'political theology' . . . of the twentieth century has not been written, though there have been glancing efforts here and there.
But it exists—or, more exactly, various forms of it exist—and until it is understood at least as
well as that of the Tudors, the Majapahits, or the Alawites, a great deal of the public life of
our times is going to remain obscure. The extraordinary has not gone out of modern politics,
however much the banal may have entered; power not only intoxicates, it still exalts" (143).

[24] Local studies of fascism to date pay little attention to the cultural dimensions of public
life and concentrate on political economy and labor problems. In general, regional studies
focus on the regime's seizure of power, and their narrative accounts end in the mid-twenties;
see, for example, Frank M. Snowden, *Violence and Great Estates in the South of Italy: Apulia,
1900–1922* (New York: Cambridge University Press, 1986); Frank M. Snowden, *The Fascist
Revolution in Tuscany, 1919–1922* (New York: Cambridge University Press, 1989); Simona
Colarizi, *Dopoguerra e facismo in Puglia, 1919–1926* (Bari: Laterza, 1971); Anthony L.
Cardoza, *Agrarian Elites and Italian Fascism: The Province of Bologna, 1901–1926* (Princeton: Princeton University Press, 1982); Paul Corner, *Fascism in Ferrara, 1915–1925* (London: Oxford University Press, 1975); Alice Kelikian, *Town and Country under Fascism: The*

In 1942, the central office of the Fascist Party, in preparation for the third staging of the Mostra della Rivoluzione Fascista, requested local Fascist Party heads to prepare reports listing fascist war dead, public works created during the regime, and local newspapers and party organs. The fascist representative in Verona was excessively diligent and produced a typewritten calendar that recorded all public events sponsored by the Veronese Fascist Party from 1922 to 1942. This accidental data trove provides a picture of fascist public life in Verona.[25] The typewritten log illustrates how the Fascist Party colonized the public sphere in Verona and redrew the boundaries of civic and communal life to include the repeated experience of public party activities.

Fascism and Civic Life in Verona

Geography and political history are often inextricable. Verona, a Roman fortress city, has had military importance from antiquity. Located in the northeastern corner of Italy at the foothills of the Dolomite Mountains near the Italian, Austrian, and German borders, the province of Verona was the site of battles that set the course of contemporary Italian history. Napoleon III and Emperor Franz Joseph signed the treaty that led to Italian unification without the Veneto at Villafranca in 1859; the battle of the Piave, which resulted in the postwar humiliation of Italy at Versailles, was fought in the Veneto. But Verona is more than a military bastion. Lying in the fertile Po basin, it is a major agricultural and wine producer. The Roman Arena is only one example of an architecture that spans centuries of Italian history. Shakespeare set *Two Gentleman of Verona* and *Romeo and Juliet* in the city,

---

Transformation of Brescia, 1915–1926 (New York: Oxford University Press, 1986). A dated but still useful study that incorporates issues of civic life is "Convegno di studi promosso dall'Unione Regionale delle province Toscane, della provincia di Firenze e dall'Istituto Storico per la Resistenza," in Toscana, *La Toscana nel regime fascista (1922–1939)* (Florence: Olschki, 1971). Regional studies of the Veneto are sparse. Michele Risolo, *Il fascismo nella Venezia Giulia: Dalle origini alla Marcia su Roma* (Trieste: La Vedetta Italiana, 1932), was written during the fascist period to garner support for the regime and only 650 copies were printed. Among postwar studies, see Elio Apih, *Italia fascismo e antifascismo nella Venezia Giulia (1918–1943)* (Bari: Laterza, 1966); Silvio Tramontin, *Cattolici, popolari e fascisti nel Veneto* (Rome: Cinque Lune, 1975); and Ernesto Brunetta, "Della grande guerra alla Repubblica," in *Il Veneto*, ed. Silvio Lanaro (Turin: Einaudi, 1984), 913–1035. Maurizio Zangarini, *Politica e societa a Verona in epoca fascista: Studi e ricerche* (Verona: Cooperativa Editrice Nuova Grafica Cierre, 1986), the only full-length study of Veronese fascism, is highly schematic.
[25] See note 2 for a complete citation to the log, hereafter cited as "Documentario manifestazioni," *ACS, PNF, MRF*, b. 12 (Verona). For a discussion of the log as a data source, see Methodological Appendix.

suggesting Verona's reputation and place in Renaissance literary imagination.

During the twenty years between the first and second world wars, politics took precedence over aesthetics. The Soave and Valpolicella wine continued to flow, the strains of lyric opera still echoed forth from the Arena, and tourists continued to visit Juliet's tomb. But Verona's location on the last express railway stop before the Brenner Pass and Germany made it a frequent destination for German and Italian visitors and an ideal location to enact the theater of state. The morning of January 11, 1944, ensured Verona's place in the history of fascism. With the fascist regime gone and Mussolini's puppet government at Salo crumbling, Il Duce gave the order to execute the five members of the Grand Council, including his son-in-law Galeazzo Ciano, who had voted against him in the meeting of July 25, 1943, that forced the king to ask for Mussolini's resignation. Verona was chosen as the site of the sham trial, the *processo di Verona*, that led to the executions, because of its proximity to Salo. This accident of geography left an ambivalent legacy.[26] Verona was "fascist" as all Italy was "fascist" during the period of the regime, but its level of commitment was weaker than that of other fascist cities. In 1930, when the local Federal secretary, Giuseppe Righetti, gave the report from his annual inspection tour to Mussolini, Il Duce asked when Verona would be placed "in the hands of true fascists."[27]

Verona's traditional "white" culture determined the short supply of "true fascists"—as well as "true" socialists.[28] An agrarian social structure with a weak industrial base and a strong commitment to Catholicism shaped the political affinities of the Veronese. The few histories of Verona that exist for the fascist period agree that it was "a-fascist" rather than anti-fascist.[29] Yet in the pre-1922 period, Verona had the first rural fascist organization in Italy and a larger number of supporters than Rome and Milan.[30] The Italian campaign during the First World War was fought largely in the Veneto. Former

[26] On the events leading up to the *processo*, see Mack Smith, *Mussolini*, 342–55. For a popular account written by Ciano's lawyer, see Vincenzo Cersosimo, *Dell'istruttoria alla fucilazione: Storia del processo di Verona* (Milan: Garzanti, 1963).

[27] Rapporti del Duce ai Segretari Federali, February 1930. "Relazione dell'On Giuseppe Righetti (Commissario straordinario) della Federazione Fascista di Verona," 5, *ACS*, *PNF*, *MRF*, b. 53, f. 123, sf. 3.

[28] On the "white culture" and Catholicism's long-term effect in Verona, see Silvio Lanaro, "Genealogia di un modello," in *Il Veneto*, ed. Silvio Lanaro (Turin: Einaudi, 1984), 24–60; on the conflict between socialism and Catholicism, see Emilio Franzina, "Operai, braccianti e socialisti nel Veneto bianco," in *Il Veneto*, 701–59.

[29] I rely principally on Zangarini, *Politica e societa a Verona*, and Tramontin, *Cattolici, popolari e fascisti*, as secondary sources in the account that follows.

[30] Zangarini, *Politica e societa a Verona*, 30; this statement seems at variance with standard accounts. See, for example, Adrian Lyttelton, *The Seizure of Power: Fascism in Italy, 1919–1929* (rpt., Princeton: Princeton University Press, 1987), 42–76, 443–44.

battlefields did not immediately return to fertile farmland, and this led to a sharp drop in agricultural production and high unemployment rates in the postwar period. The "red" leagues' rhetoric of revolution appealed to the lowest level of agricultural workers (*braccianti*), whereas the "white" leagues' promise of upward mobility attracted the sharecroppers (*mezzadri*) and tenant farmers (*fittavoli*). Conflict arose between the red and white leagues, and random acts of violence occurred.[31]

The elections of 1919, in which the socialists won the majority of votes in the city and the countryside, demonstrated that Catholicism was a cultural and not a political force.[32] On April 3, 1919, in response to violence and conflict, a group of soldiers, *arditi*, students, professionals, and workers founded the Veronese Fascist Party. The reporter from *Il Popolo d'Italia* who was present at the founding meeting noted that "the greater part of the adherents *did not have a clear idea of fascist directions* [emphasis added]; they were liberals, democrats, conservatives; they had instead the word 'Fascio' only in their sense of physical union and aimed at an alliance of all those considered the 'forces of order,' to confront the future elections under a new formula and with a new lineup."[33]

The 1930 federal secretary's report suggests that eleven years after its founding the Veronese Fascist Party still lacked clear ideas. Mussolini was troubled by this absence of focus, which he described as insufficient emotional commitment. Righetti began with a statistical report. In 1930, the province of Verona had a population of 583,569 distributed among ninety-three communes. There were 105 units of the Fighting Fascists (Fasci di Combattimento), consisting of approximately fourteen thousand members, of which only four thousand belonged to the "Old Guard" (men who were in the Fascist Party before 1922).[34]

The federal secretary took comfort in the fact that "the statistics on positions occupied by fascists demonstrate that in reality a true work of penetration has been completed." He painted a similarly optimistic picture of the fascist commitment of women and university students. The fascist women's organization, with 1,294 members, was "particularly useful in the country-side," where it provided instruction to peasant women. The 322 members of the fascist university group (Gruppo Universitario Fascista [GUF]), which the federal claimed represented 90 percent of Veronese university students, actively participated in syndical meetings and remained in close contact with

[31] Zangarini, *Politica e societa a Verona*, 101–24.
[32] Tramontin, *Cattolici, popolari e fascisti*, 11–12.
[33] *Dux-Fascismo veronese*, 10.
[34] "Relazione dell'On. Giuseppe Righetti," 1.

the federation. The university students were preparing themselves for "future tests" and the assumption of party leadership roles.[35]

According to Righetti, children and laborers posed a particular problem for Veronese fascism. Loyalty to Catholicism among schoolteachers and group leaders colored the fascist socialization process in the Veronese children's organizations—the Balilla, the Avant-Gardes, the Young Italians, and the Little Italians. The domination of Catholicism was more pronounced in the countryside than in the city, but there it was nonetheless real. Catholicism was an enemy that the regime was continually co-opting. Commitment to socialism and popularism, the forerunner of Italian Christian Democracy, was a never-ending threat to Veronese fascism, in which emotional attachment lagged behind organizational membership.

The fascist unions managed to enroll only 60 percent of the provincial workforce, but Righetti optimistically noted:

> As to the efficiency of organizing, we can say that we are able to organize, to enroll, to *interest*; however are not able to say that the spirit is yet completely syndical; relics of populism and communism persist, but it is of little importance; the syndical world will be persuaded little by little and I judge that its complete *spiritual transformation* [emphasis added] will not be far.

Agricultural landowners were more committed to fascism, and Righetti boasted that the conclusion of the agricultural pact was excellent and that 96 of the 110 directors of the agricultural federations (federazione agricoltori) were "true fascists, of ancient enrollment."[36]

The federal displayed less optimism about economic matters than he had about spiritual. Verona lacked "a practical industrial leadership class, perhaps in consequence of its *military servitude* that only today has been completely broken away, but for many years held Verona and its hinterland locked in an unbreakable circle."[37] The general absence of industrial expertise contributed to financial problems within the debt-ridden Fascist Party and weakness in the local economy. The previous federal secretary, Mutto Plinio, had prepared a lengthy memorandum for the administrative secretary of the Fascist Party in Rome to explain why the accounts in Verona appeared disorderly. While protesting the honesty of the local party officials, he asked for increased subsidies from the national fascist party in Rome.[38]

[35] Ibid.
[36] Ibid., 2.
[37] Ibid., 3.
[38] Federazione Provincial Verona, 16 December 1929, *ACS, PNF*, Direttorio Serie I, b. 1202.

The issue of national party subsidy made the financial situation of local parties particularly important. For example, the National Fascist Party contributed 50,000 lire to defray the costs of Mussolini's visit and 250,000 lire to build a Balilla House (Casa del Balilla).[39] In addition, the numerous public events and ceremonies were costly affairs. For example, in 1927, the celebration of the fifth anniversary of the March on Rome required 28,000 additional lire and represented 10 percent of the Veronese party's expenditures for that year. The Commune of Verona and the National Fascist Party each provided half the money.[40] In 1930, the Veronese party allocated 104, 241 lire to "large meetings" (adunate). The largest expenditures were for "artistic" items, such as medals, prizes, albums, and promotional posters, and the transportation of squads of participants from other parts of the Veneto.[41]

Verona employed about 25,000 workers, but the wool, furniture, and cotton industries were in crisis. Industrial salaries were going down and the situation was worsening. Unemployment was reported as 6,686 persons in industry and 3,000 persons in agriculture. The cost of living was too high, as measured by the price of bread at 2.30 lire per kilogram. Mussolini and the federal secretary agreed that the presence of opportunistic fascist businessmen, men who had enrolled in the party after 1927 to enhance their career prospects, was contributing to Verona's financial problems. The federal's solution was to find "old fascists," to throw the "profiteers" out of government, and to train a new generation of fascist leaders. In a conference held in July of the same year on "Veronese economic problems," Righetti argued that Verona needed to learn

> the necessary concordance of spirit and intentions—to use all the resources that derive from this concordance: from its topographical position, from its productive and agrarian capacity, from the technical skill of its inhabitants and from their financial availability, it will be able, in a relatively brief cycle of years, to completely transform itself and become one of the richest, most industrious and truly fascist provinces, in dynamic expression, in all Italy.[42]

If local industry and government suffered from a lack of true fascists, the Catholic Church posed a more challenging problem. For indeed, its pro

[39] Provincia di Verona, Un quadriennio di amministrazione fascista: Marzo 1935–XIII– marzo 1939–XVII (Verona, 1939), 11.

[40] Partito Nazionale Fascista Federazione Provinciale Fascista Veronese, "Rendiconto dei proventi e della spese dell'anno 1927," ACS, PNF, Direttorio Serie I, b. 1202.

[41] Federazione di Verona, "Bilancio consuntivo al 28 ottobre 1930–VIII," ACS, PNF, Direttorio Serie I, b. 1202.

[42] Partito Nazionale Fascista, Federazione dei Fasci di Combattimento della Provincia di Verona, Problemi economici veronesi, Convegno Tenuto Nella Casa del Fascismo il 14 Luglio 1930–VIII, Processo Verbale Riassuntivo, 4, ACS, PNF, Direttorio Serie I, b. 1202.

forma support of fascism could not be rectified by simply replacing the hierarchy. The bishop and the federal exchanged visits, but the bishop was
"anti-fascist" and also "anti-populist." The bishop's antipathy to both parties gave the fascists a free rein to wrest the youth organizations from the
hands of Catholic Action in the countryside. Catholic Action was not formally allied to the Popular Party. It was a lay organization of Roman Catholic moral activists founded in 1914 as an alternative to socialist voluntary and
civic organizations.[43] It sponsored leisure-time activities with a Catholic
moral focus for youth, women, and men. Until fascism came to power in
1922, the Socialist Party was its principal competitor. But in 1931, the Veronese Fascist Party targeted Catholic Action for surveillance and acts of violence because it was associated with the National Alliance (Alleanza
Nazionale), a group of militant anti-fascist Catholics with a strong organizational presence in Verona.[44] Their leader was Lauro De Bosis, who publicly
argued that Catholic Action was a powerful tool of organizational opposition to fascism. The Alliance's propaganda stated:

> The Pope is in continual conflict with Fascism over the fundamental prob-
> lem of the education of the young and the self-styled "Catholic" but really
> anti-Christian character of Fascism. . . . Catholic Action is the greatest orga-
> nization outside of Fascism and is covertly anti-Fascist. At the moment of
> crisis it will be a valuable liaison and rallying point, not only against Fascism
> but also against possible subversive agitations let loose by the crisis itself. It
> is necessary to act in agreement with Catholic Action, not against it.[45]

De Bosis believed that propaganda statements should be scattered in the
streets of a targeted locale (he died dropping leaflets from an airplane over
Rome). The strong presence of the Alliance in Verona served to focus fascist
attention on Catholic Action and exacerbated the regime's long-standing
hostility to the organization.

The country priests also were problematic, for they were hostile to fascism
and frequently did not pay attention to fascist ceremonial orders. Their hostility took the form of a retreat to the more puritanical aspects of Catholic
social practice. For example, in the municipality of Terrazzo, a parish priest

---

[43] See Gianfranco Poggi, *Catholic Action in Italy: The Sociology of a Sponsored Organization* (Stanford: Stanford University Press, 1967), 14–29.

[44] See Tramontin, *Cattolici, popolari e fascisti*, 157, 257–303. The fascist attack on Catholic Action was a national, and not a purely local, initiative; see Edward R. Tannenbaum, *The
Fascist Experience* (New York: Basic, 1972), 193–94.

[45] Lauro De Bosis, *Storia della mia morte*, 9–10, cited in Richard A. Webster, *The Cross
and the Fasces: Christian Democracy and Fascism in Italy* (Stanford: Stanford University
Press, 1960), 126–28. Webster describes Verona as a "strong point of militant Catholicism"
and focuses on it in his story of De Bosis and the Alliance.

was reported to the prefect because he refused to allow his parishioners to participate in a people's dance held to celebrate the Vittoria. The priest claimed that dancing was a form of immoral public behavior of which his bishop disapproved.[46] A fringe benefit of the strong Catholic culture was that the "demographic" situation was "excellent."

Civic life in Verona provided a fertile terrain in which to cultivate a fascist public sphere and to offset the lack of emotional commitment that tarnished the Veronese Fascist Party in the eyes of the regime. The cityscape was an ideal setting for fascist public events on a grand scale, and Verona was small enough that even minor public events were impossible to avoid. A major street leads from the train station to the grand Piazza Bra in front of the Arena. Another street winds in front of the Arena to the Piazza dell'Erbe, a daily agricultural market that could be cleared at a moment's notice for fascist spectacle, and another turn leads into Piazza Dante in front of the prefect's offices. Verona also has a cathedral in a very narrow piazza and a magisterial military fort on the periphery. There were three major theaters, six amateur theater groups that included a (*dopolavoro*) company at the military fort, a philharmonic hall, and eight cinemas. Verona had two daily newspapers, *L'Arena* and the *Gazzettino*. *L'Arena*, founded in 1866, was the principal daily, and in 1925, it became the official organ of the Fascist Federation of Verona. In addition, there were numerous small weekly and monthly papers associated with either the Fascist Party or Catholic organizations.[47]

The citizens of Verona were accustomed to a public communal life and had a rich network of voluntary organizations that included sports clubs, literary clubs and choral societies, and various philanthropic associations allied with Catholic Action. These organizations provided a structure on which the fascists could graft their activities.[48] Although it is convenient to speak of the Fascist Party as though it was a unit, it was essentially a matrix of diverse organizations with different constituencies—women, children, youth, veterans, paramilitary groups.[49] In 1942, the Veronese federal secretary, Antonio Bonino, reported that 187,423 youth, 62,219 women, 1,729

[46] Letter dated 7 November 1933, *ASV, GP*, 1929–40 (Verona 1933.480).
[47] Zappi, *Guida generale*, 396–99.
[48] Zappi, *Guide generale* (400–406), lists forty-four organizations that are not directly affiliated with the Fascist Party. Scholars have never examined the well-known Tocquevillian proposition that relates civic association and democratic political practice with respect to nondemocratic political practice. Robert Putnam has recently developed an index that measures civic traditions and civic engagement in contemporary Italy (*Making Democracy Work* [Princeton: Princeton University Press, 1993], 120–62). Not surprisingly, the Veneto ranks high on civic virtue.
[49] See *The Fascist Party* (Florence: Valecchi, 1937), 77–125, for a description of the fascist suborganizations.

university students, and 77,785 Fighting Fascists were enrolled in the local party.[50]

Civic is the adjective that best captures the nature of the activities described in the annual reports of the various Veronese fascist organizations. For example, in 1926, the Veronese Federation of the National Association of Fighting Fascists (Associazione Nazionale Combattenti) collected money to provide aid to veterans and the unemployed and sponsored exhibits of the products of small industries to help promote them.[51] In 1928, the same organization subsidized the travel of Veronese artisans to local fairs in other parts of Italy to display their goods, completed a census of fifty-four hundred artisans in the province of Verona, distributed free milk and anti-malarial drugs, gave birthday presents to war orphans, sponsored the showing of war movies, gave out free books on the association, and participated in local and national public ceremonies. This pattern of activities remained the same throughout the 1930s.[52]

The types of activities varied only slightly according to the constituency addressed. For example, as late as 1941, when Italy was already at war, the Veronese fascist youth organization maintained a full calendar of activities. There were summer camps for soldiers' children, home economics exhibits for young women, gymnastic contests, and amateur theatricals and musicals.[53] Choral singing was a favored activity. The organization's commander general compared singing to a sporting event in his description of a musical competition:

> It was a competition in which the values that characterize poetry and music ought, also and above all, to reflect other elements, that in music refines and tests itself, indispensable in the social life of a collectivity: those of profound intimate discipline that tying more voices, more sounds and personality, blending and enriching in the will of composition, without which no one attracts and no one gets lost or suppresses, brings to a more elevated

[50] Partito Nazionale Fascista Federazione dei Fasci di Combattimento—Verona, "Numero degli inscritti alla Federazione dei Fasci di Combattimento per ciascuna categoria," *ACS, PNF, MRF,* b. 12 (Verona).

[51] See Associazione Nazionale Combattenti, *Relazione sul lavoro compiuto dalla Federazione Provinciale di Verona nell'anno 1926* (Villafranca di Verona: Massagrande, 1926).

[52] Associazione Nazionale Combattenti, *Relazione schematica del avoro compiuto l 31-12-1928-VII E.F.* (Verona: Federazione Provinciale di Verona, 1928); Associazione Nazionale Combattenti, *Consiglio provinciale della Federazione Provinciale di Verona dell'Associazione Nazionale Combattenti* (Verona: Federazione Provinciale di Verona, 1932); and Associazione Nazionale Combattenti Federazione provinciale di Verona, *Rapporto Provinciale—15 ottobre 1933-XI* (Verona: Arena-Verona, 1933).

[53] Partito Nazionale Fascista—Gioventu italiana del littorio, *Ordine del giorno federale* (Verona: Arena, 1941), 10, 15, 16.

harmony that in every expression, submissive or powerful, gentle or rough, has the sense and the force of solidarity.[54]

The virtues the commander general ascribed to choral singing might also be found in the repeated experience of fascist public events. As the singing in unison generated a feeling of solidarity and collectivity, so too the daily, weekly, and monthly anticipation of Fascist Party events created a rhythm of ritual that had the potential to be more powerful than any single ritual event.

Classifying and Reclassifying Verona's Fascist Ritual

The Contours of Ritual

Using the commander general's musical metaphor, we might say that all of Italy engaged in public acts of choral singing during the fascist period. Public political events that took the form of ritual—repeated, expected, and stylized expressive actions—were the National Fascist Party's favored vehicles of solidarity. Local orchestrations with their variations in form and content suggest how the fascist cultural project played when away from the pomp and ceremony of the Roman center.

The problem with fascist commitment in Verona induced the local party head to pay particular attention to public political events. Thus, in the years between 1922 and 1942, a distinct pattern of ritual emerged that set Veronese public life to a fascist rhythm.[55] During this period, the Veronese Fascist Party staged 727 events, ranging from small mundane affairs such as a local official's speech on a feature of fascist ideology to huge public spectacles such as Mussolini's visit. Of these events, relatively few exhibited the characteristics that popular culture and fascist propaganda have come to associate with fascist spectacle (see Table 1). For example, only 16 percent (118) were either described as large or had more than a thousand persons present. The log explicitly listed only 101 events (14 percent) as taking place in public spaces. The favored public places for fascist events—the Arena, the central piazzas, the cathedral, and the train station—figured in only 15 percent of fascist events; 20 percent took place in the local Fascist Party building or the military fort. There was no notation as to location of event in 50 percent (369) of the calendar entries, suggesting that the person who en-

---

[54] Ibid., 1.

[55] The typewritten log (see note 2) provided the data for the quantitative material in this section. For a description of coding procedures and the reliability of the log as a source of evidence, see Methodological Appendix.

Table 1. Contours of fascist public events in Verona, 1922–1942 *(n = 727)*

	n	*percent*[a]
Event > 1,000 persons present	118	16
Spatial location		
Public space	101	14
Central piazza	44	6
Antiquity	19	3
Church	29	4
Train station	15	2
PNF building	93	13
Military building	48	7
Temporal location		
Sunday	243	33
Fascist holiday	51	7
National holiday	54	7
Ritual activity		
Parade	33	5
Military review	35	5
Rally in piazza	84	12
Roman Catholic Mass	35	5
Unveiling monument	40	6
Ritual actors present		
Clergy	45	6
Women	29	4
Youth	118	16
War veterans	119	16

[a] Percentages do not add up to one hundred.

tered events in the log viewed many as ordinary and that their location was not noteworthy.

The type of ritual activity displayed a similar pattern. Parades and military reviews each accounted for 5 percent of Veronese fascist activities, and rallies for 12 percent. Commemorative actions such as special Roman Catholic masses and the unveiling of monuments to local heroes accounted for 6 and 5 percent of activities, respectively. The presence of youth and war veterans at events was considered noteworthy and was reported in 16 percent of events, whereas women and clergy took center stage in 4 and 6 percent of events, respectively.

The dates of events offer a mirror of how the activities broke up the daily pattern of life in Verona. Thirty-three percent took place on a Sunday, a day with secular and religious meaning. The Italian state mandated that Sunday was a day of rest from labor; the Roman Catholic Church obligated its members to attend Mass on that day. Thus the events that occurred on Sunday interrupted customary leisure and religious practices. In a country such as Italy where even schooling was often an ad hoc event and truancy rates were high, weekly participation in the Roman Catholic Mass was one of the few cultural practices that had any ability to command a constituency.[56] Only 7 percent of events occurred on a specifically designated fascist or national holiday, suggesting that the Sunday events, a usurpation of religious ritual time, were part of a fascist strategy to undermine the hold the Catholic Church had on the mental lives of Verona's citizens.[57] The temporal location of the majority of the events on what would ordinarily be work days indicates that the routine activities of the participants were often disrupted.

Genre

The brief narratives recorded on each calendar entry were sufficiently descriptive and discrete to permit a classification of events according to ritual genre. Of the 727 events, celebrations made up the largest type (29 percent), followed by symposia (22 percent), commemorations (21 percent), demonstrations (17 percent), and inaugurations (11 percent) (see Table 2).

Veronese commemorations included ceremonies for national events such as the Vittoria and the March on Rome as well as funerals for public figures. The public event that marked the death of Michele Bianchi provides an example. On February 9, 1930, the log entry read: "In the Piazza dei Signori with austere and emotional displays the Black Shirts, the official representatives, and the people commemorated the admirable and exemplary figure of an Italian and a fascist of the Quadrumvirate Michele Bianchi. The Federal Commissioner Giuseppe Righetti spoke and after his speech the fascist appeal to the Dead was made."[58] Two days later the fifth page of *L'Arena* featured a report on the commemorative event. The "austere" and "solemn" "rite" was a "commemoration" of Bianchi, who was the "apotheosis" of fascist manhood and, according to Righetti, "a Man of the Revolution." Brigades of local fascist notables were present at the ceremony in the Piazza Dante, which faces the Veronese seat of government (Palazzo del

---

[56] Verona is located in the northern corner of Italy, where education rates have been historically high in contrast to the center and the south. For statistics on schooling by region, see Marzio Barbagli, *Educating for Unemployment* (New York: Columbia University Press, 1982), 71–101, and the dated but still useful Bolton King and Thomas Okey, *Italy To-Day* (London: James Nisbet, 1904), 236, and Herbert W. Schneider and Shephard B. Clough, *Making Fascists* (Chicago: University of Chicago Press, 1929), 83–85; on the Catholic Church and ritual space, see Herbert W. Schneider, *Making the Fascist State* (New York: Oxford University Press, 1928), 216–17, and David I. Kertzer, "The Role of Ritual in State Formation," in *Religious Regimes and State Formation*, ed. Eric R. Wolf (Albany: State University of New York Press, 1991), 85–103.

[57] "Pro-Memoria," *ACS, PCM* 1937–39 3.3.3/f. 1558, sf. 8, summarizes the fascist legislation on holidays.

[58] "Documentario manifestazioni," 30, *ACS, PNF, MRF,* b. 12 (Verona).

Table 2. Distribution of ritual events in Verona, 1922–1942 ($n=727$)

	n	*percent*
Genre		
Commemoration	154	21
Celebration	208	29
Demonstration	122	17
Symposium	159	22
Inauguration	84	11
Local/national interaction		
Local event/Local leader	263	36
Local event/National leader	235	32
National event/Local leader	196	27
National event/National leader	33	5
Period		
Matteotti (1-1-22 to 6-10-24)	38	5
Consolidation (6-11-24 to 3-24-29)	127	18
Consensus (3-25-29 to 9-8-35)	240	33
Mobilization (9-9-35 to 6-10-40)	219	30
World War II (6-11-40 to 7-19-42)	103	14

Governo). After the applause for Righetti's speech died down, sounding trumpets signaled the beginning of the "fascist rite":

> The Honorable Righetti with strong voice and serious accent called: *Comrade Michele Bianchi!* The crowd responded with a single powerful shout: *Presente!*
> A minute of remembrance followed the call. Soon after, three drumbeats echoed and finally a bugle sounded announcing the end of the ceremony.[59]

As the band played the anthem of the battle of the Piave, the crowd filed slowly out of the piazza and the members of the various fascist organizations returned to their party offices.

Fascist celebration in Verona during 1932, the year of the tenth anniversary of the March on Rome, provides an example of the range of events that this genre subsumed on the local level.[60] In March, Luigi Razza, the head of the National Fascist Agricultural Union, visited Verona to celebrate a day dedicated to the Rural Housewives (Massaie Rurali). In April, eighteen propaganda meetings were held throughout the province by order of the National Fascist Party head. Verona celebrated the Birth of Rome (Natale di Roma) on April 21 with the "symbolic rite" of the *leva fascista.* In May,

---

[59] "La Commemorazione del Quadrumviro Michele Bianchi," *L'Arena* (Verona), 11 February 1930, 5.
[60] "Documentario manifestazioni," 46–53, *ACS, PNF, MRF,* b. 12 (Verona).

veterans, fascists, and the "people" enthusiastically participated in propaganda meetings (raduni di propaganda). On July 3, there was a "vibrant day of fascist faith." August saw the *carabinieri* (the military and civil police) march, a display of tactical maneuvers, and a military parade. On September 8, there was a "powerful fascist manifestation" to signal the changing of the guard at the Federation of Fighting Fascists. On October 9, an "extremely grand meeting" (*grandiosa adunata*) of youth was held to celebrate the presence of high-level National Fascist Party members at the annual young fascist celebration. On October 30, members of the fascist youth organization again staged a "vibrant patriotic manifestation" at the Teatro Nuovo.

The last celebratory event of the year was the departure on December 9 of six hundred Veronese peasants (*rurali*) for the fascist province of Littoria. Exporting unemployed peasants and workers to either the African colonies or planned communities in Italy was a standard fascist strategy for dealing with the economic distress of the 1930s.[61] The farewell event included a mass in the cathedral, where the bishop imparted his blessings, and a ceremony at the train station, where the local Fascist Party head and the local leader of the agricultural union delivered speeches.[62]

The Birth of Rome, April 21, was a national fascist holiday that subverted Catholicism and socialism; it was celebrated every year in Verona through 1942. It was one of two holidays that the regime created, the second being the celebration of the founding of the Fascist Party observed on March 23. The timing of these holidays ensured that in some years they would conflict with Easter.[63] The fascist "feast of labor" aimed to attenuate whatever feelings remained for the socialists' celebration of labor on May 1.[64] In a book on fascist holidays, two regime publicists drew an explicit comparison between the socialist and fascist celebrations:

> The feast of labor was celebrated in Italy—and is still celebrated in many countries—on the first of May. This feast, inspired by strangers, was in Italy, and is elsewhere, a day consecrated to the apology for class struggle: groups of workers with red flags, harangues of revolutionary agitators, and various incitements to indiscipline and disorder. Fascism, abolishing class struggle, necessarily had to cancel from the calendars the revolutionary feast of the first of May, but not to suppress from this feast of labor the blessing of God: fascism changed the date, making it coincide with the Birth of

[61] On Veronese immigration to fascist colonies, see Zangarini, *Politica e societa a Verona*, 24–46.

[62] "Documentario manifestazioni," 40–45, ACS, PNF, MRF, b. 12 (Verona).

[63] "Pro-Memoria," 3–4.

[64] May 1 had become a legal holiday in Italy in 1921. The fascists outlawed it in 1923, three months after assuming power. See "Comunicato per Stafani e per la stampa," ACS, PCM 1923 2.4–1/f. 1123.

Rome, and bestowed upon it a new significance, because in human labor, as in the birth of the City, is the origin of all progress.

On the occasion of the Italian Feast of Labor all work in offices and laboratories is suspended and intellectual work is interrupted, to participate in the celebrations of the Birth of Rome that take place with diverse and significant manifestations everywhere.[65]

The ceremony of the *leva*, an integral part of the April 21 events, underscores how celebration and commemoration diverged as ritual genres.[66] The *leva* was a rite of passage in which fascist youth passed from one level or suborganization of the Fascist Party to the next. The party strictly specified the ages at which one proceeded to the next stage: a youth became a member of the Balilla at age fourteen, an *Avanguardista* (Avant-Garde) at age eighteen, and a *Universitario fascista* (fascist university student) or *Giovane fascista* (Young Fascist) at age Twenty-one. The *leva* ceremony took place throughout Italy, with the largest one occurring in Rome before Mussolini; in Verona it was held in the Piazza Bra, the central square and next to the Arena. It began the local heads of the diverse fascist groups provided a list of the initiates to the federal secretary, who administered the "fascist oath" to the assembled youth. The secretary intoned the oath: "In the name of God and of Italy I swear to follow the orders of the DUCE and to serve with all my force, and if it is necessary, with my blood, the cause of the fascist Revolution." He then asked the youths, "Do you swear it?" and they responded in unison, "I swear it!"[67] This ceremony treads on Roman Catholic ritual turf. Historian Emilio Gentile compares the *leva* to Roman Catholic confirmation: "From Catholic liturgy, for example, was taken the rite of the 'leva fascista,' instituted in 1927: a 'rite of passage' similar to confirmation [*cresima*], with which youth coming from the youth organizations, confirming their faith in fascism, they become 'consecrated fascists,' members of the party."[68] This analogy, though probably correct, fails to capture the temporal dimension of the Catholic and the fascist rite. Both are actions that signal the end of youth and the passage to active commitment in an ideological program. In the Catholic rite, the young person becomes a "soldier of Christ"; in the fascist rite, a "soldier of the regime."

The second part of the fascist ceremony, the initiation rite, dramatized the linking of generations that was a vital part of fascist, as well as religious,

[65] Ezio Bonomi and Arnaldo Caro, *Celebrazioni patriottiche fasciste religiose* (Milan: Nuova Italia, n.d.), 82.

[66] Schneider and Clough, *Making Fascists*, 194, and Emilio Gentile, *Il culto del littorio* (Rome: Laterza, 1993), 129–30.

[67] The description of the ceremony is found in Montemaggiori, *Dizionario* della doctrina fascista (Rome: G. B. Paravia, 1934), 449–50.

[68] Gentile, *Culto del littorio*, 129.

continuity. Paragraph 84 of the regulations of the Young Fighting Fascists described the initiation ceremony:

> The symbolic form of the passage of ranks takes place in the following manner:
> a Black Shirt bestows on a Young Fascist, chosen from the ranks, a musket [*moschetto*];
> a Young Fascist, from among the oldest, bestows on an *Avanguardista* a scarf made of Roman colors.
> The bestowing of the musket and the scarf occurs simultaneously.
> Then the chosen youths exchange an embrace. In the name of the Duce, the Legions salute in one voice.[69]

The annual performance of the *leva* drew Verona to the Roman center, created a new political generation of young Veronese fascists, and competed for ritual space with the Catholic Church. *L'Arena*'s description of the 1930 *leva* as a "rite of youth" suggests these themes: "For spirit of discipline, for fervor of enthusiasm, for rigid military austerity, the ceremony offered a spectacle of grand pride and truly assured the high character of the rite that formed the spiritual content of the celebration."[70]

Demonstrations figured in Veronese ritual life, but they were slightly less spectacular and somewhat more frequent than in the Roman center. For example, in 1925, there was an assassination plot against Mussolini. The calendar entry on November 5, 1925, read: "With a meeting of the masses in the Piazza dei Signori the Black Shirts and the people of Verona express their sentiments of indignation against the conspiracy against Mussolini."[71] A day later, *L'Arena* recorded the event in its "Daily Chronicle" page Noting the "indignation of the Veronese people" over the plot against Mussolini, Federal Secretary Giovanni Eliseo announced a rally at nine in the evening of "fascists" and "citizens" in the Piazza Dante.[72] Two features of *L'Arena*'s relatively short account are worthy of attention. First, the language in the newspaper and the log are strikingly similar, indicating that the party secretary may have used the newspaper to create the log. Similarities in phrasing occur repeatedly between the log and *L'Arena*. Second, the distinction between "fascists" and "citizens" appears consistently in the log, suggesting that the party was aware of its need to create a constituency.

Demonstrations flourished in the mid-1930s, and as a genre of event,

[69] Montemaggiori, *Dizionario*, 450.
[70] "Il rito della giovinezza," *L'Arena*, 22 April 1930, 4.
[71] "Documentario manifestazioni," 13, ACS, PNF, MRF, b. 12 (Verona).
[72] "L'indignazione del popolo veronese," *L'Arena*, 6 November 1925, Cronaca Cittadina, unpaginated.

they took many forms. The calendar entry recorded on October 3, 1935, the day Mussolini declared war against Ethiopia, captured the spirit of fascist demonstration as it evolved, as well as mimicking the demonstration held in the Roman center: "With a powerful manifestation of fascist fierceness and faith all the people of Verona participated in a gigantic rally [*gigantesca adunata*] on the occasion of the historic speech of the DUCE that declared war against Ethiopia."[73] The passage of heads of state through Verona might also trigger a demonstration. On May 3, 1938, when Adolf Hitler passed through, the calendar read:

> With the largest meeting [*grandiosa adunata*] of the people—the crowd present was calculated at 30,000 persons—Verona gave its homage and offered its salute to the Chancellor of the Reich Adolf Hitler who came from the Brenner and was going to Rome for his historic meeting with the Emperor King and the DUCE. Also the little cities of the province welcomed the Head of the new Germany with sympathetic manifestations.[74]

As a genre of event, demonstrations were eclectic as to content. What sets them apart as a distinct type is that they claimed the appearance of spontaneous collective emotion and tended to be large events.

Symposia served as the ritual glue of fascist civic life in Verona, followed by inaugurations. The local Institute of Fascist Culture was frequently the scene of these typically small events where local notables offered lectures such as "The Mission of Rome in the World," author Ezio Maria Gray evoked the past in a discussion entitled "The Lessons of Zama," and an Italian senator addressed the women of Verona on "the Italian woman and the sanctions."[75] On September 16, 1934, the calendar noted a representative local inaugural event: "In the presence of the excellent Lojaconi, Undersecretary of State for Communications, and of the honorable Del Croix and Malusardi with a great manifestation of the people the House of the Wounded [Casa dei Mutilati] was inaugurated."[76] On the day before the event, the *Gazzettino* described it in detail. The "patriotic ceremony" would "consecrate one of the most beautiful and holy works of [our] Province." Twelve thousand war wounded would descend on Verona after a pilgrimage to the nation's battlefields. Arriving at the train station early in the morning, the group would proceed to the Ristori Theater to hear speeches by local military leaders; then there would be a parade to the House of the Wounded for the inauguration ceremony; and the last part of the "rite" would be a

[73] "Documentario manifestazioni," 68, *ACS, PNF, MRF*, b. 12 (Verona).
[74] Ibid., 92.
[75] Ibid., 17, 54, 71.
[76] Ibid., 58.

huge assembly (*immensa adunata*) in the Arena.[77] The inauguration of the House of the Wounded was a relatively large event for this genre of activity. The modest calendar entry on June 11, 1936, was more typical: "With a solemn ceremony the Federal Secretary inaugurated the flags and flames of the women's regional organizations."[78]

Symposia and inaugurations made up the largest proportion (34 percent) of Fascist Party activity. Small ceremonies that brought together discrete subsections of the party constituency were thus the core of Veronese fascist ritual. In contrast to the other genres of ritual activity, the prevalence of symposia and inaugurations depends on local conditions. Verona's long-standing civic culture suggest a general eagerness to participate in the public sphere which made its citizens receptive to symposia.[79] In March 1936, the National Ministry of Press and Propaganda asked local prefects to identify private citizens who would be willing to speak on behalf of the regime "in the event of mobilization."[80] The prefect of Verona did not have difficulty finding a cadre of "good" and "excellent" speakers who were willing to volunteer their oratorical skills to work in local propaganda centers. In general, the volunteers came from the educated professional middle classes. A corp of Veronese lawyers, professors, teachers, and a few "war wounded" formed a circle of propagandists-in-waiting.

The reconstruction of the Italian infrastructure was a regime directive that was dependent on local resources and capacities. Verona's massive rebuilding program between 1922 and 1942 contributed to the flourishing of inaugurations as a ritual genre. Verona built bridges, roads, hospitals, and schools; expanded its cemeteries; and restored artistic monuments such as Juliet's house and the medieval tower in the Piazza of Herbs. This physical transformation generated civic enthusiasm. For example, in March 1935, *L'Arena*'s headlines boldly proclaimed, "For a greater Verona: THE TRANS-FORMATION OF THE PHYSICAL PLAN OF URBAN TRAM LINES: The Communal Council approved with a fervid manifestation of applause the deliberation of the Podesta that confronts and resolves this annoying problem."[81] In addition, certain forms of Fascist Party activity required new buildings. During this period, the Veronese Fascist Party built eleven summer colonies for fas-

---

[77] "La casa del mutilato verra inaugurata domani presenti S.E. Lojacono e l'on. Delcroix," *Gazzettino* (Verona), 15 September 1934, internal page.

[78] "Documentario manifestazioni," 75, *ACS, PNF, MRF*, b. 12 (Verona).

[79] Putnam traces the roots of civic community in contemporary Italy from patterns established in the Renaissance. The Veneto is in the top third of Putnam's index of civicness. See *Making Democracy Work*, 97, 150.

[80] See "Propaganda all'interno in caso di mobilizazione," N.U.P.I.E., *ACS, MCP*, b. 241, f. 91.

[81] "La trasformazione dell'impianto tramviario urbano," *L'Arena*, 27 March 1935, 1.

cist children, three federal headquarters, ten Fascist Houses, and two regional headquarters.[82]

Local/National Interaction

The interaction between the local and the national—the "exemplary center" and the periphery—requires its own classification scheme. An analysis of Veronese events that determines whether they were local or national in scope and whether national leaders attended them elucidates the interaction between the central state, as represented by the National Fascist Party and regime in Rome, and local variations of national directives, yielding a fourfold classification scheme. Veronese events were (1) local with only local leaders participating; (2) local with national leaders present; (3) national with only local leaders present; (4) national with national leaders present.

Genre did not necessarily determine an event's classification in the local/national scheme.[83] A local event was restricted to Verona, such as a local religious holiday, an investiture in the Fascist Party, or a demonstration. A national event tied Verona to Rome and was celebrated throughout Italy, such as the annual commemorations of the March on Rome and the Vittoria and the celebration of the Birth of Rome. By the mid-1930s, the regime had developed a full calendar of secular holidays that required observance. In addition, Roman Catholic ritual days such as Christmas, All Saints' Day, the Immaculate Conception, and the Birthday of Saint Joseph were legal state holidays and fell under the rubric of a national event. Unique events such as demonstrations to support a national policy such as the invasion of Ethiopia also fell within this classification. A local leader was a member of the Veronese Fascist Party or local notable such as the mayor or the bishop. A national leader was a member of the fascist regime or National Fascist Party who either led or participated prominently in the event. Regime members varied from Mussolini to the heads of government ministries and fascist corporative bodies (see Table 2).

The largest proportion of events (36 percent) were local. Many of the symposia fell into this category. For example, on January 9, 1930, "Professor Chinigo, noted student of Albanian problems, spoke at the Institute of Fascist Culture on the future of Albania." Commemorations also were

[82] "Elencazione opere del regime realizzate nella circoscrizione territoriale della Federazione," memo prepared by Federal Secretary Antonio Bonino, ACS, PNF, MRF, b. 12 (Verona).
[83] A cross-tabulation of genre with local/national interaction showed a statistically significant relation between the two (p = 0.000). In general, 66 percent of commemorative events tended to be national with local leaders present; 40 percent of celebratory events and 48 percent of symposia tended to be local with national leaders present; and demonstrations (54 percent) and inaugurations (42 percent) tended to be purely local events.

frequently local, such as the entry on December 20, 1930: "In the salon of
the Fascist House a solemn remembrance of Guglielmo Oberdan was held
for the young Fighting Fascists: orator Carlo Cilione." Demonstrations
might be local events as well. For example, on September 2, 1933, the log
reported a "powerful nocturnal mobilization of 50,000 young fascists. The
Prefect and the Federal reviewed the mobilized."[84] National events celebrated locally made up 27 percent of all events. These were frequently fascist
holidays to which the National Fascist Party did not send representatives.
For example, the 1933 commemoration of the March on Rome in Verona
was celebrated with the reading of Mussolini's message to the nation by a
local leader.[85]

The official visit was the principal symbolic vehicle that the regime and
party used to draw the periphery to the center. Mussolini's 1938 visit was
the apogee of this political form. From the days that Roman emperors made
their grand ceremonial entrances, the visit was a powerful ceremonial tool
that disseminated authority from the center.[86] The presence of regime and
national party leaders at purely local events stamped these occasions with a
national and fascist character. National leaders were present at 268 Veronese
Fascist Party events (37 percent of the total), only 33 (5 percent) of which
were national events. The presence of the head of the Fascist Industrial Syn-
dicate at the national convention of industrial leaders held in Verona on
August 6, 1931,was in this category.[87] More typical was the 1934 commemoration of the founding of the Fighting Fascists. The March 23, 1934, calendar noted the presence of a government minister:

> Before a grand crowd of fascists and people the Honorable De Francisci,
> Minister of Grace and Justice, spoke in the Arena celebrating the anniver-
> sary of the Founding of the Fighting Fascists. Before the celebration the
> Minister rendered homage to the Fallen fascists and with the Prefect and
> the Federal Secretary as guides visited the House of Fascist Assistance.[88]

The visits to local events far outweighed the visits to national events. Local
events with national leaders present represented 32 percent (235) of all

[84] "Documentario manifestazioni," 30, 34, 51, ACS, PNF, MRF, b. 12 (Verona).
[85] The absence of a national representative on this particular occasion does not signify
regime indifference to local celebrations of national events. The prefects throughout Italy
were required to file reports of these events with the Ministry of Internal Affairs; their reports
are a rich archival source of local celebration.
[86] Scholars of symbolic politics have tended to neglect this form of ritual action. On the
Roman use of "triumphs and ovations," see H. H. Scullard, Festivals and Ceremonies of the
Roman Republic (Ithaca: Cornell University Press, 1981), 213–18; on visits in Renaissance
Venice, see Edward Muir, Civic Ritual in Renaissance Venice (Princeton: Princeton University Press, 1981), 135–56.
[87] "Documentario manifestazioni," 37, ACS, PNF, MRF, b. 12 (Verona).
[88] Ibid., 55.

events staged between 1922 and 1942. The regime and the party sent its most visible representatives to purely local events.

In the years between 1922 and 1942, National Fascist Party leaders and prominent government ministers paraded in and out of Verona. The panoply of leaders that arrived in 1933 provide an example. Giacomo Acerbo, the minister of agriculture, visited the agricultural fair; Achille Starace, national secretary of the Fascist Party, came to "celebrate" Veronese fascism; Luigi Razza, head of the Fascist Agricultural Union, presided over a meeting of national agricultural unions; the undersecretary of state for war made two visits, the first to participate in a military training session and the second to attend a local commemorative ceremony; and the national president of the Balilla visited the Veronese Balilla.[89]

The average Veronese citizen would find it difficult to avoid a national leader's visit, which created spatial and temporal disruption as the leader paraded into the center of the city from the train station. *L'Arena* announced impending visits in front-page stories with bold headlines and reported on them afterward. National leaders invariably made speeches, laid commemorative stones, and cut ribbons, but it was their presence at an event which transformed it from a local expression of fascist solidarity to a symbolic occasion that bound Verona to Rome, periphery to center, and reinforced the idea that the fascist collectivity was the nation and the state.

Rhythms of Veronese Fascist Ritual

Temporal Patterns

Historical period affected ritual action in Verona as it did in the Roman center. The greatest proportion of events occurred during the consensus and mobilization periods (63 percent versus 23 percent in the two earlier periods and 14 percent in the World War II period; see Table 2). The periodization of events provides a useful shorthand to the interplay of history and ritual events, although it distracts from the pattern of ritual repetition.

A mapping of fascist events in Verona on a yearly basis reveals a distinct temporal pattern and suggests a momentum behind them (see Figure 11). Public events came in waves and displayed a generally bimodal distribution.[90]

[89] Ibid., 46–53. During this period there were twelve National Fascist Party heads. Starace occupied the post from 1931 until 1939 and made two additional visits to Verona, in 1938 to assist at commemoration ceremonies and in 1939 to inaugurate a *dopolavoro* sports arena.

[90] I have not been able to attribute the anomalous drop in the number of events in 1939 to exogenous variables such as historical events, change in National Fascist Party leadership, or change in local party leadership. The typewritten log (see note 2) provided the data for the quantitative material in this section.

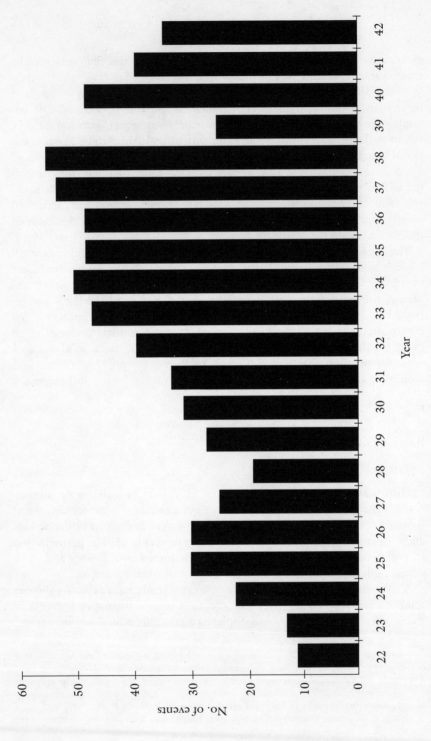

Figure 11. Number of fascist-sponsored public events per year, 1922–1942

The first peak occurred in the mid-1920s when the regime was consolidating its political, social, and cultural agenda; the second peak occurred in the mid-1930s when it was beginning to create a new Roman empire in Ethiopia and to mobilize for war. The largest number of events occurred in 1937 and 1938, the height of the mobilization period. In general, the pattern showed an increase in the absolute number of events over time with a decline during the war years (1940–42).

National and international forces drove the accelerating number of events and established the rhythm of ritual in Verona. Local exigencies shaped the formal patterning of ritual events. Commitment, Catholicism, and the necessity of creating new generations of fascists were the three problems Righetti outlined in his report to Mussolini.[91] Temporal variations in the size and genre of events, the local/national interaction, and generational presence suggest ritual corrections to the problems of Veronese fascist identity.

Extraordinary events punctuated the rhythm of fascist ritual. Large public spectacles, where more than a thousand persons were present, represented a relatively small proportion of all events (see Figure 12). They began to increase during the consensus period and reached a plateau during the period of mobilization and the war. Between 1922 and 1935, Verona staged an average of three spectacles a year (range two to seven); between 1936 and 1942, the city staged an average of nine spectacles a year (range four to fourteen). In 1936, the first year that events increased, from five to twelve, the Veronese party sponsored an array of diverse events. In February, "a spontaneous and huge popular meeting of Black Shirts and citizens expressed their jubilation" over a military victory in Africa.[92] Two months later, a "picturesque parade" of seven thousand peasants filled the Piazza Vittorio Emanuele to celebrate the Birth of Rome.[93] On May one hundred thousand persons convened in the same piazza to hear a radio broadcast of Mussolini's proclamation that the Italians had achieved a military victory in Ethiopia. The log entry read:

[91] The problem of creating a new political generation was not unique to Verona. Bruno Wanrooij makes the point that Italian fascism in general found it difficult to create a replacement generation of fascists: "Despite the introduction of the propaganda slogan 'Make Way for Youth,' the problem of the renewal of the ruling class remained substantially unsolved. Eighty of the 145 new deputies appointed in 1934 had entered the fascist party before 1922; twenty-seven had joined that year, and only thirty-eight had become members at a later stage. Even among the leaders of the fascist student groups in 1931, 57.3 per cent had entered the party before 1923 whereas only 13 per cent had come from the fascist youth organizations" ("The Rise and Fall of Italian Fascism as a Generational Revolt," *Journal of Contemporary History* 22 [1987], 410).

[92] "Documentario manifestazioni," 71–72, ACS, PNF, MRF, b. 12 (Verona).

[93] Ibid., 73–74.

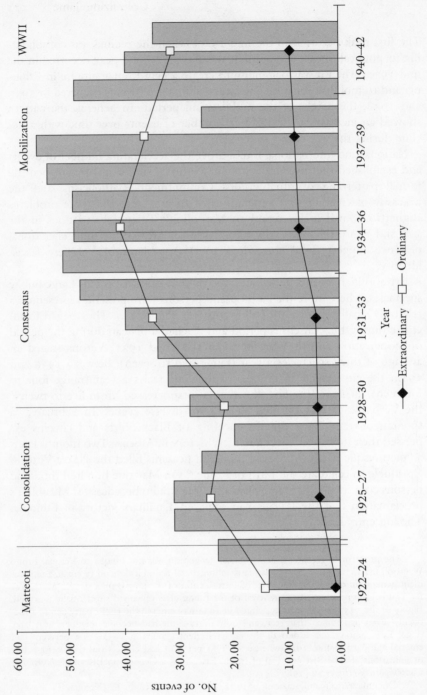

Figure 12. Number of extraordinary and ordinary events, averaged over three-year periods, 1922–1942

A multitude of 100,000 persons, convened in the Piazza Vittorio Emanuele from the most distant parts of the city, listened to the announcement of the Victory of the armies of Rome over the Ethiopian hordes and repeated with formidable impetuous emotion the shout of the DUCE. After the discourse of the DUCE a long parade gathered in the historic Piazza dei Signori, where the Prefect and the Vice Federal addressed the organizations and the people with inflamed words.[94]

A few days later, on May 9, church and party united with a mass in the cathedral to give thanks for the Italian victory. The head of the diocese of Verona spoke with "noble eloquence" of the "sacrifice and faith of the Italian people" and proclaimed that the Ethiopian victory marked Italy and Rome as the center of "Roman-ness [*romanita*], latin-ness [*latinita*], and civilization."[95] In the evening, a huge crowd gathered in the Piazza Bra to listen to Mussolini's radio broadcast proclaiming the new Italian empire; the remainder of the evening was spent in the singing of patriotic songs and torchlight parades. International and national events were the catalysts for the Veronese spectacles of 1936, Mussolini's 1938 visit, and extraordinary events in general.

Genre Patterns

Commemorations and celebrations varied inversely during the fascist period (see Figure 13). Commemorative events as a proportion of all events peaked between 1931 and 1933, began to decline in 1935, and dropped off sharply in 1940. Commemorations that focused on the fascist past were salient at the end of the period of regime consolidation but a less useful form of ritual in the period of mobilization; they dropped to 1922 levels during the war period. The fascist past gave way to the fascist future as a ritual vehicle.

Celebratory events followed a steep upward trajectory, dipped briefly in 1935 probably in response to the increased number of demonstrations, continued a sharp rise in the late 1930s, and remained stable throughout the war period. Demonstrations, purely expressive events, were not the most prevalent form of Veronese public event, although they had a sharp rise from 1932 to 1935; then they leveled off and in 1938 began to decline sharply. During this period, the regime began to lay the groundwork for international aggression, and it is not surprising that demonstrations were a favored vehicle of mobilization and emotional commitment. The regime waged war on Ethiopia, declared Italy an Empire, withdrew from the

[94] Ibid., 74.
[95] Ibid.

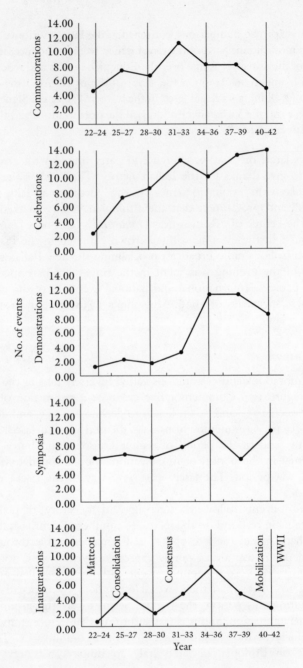

Figure 13. Relative prominence of genres of fascist public events, averaged over three-year periods, 1922–1942

League of Nations, formed the Rome/Berlin Axis and intervened in the Spanish Civil War. Demonstrations may have become a habitual part of Veronese life between 1935 and 1938, but their relative frequency declined markedly beginning in 1938, when Italian military aggression accelerated, and continued to drop through the war years. In contrast, celebrations increased.

Symposia occurred at a relatively stable rate throughout the period and experienced a slight increase between 1932 and 1935. As symposia were frequently lectures on current Fascist Party lines, their sharp decline between 1935 and 1938 is probably related to the significant rise in demonstrations during the same period. Taking to the streets is always a more potent method of displaying an ideological point than attending a lecture. Inaugurations show a fluctuating pattern that is sensible in terms of the type of activity they represented and the exigencies of fascist policy making. Inaugurations often consisted of the laying of commemorative stones on graves of fascist heroes or the opening of a regime- or party-subsidized Veronese building. Both types of activities peaked in 1935. Building the fascist state required time, which suggests an explanation for the long rise during the late 1920s and 1930s; beginning in the mid-1930, war efforts probably drained energy and financial resources from infrastructure and past heroes.

Commemoration and celebration represented the greatest overall proportion of events (50 percent), and the inverse relation between their relative frequencies suggests a meaningful pattern. Commemorations were stagings around history that were firmly rooted in the fascist and Italian past. They began their marked decline in the middle of the consolidation period and continued into the mobilization period, when they again dropped sharply. Memory is frequently a rallying cry for war but usually requires a historical trajectory of long duration. Italian and fascist history was short: unification occurred in 1860, and fascism came to power in 1922. The seventy years between 1860 and 1932 were not filled with glorious events but instead were dominated by labor unrest, political instability, and economic distress. The attenuation of the Italian victory in the Veneto at Versailles may have been the focus of postwar resentment and a rallying cry for the fascist movement, but it had limited appeal as an impetus to future greatness.

A regime that was embarking on a major project of political and cultural creation required a ritual form that focused on the present or on events that were so distant in time, such as the Roman Empire, as to constitute myth rather than memory. Events that used theatricality to draw attention to the fascist present were powerful crucibles in which to forge a community of citizens with emotional commitment to the fascist project at home and abroad. The repeated experience of fascist public events that were annual and ongoing—events surrounding new fascist projects, annual rituals such as the *leva*—provided a sense of futurity. The memories of past events, especially those whose outcomes were ambiguous, sometimes serve as rallying cries, but they are incapable of providing the sense of hope and belief that mobilizes citizens to support their governments in whatever paths they choose to take.

With the exception of the brief drop in 1935, celebratory events exhibited a steady rise throughout the twenty-year period, suggesting the colonization of time as fascist in Verona. The repeated experience of celebration made fascism appear usual, customary, necessary, and ultimately worth dying for. Commemoration took second place to celebration as the regime and party worked on consolidating emotional commitment. The decrease in commemoration served to attenuate the ritual power of the Catholic Church. Masses for the dead ensured the church's presence at commemorations, whereas its presence at celebrations was optional. The relative decline of commemoration chipped away at the emotional hold of the church in Verona as the Veronese party attempted to replace traditional religious identities with fascist identities.

Patterns of Local/National Interaction

The interaction between Verona and the Roman center suggested the extent to which feelings of national and fascist solidarity radiated outward from the core (see Figure 14). National leaders and national events drew Verona to Rome. The presence of local leaders at national events increased sharply until 1935, when it dropped off. The calendar of national events, mainly annual national holidays as specified by the state law, provided a cyclical structure to Verona's relation to Rome, as these events could be fascist, national, or religious. The presence of local leaders was not as significant as the mere existence of the events themselves; the patterning of events is reflective of changes in the laws on holidays, which diminished in the late 1930s. The presence of national leaders at national events in Verona was a relatively rare occurrence, so the pattern lacks meaning in terms of ritual habituation.

The changing pattern of local events (68 percent of all events) suggests a more ideologically potent pattern of local/national interaction. Like the relation between commemoration and celebration, local events with local leaders present varied inversely with local events with national leaders present. Purely local events peaked in 1935 at the end of the consolidation period and declined steadily through the mobilization and war periods. In contrast, local events with national leaders present increased steadily until 1932, reflected a slight decline in 1935, and then increased again to 1938, when they leveled off. As the consolidation period turned into the mobiliza-

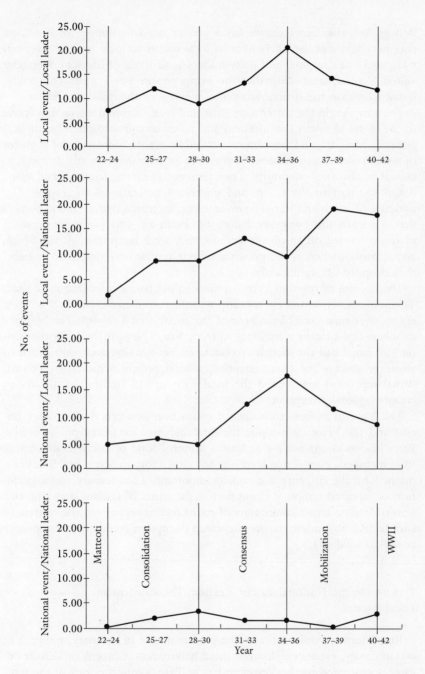

Figure 14. Interaction between the local and national in Veronese fascist public events, averaged over three-year periods, 1922–1942

tion period, the fascist center felt a greater need to impose itself on the periphery and was less likely to trust local events to local leaders. Between 1935 and 1942, regime and party leaders at all levels of the state hierarchy visited Verona, suggesting that the living person was a more compelling fascist icon than the structured cyclical message of the holiday calendar.

The variation in the patterns of genre and local/national interaction spoke to the issues of fascist commitment and religious competition. The physical presence of youth and war veterans at public events addressed the problem of fascist political generations. Youth and war veterans were visual representations of historical continuity. Their presence at events, together and apart, linked the past to the future and suggested generational succession. The presence of youth and war veterans at events increased sharply and in parallel between 1928 and 1935 (see Figure 15) From 1935 to 1942, the presence of youth leveled off (probably because they were fighting in Africa, Spain, and Albania), whereas the presence of war veterans continued to rise and then dropped off significantly.

The rhythm of ritual in Verona points to the fascist colonization of time. The public repetition of ritual events and the cumulative experience of these events over time created patterns of familiarity that Veronese Fascist Party members and citizens were likely to recognize. The form, and not the content, of ritual had the capacity to create fascist meaning and contributed to whatever success the fascist identity creation project achieved in Verona. Ritual repetition legitimated the local party's, and fascism's, authority to create temporal disruption.

The log entries frequently drew a distinction between the Veronese fascists and the Veronese people, the dual audience for fascist public events. Party leaders could assume at least a minimal level of fascist commitment from members, even if that level was not satisfactory to Mussolini. The commitment of the citizenry was equally important. The memory and expectation of repeated temporal disruption in the name of fascism drew the citizens of Verona into a community of fascist feeling. However, the content of such feeling was indeterminate. Repeated disruption could create annoyance as well as solidarity.

Performing the National Fascist Agenda: The Content of Local Events

Ritual form colonized time. The predominance of ordinary, rather than extraordinary, events emphasized ritual habituation. Citizens of Verona became accustomed to the Veronese Fascist Party's interruptions of the temporal rhythms of work, leisure, and religious observance. National and inter-

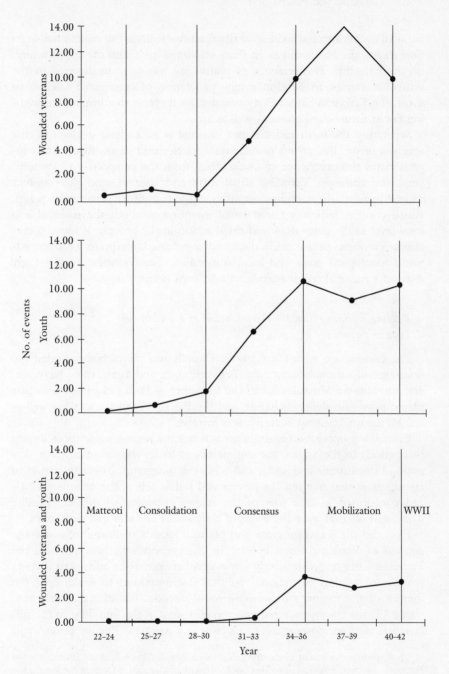

Figure 15. Presence of youth and wounded veterans, averaged for three-year periods, 1922–1942

national events affected local-level ritual action. Even as the regime was in its final stages, the National Fascist Party impinged itself, and the fascist future, on the citizenry. The presence of youth and war veterans attested to the symbolic attempt to develop a new generation of committed fascists. In short, the Veronese Fascist Party oriented local events to affirming an ongoing fascist future for Verona as well as Italy.

Separating the form and content of ritual is an analytic distinction that acts as a prism. But prisms provide only fractionated views. Ritual form approximates the experience of fascist ritual from the perspective of its audience, the citizenry. Veronese ritual form had content, and that content viewed against salient regime activities suggests another turn of the prism. Ritual content indicates fascist ritual intention on both the national and local level as the party deployed ritual action in the process of identity creation. Veronese fascist ritual displayed a point-counterpoint between national ideological goals and local constraints. The Veronese Fascist Party enacted a national fascist agenda with its own peculiar stamp.

Regime Building and the Articulation of a Fascist Self (1922–1929)

The conciliation with the Catholic Church and the plebiscite ended the first stage of national fascist rule. Between 1922 and 1929, there were several attempts on Mussolini's life; the Chamber of Deputies passed laws that placed power firmly in his hands; and the Fascist Grand Council, as well as the Militia for National Security, was formed.[96]

Containing opposition and dissent was not the regime's sole focus during this period. In the 1920s, the regime began to lay the foundation for new political institutions and social and economic programs. The articulation of fascist values that merged the private and public self of the new fascist citizen constituted a large part of the regime's ideological project. Family, work, and religion were the focus of early policy agendas and discourses.

How did the social program and political agenda of Rome influence the content of Veronese ritual events? In comparison with later periods, the Veronese party staged relatively few events between 1922 and 1930. Events tended to respond to national political dilemmas and to underscore the themes of the regime's developing social agenda. For example, in 1925, fascist Verona commemorated anniversaries such as the founding of the militia, attended symposia such as "Fascism as a Religious Phenomenon," and

[96] I summarize the salient events from *Il primo e secondo libro del fascista* (Rome: Partito Nazionale Fascista, 1941), 3–15. This book, a fascist propaganda document for youth, has the advantage of highlighting what the regime thought was important, rather than what history later judged to be of importance.

displayed public outrage at an attempt on Mussolini's life.[97] Purely Veronese
events included the inauguration of a new Directorate of the Provincial Fascist Federation and a celebration of the one hundredth anniversary of the
Bank of Verona.

The extraordinary event in Verona in 1925 was the May 25 rally in the
Arena of wounded Italian war veterans. Carlo Del Croix, president of the
National Association of War Wounded and Invalids, presided over the audience of twenty thousand persons. The headlines of *L'Arena* boldly proclaimed, "The Grand Rally of Glorious Wounded Italians in Verona." May
23 was the anniversary of Italy's entrance into the First World War. Del
Croix's carefully crafted speech to the assembled masses in the Arena emphasized historical continuity. Invoking ancient "Roman potency" and the
"Christian martyrs," Del Croix argued that the "revolutionary deed of May"
signaled the "entry of the people [Italians] into History." The image of
generations of Italian soldiers marching forth to capture national and international glory foreshadowed the rhetoric of generational linkage that dominated public commemorative events in the 1930s.[98]

In May 1926, the visits of Augusto Turati, national secretary of the Fascist
Party, and Edmondo Rossoni, president of the Fascist General Confederation of Syndical Corporations, linked national goals to local Veronese conditions. The Provincial Congress of Veronese Fascist Organizations was the
occasion for Turati's visit. The problem of Verona's "commitment" that
Righetti discussed with Mussolini in 1930 first manifested itself in the
1920s. The day before Turati's visit, *L'Arena* reminded the citizenry that
Verona's geographical location gave the city a special place in the fascist
project: "The Party and the Government has always understood the excep-
tional mission of Veronese fascism and it is necessary here in our province to
create a solid and unbreakable block of Black Shirts because Verona is considered a sentinel of Italy before the border of the Brenner." Addressing the
internal bickering and power plays between "old guard" intransigent fascists
and those of a more parliamentary disposition which plagued the leadership
of the Veronese Fascist Party, *L'Arena* warned, "For the superior interests
of the Nation and fascism—a more rigid and conscious discipline is now
necessary." The paper added, "It is not a mystery to anyone that Veronese
internal quarrels have provoked the most intense sorrow and the strongest
and most justifiable disappointment in the soul of the Duce."[99] Turati's presence at the local fascist congress kept the local party in line, warned that the

[97] "Documentario manifestazioni," 9–13, ACS, PNF, MRF, b. 12 (Verona).
[98] "La grande adunata dei gloriosi mutilati italiani a Verona," *L'Arena* 26 May 1925, 1.
[99] "L'Odierno Congresso Provinciale Fascista Veronese," *L'Arena*, 2 May 1926, 1. On
power plays within the Veronese Fascist Party, see Zangarini, *Politica e societa a Verona*,
125–69.

regime was watching, and provided a forum to articulate fascism's developing social vision.

Turati's speech in the Arena emphasized the unity of the new fascist people and blurred the boundary between public and private self, family and nation. Turati began with the familiar myth of postwar disarray brought on by the evils of socialism and argued that the fascist "crowd" represented the unitary soul of the fascist heart and mind. The crowd was the physical manifestation of the mental union of public and private self that would create a committed fascist. For Turati, the crowd of a million arms, legs, and faces had a "single soul, a single song, and a single hope: Italy in every heart, Italy above every heart."[100]

The family and the identification of the nation with the family collapsed the public and private self in fascism. Turati called for the waging of new battles against democracy and liberalism as well as socialism and bolshevism. The Patria—the new Italian family—would be the institutional location of this battle. The personal tie between citizen and nation made fascism morally superior to other modern political ideologies. Turati repudiated romantic visions of nationalism that defined the Patria in terms of poetic agony and painted a "new" image of a nurturing family that more than slightly evoked Mazzini:

> The Patria ought to be the nation despite the tears of its children, despite the pride of its children. If the Patria is this, then its work is in the future and its construction. If the Patria is in the memory of our Dead, then the Patria lies in the will of rebirth and transformation. If the Patria is in the smile of our children, in the serene light of our houses, in the memory of the saintly face of our mothers, the Patria is a reality whose reason for being touches the greatest reasons for life of the whole people. (*Vigorous applause*)
>
> But because the Patria is a nation and because the nation is a living thing and not a bureaucratic organism, not a heavy discipline, but truly something that is inside ourselves, we need to conquer the useless, grating, miserable liberal-democratic mentality, for which the Nation and the Patria and the State are things torn out of the very life of the country.[101]

Two weeks after Turati's visit, Edmondo Rossoni came to Verona to address a provincial congress of fascist syndicates. During this period, the re-

---

[100] "Il forte discorso dell'on. Augusto Turati in Arena," *L'Arena*, 4 May 1926, 1. The recurring newspaper description of the emotional and physical unity of crowds suggests the popular diffusion of Gustave Le Bon's theories of crowd behavior. See, for example, Le Bon's discussion of the "mental unity of crowds" in *The Crowd*, 2d ed. (Athens, Ga.: Larlin, 1982), 2–14.

[101] "Il forte discorso," 2.

gime was busy designing a fascist labor policy that replaced socialist unions with fascist syndical organizations. On the occasion of the congress, *L'Arena* defined commitment to fascism as commitment to labor. The newspaper's opening narrative stated that the "solid organization within the ranks of Fascism" of the "people who labor, suffer, and produce the wealth and power of the Nation" was more important than "sociological treatises" on politics. Trying to show the commitment of Veronese fascism to the regime, *L'Arena* gushed, "Spectacle without precedent for our city! Spectacle that does not leave a doubt of our future."[102]

In contrast to Turati's speech, which concentrated on the moral and spiritual goals of the nation, Rossoni's speech sought to juxtapose a fascist vision of labor against a liberal or socialist vision. Using the Arena as his forum, Rossoni spoke to a crowd of twenty-five thousand, emphasizing the importance of work for the nation.[103] According to Rossoni, the Fascist Party was not the exclusive domain of either the rich or the workers; rather, it was a party of "all Italy and all Italians" which did not seek its political inspiration in "Moscow, London, or Paris." In contrast to socialism, which saw its center in class struggle, and democracy, which found its center in the power of the rich (or the "plutocrats," as the fascists referred to the bourgeoisie), fascism located its center in the nation. In order to achieve its "spiritual" goals, fascism would have to transcend economic struggle. Fascist syndicalism, which included all citizens, whether workers or owners, was the organizational vehicle that would render class struggle obsolete.[104]

Rossoni's speech, given a year before the regime introduced the Labor Charter, the document that formalized the fascist relation of work, self, and society, articulated many of the charter's themes.[105] Fascist Verona did not ignore the Labor Charter. On April 21, 1927, the Birth of Rome and the day of the formal introduction of the document, the Veronese syndical delegate gave a speech in the New Theater (Teatro Nuovo) to "fascists and laborers, on the significance of the feast, exalting the realization in the field of labor that the institution of Mussolini's Labor Charter brought."[106] Later in the day in the provincial town of Malcesine, a convention of syndical organizers and delegates convened for yet another set of celebrations of this new fascist document.

[102] "La imponente manifestazione sindacale fascista di ieri a Verona," *L'Arena*, 23 May 1926, 1.

[103] Ibid.

[104] "L'On. Rossoni illustra al popolo veronese i benefici della nuova concezione sindacale fascista," *L'Arena*, 23 May 1926, 2.

[105] On the political maneuverings behind the formulation of the Labor Charter, see Alberto Aquarone, *L'organizzazione dello stato totalitario* (rpt., Turin: Einaudi, 1974), 111–68.

[106] "Documentario manifestazioni," 20, *ACS, PNF, MRF*, b. 12 (Verona).

In February 1929, the regime signed the Concordat with the Catholic Church. Verona marked the "conciliation," as the Concordat was popularly known, with ceremonial pomp that belied the conflicts with the bishop and Catholic Action that plagued the region and the city. The calendar entry for February 17, 1929, read:

> In the Cathedral, authorities, higher-ups, fascists, and the people, the Bishop assisted by a group of clerics, elevated to God a hymn of thanks for the uniting accord between Church and State, which consecrates in imperial Rome and Christianity the political greatness of Mussolini and the faith of the Italian. The Bishop made a lofty speech; after the solemn rite a parade formed that ended in the Governing Palace, the seat of the Commune where the Mayor [*Podesta*] made a brief proclamation on the historic event. Acclamations followed to the King, the DUCE, the Pontiff, Italy, and Rome.[107]

The celebration of the conciliation turned into a local feast in Verona. Parish priests dined festively with local fascist leaders from the afternoon until the early evening; local leaders issued manifestoes that gave a Veronese gloss to the importance of events.[108]

The plebiscite of March 24, 1929, which eliminated participatory democracy (ironically, by popular vote), was also celebrated in Verona.[109] On March 19, Gino Cacciari, president of the Agricultural Confederation and member of the Fascist Grand Council, lectured on the significance of the vote. Given the dependence of the region on agricultural production, it was not surprising that Cacciari framed his support of the plebiscite in terms of the benefits that absolute political stability would bring to Italian agriculture.[110] A week later, Verona celebrated the passage of the plebiscite with a "rally of fascists and people" in the Piazza dei Signori.

Living Fascism: The Underside of Veronese Public Ritual
(1930–1935)

During the 1930s, Veronese ritual events increased and a pattern developed that emphasized political commitment and the formation of a replacement generation of young fascists. Achille Starace, secretary of the National Fascist Party, visited Verona on June 18, 1933. He engaged in commemorative and celebratory activities that linked the old and new generations of Veronese fascists. Starace laid commemorative stones, inaugurated the Sacri-

---

[107] Ibid., 26–27.
[108] "Il solenne Te Deum di domani in Duomo," *L'Arena*, 16 February 1929, 2.
[109] "Documentario manifestazioni," 27–28, ACS, PNF, MRF, b. 12 (Verona).
[110] "Questa mattina in Piazza Dante, Gino Cacciari parlera ai veronesi illustrando il significato del plebiscito," *L'Arena*, 19 March 1929, 1.

sty of Fascist Martyrs, reviewed a parade of Young Fascists, and met with the mayor and leaders of Veronese fascist youth organizations. A "magnificent gathering [*superba adunata*] of fascists and people" heard his speech in the Arena. Starace's inspection of the local "Home Economics Exhibit" emphasized fascist commitment to family, and his inauguration of a local leisure (*dopolavoro*) organization gave ceremonial recognition to fascist labor policy.[111]

Starace's visit encapsulated themes that dominated fascist ritual action during the consensus period. In 1930, the Vittoria was celebrated with a "powerful parade" that included "3,500 young fascists."[112] In 1933, veterans attending the annual meeting of Veronese war wounded laid the cornerstone of the local Club of the Wounded (Casa dei Mutilati).[113] In 1934, the headlines of *L'Arena* focused on youth as it marked the anniversary of Italy's entrance into the First World War: "Fascist Verona celebrated the anniversary of the Intervention: the redeemed Patria, exalting the youthful forces of the Regime."[114] Youth parading in public space suggested a new fascist generation and underscored the importance of the fascist past that the veterans represented to the fascist future.

When the Casa dei Mutilati was opened in 1934, the inaugural ceremonies included a rally in the Arena that arrayed the principal figures in the new fascist polity in order of cultural and social significance. The diagram that *L'Arena* printed displayed the following spatial arrangement in the amphitheater: wounded of Verona and the Veneto, armed forces, syndical organizations and women's fascist groups, young fascists and fascists of Verona, the public, soldiers, and the "wounded pilgrims" of Lombardy (veterans who were transported across northern Italy for the event). The circular center of the amphitheater was divided along the diameter. Members of the Balilla filled half the circle, and the flags of the wounded filled the other. The militia remained on the circumference.[115] The wounded, the women and syndical organizations, the youth, and the pilgrims were allotted the largest space on the steps of the Arena. The children filled the center of the Arena, suggesting where the symbolic core and future of fascism lay.

L'Arena announced Starace's 1933 visit with the headline "A Grand Day for Veronese Fascism: The Ardent Passion of Verona for the Duce Expresses

---

[111] "Documentario manifestazioni," 50, *ACS, PNF, MRF*, b. 12 (Verona); "Regia Questura di Verona, 16 giugno 1933," *ASV, GP* 1929–40 Verona (1933.480), describes Starace's visit in detail.

[112] "La grandiosa celebrazione dell'annuale della Vittoria," *L'Arena*, 5 November 1930, 2.

[113] "Regia Questura di Verona, 23 giugno 1933," *ASV, GP* 1929–40 Verona (1933.480).

[114] "Verona fascista ha celebrato nell'anniversario dell'Intervento," *L'Arena*, 25 May 1934, 1.

[115] "L'inaugurazione della Casa del Mutilato Verona alla presenza di S. E. Lojacono e dell'on. Delcroix," *L'Arena*, 9 September 1934, 2.

Itself in Its Triumphal Welcome to Starace."[116] *L'Arena's* narrative of Starace's visit indicated that the emotionally charged language of fascist journalism, which spoke of the "single palpation of love" that united the "beating hearts" of Verona's citizens, was not restricted to Mussolini. When Starace entered the Arena to give his speech, the assembled crowd shouted, "Duce, Duce, Duce!" *L'Arena* described "delirious enthusiasm" as "thousands and thousands of red and yellow handkerchiefs displaying the colors of Rome waved" in greeting at Starace. The newspaper account interpreted this "enthusiasm" as a sign of the strength of Veronese fascism and reported:

> But the crowd, not yet satisfied to acclaim and to manifest its joy, the joy of a reconquered and resolidified unity of Veronese Fascism that wants to be and will be always more worthy of past glories and the love of the DUCE, offers to the leader [Starace] and to itself the measure of its enthusiasm, completing an expression of its vibrant faith of recognition and devotion to the Regime.[117]

An underside of Veronese political culture existed that official public discourse failed to capture. The daily morning reports that the chief of police filed in 1933, the year of Starace's visit, suggest that *L'Arena's* glowing accounts overestimate the level of fascist enthusiasm. In addition to the usual array of petty crime, car accidents, and arrests for public drunkenness, the morning police reports portrayed fissures in the smooth surface of fascist commitment.

Catholic public culture was thriving even in the face of fascist hostility and surveillance.[118] The School of Catholic Culture, a name probably chosen to mimic and co-opt the Institute of Fascist Culture, regularly gave symposia that the police recorded as having an attendance of up to three hundred and fifty persons.[119] Themes varied, but they emphasized Catholicism and not fascism. During 1933, Veronese Catholics heard lectures entitled "The City of Christ's Body—Orvieto," "The Vatican," "The Seventy-Fifth Anniversary of the Apparition of Lourdes," "The Tragic and Comic Theater of Vittorio Alfieri," and "The Position of the Cultivated Classes on the Religious Problem." In addition to lectures, Catholic Verona also hosted public events such as pilgrimages to religious shrines and special masses at which the bishop officiated.

The tenth anniversary celebration of the Catholic Men's Movement and

---

[116] "Una grande giornata del fascismo veronese," *L'Arena del Lunedi*, 19 June 1933, 1.

[117] Ibid., 2.

[118] Tramontin, *Cattolici, popolari e fascisti*, 148–59, 257–303.

[119] "Regia Questura di Verona, relazione mattinale 1933," *ASV, GP* 1929–40 Verona (1933.480). The police were responsible for maintaining public order. Their morning report described crowd activity that occurred in Verona during the previous twenty-four hours.

the Convention of Catholic University Students from the Veneto and Emilia were particular affronts to fascist fraternal organizations. Three hundred men participated in the latter event, which included a mass and a special dinner.[120] The Catholic university students met from April 18 to 20, three days before the fascist holiday of the Birth of Rome on April 21. Three hundred students attended this event, where they heard lectures on the anti-Catholicism of Russian bolshevism and made a pilgrimage to the shrine of the Madonna of San Virigilia on Lake Garda.[121] On February 27, the festival of Carnival, the secular and traditional feast on the last day of permitted excess before Ash Wednesday and the fasting of Lent, was celebrated in the Arena.[122] In contrast to fascist spectacles, the Carnival festival attracted only two thousand participants.[123] The diminished number of participants does not suggest lack of enthusiasm; rather, it highlights the documented fact that the fascists generated their large crowds by transporting participants to events from all over the region to give the appearance of enthusiastic mass support.

The failure to eradicate the Catholic public sphere was only one problem that confronted Veronese fascism. Dissent continually lurked behind the facade of fascist public events. Under orders from Rome, the police chief in Verona directed surveillance of suspected dissenters. Some police activities, such as the "sequestering" of dangerous publications, appear, in retrospect, fairly trivial. Among the dangerous books and magazines that were removed from public access were a Paris fashion review, because it displayed "women who were excessively thin and masculine acting as propaganda against the physical health of the race"; three editions of the *Tribune*, a newspaper that had excessive crime reporting (*cronaca nera*); six copies of another Parisian review because of "licentious photographs"; *Parisian Life*, another French magazine; and 112 copies of a French novel. Press censorship occupied itself with literary crimes against public morals, and Paris was the principal source of immorality.

The Veronese police department, with the help of national agents of public security, engaged in more traditional forms of public surveillance. In 1931, OVRA, the fascist secret police, began operations in Verona, and in

[120] "Regia Questura di Verona, relazione mattinale del giorno 9 gennaio 1933 = ANNO XI E.F.," *ASV, GP* 1929–40 Verona (1933.480).
[121] "Regia Questura di Verona, relazione mattinale del giorno 18, 19, 20 aprile 1933 = ANNO XI E.F.," *ASV, GP* 1929–40 Verona (1933.480).
[122] Carnival was a medieval holiday that has continued into modern times. By the early twentieth century, the culture of ribald excess was somewhat contained. On the Carnival tradition, see Peter Burke, *Popular Culture in Early Modern Europe* (New York: New York University Press, 1978), 178–204.
[123] "Regia Questura di Verona, relazione mattinale del giorno 27 febbraio 1933 = ANNO XI E.F.," *ASV, GP* 1929–40 Verona (1933.480).

1932, when a communist cell was discovered in the suburbs, persons were tried and sent to prison.[124] The local police uncovered motley groups of subversives in 1933. A French writer, Suzanne de Callias, was put under surveillance for journeying to Italy to make contact with "her anti-fascist friends residing in Italy."[125] Nine foreigners were placed under surveillance; a sixty-four-year-old man was arrested for having publicly "pronounced offensive phrases at the office of the Fascist Syndicates and the Head of the Government"; and eighteen men and women who participated in a communist cell on the periphery of the city were arrested.[126]

The problems of subversion and unemployment were linked. Italy suffered from the worldwide depression, and Verona was no exception to the general trend. The police reports regularly noted that packets of food, state alms, were distributed to about three hundred fifty persons every week. In a special memo to the prefect, the police chief warned that the approaching winter season would aggravate unemployment and that special precautions were needed to maintain public order. Workers were a particular target of police suspicion. On an especially harsh note, the police chief announced that he would prohibit unemployed workers from collectively requesting public services, such as the distribution of food or temporary employment, because any group of workers might turn from starved laborers to dangerous agitators in a matter of minutes.[127] The fear of workers as agents of collective violence suggests that the corporativist doctrine of class collaboration was at variance with local and national economic and political realities.

Communists were more dangerous to social stability than workers. In 1933, there were international communist demonstrations against war. During this period, Verona began special precautions that remained in effect for the duration of the regime. In an eight-page memorandum to the prefect, local military divisions, and agents of public security, the police chief outlined Verona's plans to monitor and prevent communist activity.[128] In addition to increasing surveillance against foreigners—hotels were under particular scrutiny and warned not to register anyone without appropriate identification—all public buildings, military barracks, fascist organizations, and roads were placed under observation. Subversive flyers, graffiti, and

---

[124] Zangarini, *Politica e società a Verona*, 172–81, 184–201.
[125] "Regia Questura di Verona, relazione mattinale del giorno 31 marzo 1933 = ANNO XI E.F.," *ASV*, *GP* 1929–40 Verona (1933.480).
[126] "Regia Questura di Verona, relazione mattinale del giorno 13, 20, 21 giugno 1933 = ANNO XI E.F.," *ASV*, *GP* 1929–40 Verona (1933.480).
[127] "Regia Questura di Verona, A.S.E. Il Prefetto della Provincia = Verona, 22 settembre 1933 = ANNO XI E.F.," *ASV*, *GP* 1929–40 Verona (1933.480).
[128] "Regia Questura di Verona, manifestinazioni internazionali comuniste pel 1 agosto contro la guerra, Verona, 26 luglio 1933 = ANNO XI E.F.," *ASV*, *GP* 1929–40 Verona (1933.480).

symbols were suppressed. On All Souls' Day, the police chief forbade mourners to leave red flowers on the gravestones, since red flowers might be interpreted as a form of communist propaganda.[129] Workers were monitored as they left factories, and the suburbs of Verona, which had housed subversive groups in the past, were declared a danger zone. Even theatrical performances in the Arena came under scrutiny.[130]

Fascist public events were particularly susceptible to subversive activity. During the 1933 celebration of the Birth of Rome, the fascist labor day, the police chief ordered special security forces to watch "workers and peasants, splinter groups from the communist party." The police chief feared public demonstrations against "unemployment and against Fascism or to demand subsidy of the unemployed and salary increases." In addition to guarding the "locales of ceremonies and parades," the police were ordered to give "special vigilance" to areas "under stairs and railroad lines, all public works in general, depositories of benzine and other flammable materials, central electric lines, post and telegraph offices, public offices and all localities and headquarters which due to their importance might be under attack by subversive anarchists."[131]

Police surveillance of ritual events expanded throughout the remainder of the year. When Verona commemorated the anniversary of Italian entry into World War I on May 24, a police order was promulgated that placed all foreigners—particularly Slavs, persons from the Balkans, Russians, and Spaniards—under special watch.[132] By the October commemoration of the March on Rome, the "suburbs" of Verona, where "workers and unemployed" were clustered together, were marked as especially dangerous.[133] By the end of 1933, security memos had lengthened and surveillance had become the routine underside of fascist public spectacle.

War Talk: Geography as Ritual Fate (1935–1940)

From the mid-1930s onward, the fascist regime expanded its catalog of enemies. Fear, fueled by an intensification of the feeling of "us versus them," helped generate fascist commitment in the hearts of Verona's citi-

[129] "Regia Questura di Verona, Commemorazione dei Defunti 30 ottobre 1933 = ANNO XI E.F.," ASV, GP 1929–40 Verona (1933.480).
[130] "Regia Questura di Verona, relazione mattinale del giorno 26 luglio 1933 = ANNO XI E.F.," ASV, GP 1929–40 Verona (1933.480).
[131] "Regia Questura di Verona, XXI aprile = Natale di Roma e servizi di vigilanza e di prevenzione, 18 aprile 1933 = ANNO XI E.F.," ASV, GP 1929–40 Verona (1933.480).
[132] "Regia Questura di Verona, 24 maggio—Anniversario dell'entrata in guerra, 22 maggio 1933 = ANNO XI E.F.," ASV, GP 1929–40 Verona (1933.480).
[133] "Regia Questura di Verona, anniversario della Marcia su Roma 23 ottobre 1933 = ANNO XI E.F.," ASV, GP 1929–40 Verona (1933.480).

zens where ceremony alone could not. But Veronese fear was grounded in
more than symbolism. Verona's geographical location in the northern corner of Italy made it vulnerable to enemy attack should a war ensue; for the
same reason, the city was also the scene of ritual visits by German soldiers
and youth groups.[134]

War and the possibility of war dominated fascist public discourse and encouraged youth to think of themselves as future soldiers. A pamphlet of
incantations that the Veronese Fascist Party distributed to youth to recite at
the 1939 celebration of the Birth of Rome displayed a singularly militaristic
cast. The booklet began with a series of predictable questions, such as "Who
is the Duce?" and "Where and when was the Duce born?" The third question begins the series of justifications for war that dominates the chants.

3. Why did the DUCE become a proponent of World War I [*Interventista*]?

—The DUCE wanted to bring the Italian people into the European war
with the idea of unifying the Patria, of bringing Italy to a rebirth, and to
give a new, virile conscience to the Nation.

The sixth question was a justification of the militaristic aspects of fascism.

6. What was the purpose of the Fighting Fascists?

—The Fighting Fascists proposed to struggle for the vindication of the
Vittoria and against the internal disorder that destroyed the Patria; they
wanted to display the goodness of the Italian people in a regime of social
justice.[135]

The booklet articulated the motto of all young fascists, "Believe, Obey,
Fight" and interpreted it to mean the willingness to give one's blood in the
name of the fascist revolution. The Labor Charter was identified as the "fundamental document of the Fascist Revolution," and the April 21 celebration
was reframed in terms of the conquest of empire:

25. Why do we celebrate April 21?

—April 21 celebrates the Birth of Rome and the feast of Labor. On the

---

[134] Typical of such events was the celebration staged to honor the visit of a nazi youth
group on October 7, 1940; "Documentario manifestazioni," 110, ACS, PNF, MRF, b. 12
(Verona).

[135] Partito Nazionale Fascista—Commando Federale di Verona, *Elementi di cultura politico militare* (Rome: Partito Nazionale Fascista, 1939), 3, 4, 5.

same day we celebrate ancient Roman potency that is reborn in imperial fascism and the grand construction of labor as a social duty.

26. When was the Empire founded?

—The Empire was founded against the opposition of the armies of Ethiopia and the odious Economic Sanctions of 52 States, with the Italian-Ethiopian war that lasted from October 2, 1935, to May 9, 1936–XIV.[136]

War talk was not the only discursive practice that was accelerating in the mid to late 1930s. During this period, ritual events in Verona increased sharply. Ritual actions in the post–1935 period were more militaristic in content than earlier actions, and there was a closer fit between national and local political rites. In the late 1930s, ritual events in Verona had become an integral part of the national drama of mobilization. The period between September 8, 1935, when Mussolini decided to invade Ethiopia, and September 26, 1938, when he visited Verona, was the most intense time of mobilization, as evidenced by the increase in the absolute number of ritual events (Figure 8).

Between 1935 and 1937, the regime staged four national rallies of the Italian people (*adunate nazionali*) in Rome to garner emotional support for its colonial and international aggression. Each occasion was celebrated with demonstrations, a speech by Mussolini, and clamorous local events. In Verona, public ritual marked each one of the *adunate*. During 1935, public events fanned the flames of war and encouraged a generally combative spirit. The annual commemoration of the March on Rome was marked with a military review consisting of youth and soldiers. In November, the duke of Aosta visited to congratulate Veronese fascists on the performance of their soldiers in the African campaign. In December, Veronese citizens demonstrated against the League of Nations' economic sanctions.[137]

In December 1935, the sacrifice of Italian women became the focus of national and local mobilization with the wedding ring campaign. Veronese women gave "50,000 wedding rings to the Patria," and the prefect lauded them with "vibrant words." Not to be outdone, a local war hero contributed his gold medal to the new war effort. The symbolic union between mothers and soldiers, present from the beginning of the regime, began to solidify during this period on both the national and local levels. Fascism imposed itself on Christmas in Verona with a special tribute on December 22 to Veronese fascist women who comported themselves properly in face of the sanctions imposed by the League of Nations, and on December 26, the

[136] Ibid., 8, 9, 10.
[137] Ibid., 69–70.

bishop offered a mass in the cathedral for Italian armies, who were engaged in a "glorious struggle to affirm the high ideals of civilization" in Ethiopia.[138]

On May 5, 1936, one hundred thousand Veronese citizens listened to a radio broadcast of Mussolini's declaration of victory in Ethiopia. The crowd then marched from the periphery of Verona into the historic center, where the prefect and the federal secretary spoke and a mass in the cathedral followed. Verona marked Mussolini's decision to exit the League of Nations on December 11, 1937, with a rally of Black Shirts who cheered the fateful move.[139]

The *grande adunate* of the mid-1930s marked the ritual height of the mobilization period. Mussolini's speech in the Piazza Bra during his September 1938 visit to Verona summarized the future of Italy as an aggressor nation and established the regime's international agenda. The commitment to the Axis that the speech reflected set the course of fascist foreign policy for the remainder of the 1930s and culminated in the disastrous decision to enter World War II. Speaking of his diplomatic triumph in Munich, Mussolini expressed his willingness to wage war to preserve what he described as the "new Europe."

Mussolini had a seductive rhetorical style which led the crowd to feel that war was morally necessary and that victory was possible. He began by addressing the issue of fascist commitment in Verona:

Black Shirts of Verona, my Verona, of this roman Verona, militaristic, fascist in spirit until the end of the vigil.

Invoking the memory of the battlefields of World War I, he placed his trip within the larger context of recent Italian history and imbued it with religious significance.

This magisterial rally of people, accompanied by a superb marshaling of force, closes my voyage among the people of the Veneto and my pilgrimage on the sacred fields of our glorious battles. (*The enormous crowd shouts with a single voice: "Return! Return!"*)

He then invokes the images of the fascist enemies using their national flags.

Our adversaries, . . . gathered under the signs of the triangle and of the hammer and the sickle (*the multitude hisses for a long time*), have in these past days given voice to their most pious hopes. (*Shout of the crowd*).

[138] Ibid.
[139] Ibid., 74, 87.

The crowds Mussolini addressed in his "sacred" voyage throughout the Veneto had recognized his role as the savior of Italy and Europe and had given their emotional commitment to him.

> These crowds that have responded in a single way to my questions demonstrate to all, I say to all, that there has never been as there is now such total, intimate, profound communion between fascism and the Italian people. (*The multitude shouts: "Yes! Yes!" and acclaims the Duce for a long time.*)

The Italian people are prepared to fight to display their commitment.

> And this Italian people is not disorganized and without spirit as many other peoples; it is powerfully organized, spiritually armed, and ready to be materially armed. (*The people again respond with a single shout: "Yes! Yes!"*)

Mussolini proceeded to discuss the international situation, which he described as subject to the "irresistible forces of history," and to explain his diplomatic maneuvers in Munich. He argued that there was still hope for a peaceful solution to the problem of national determination in the Balkans and that Europe did not need another war over the issue of borders. In a prescient statement, he argued that he expected events to move quickly, and concluded:

> Comrades!
> It is useless for diplomats to tire themselves out to save Versailles. The Europe that was constructed at Versailles, often with a monumental ignorance of geography and history, this Versailles is in its death throes. Its end will be decided this week.
> And in this week the new Europe can arise: a Europe of justice for all and of reconciliation among peoples. (*Strong acclamations*)
> Black Shirts!
> We of the Littorio are for this new Europe.[140]

The mobilization for war that dominated the 1930s somewhat belies the call for peace at the end of Mussolini's speech. Nevertheless, the speech captures the ambivalence of his position on the war, which has often been overlooked. If another European war were to be waged, Mussolini suggested, this time Italy would be prepared and not suffer the diplomatic shame of Versailles. Underlying that psychological determination was the firm belief that the united Italy was engaged in a religious mission under the leadership of a secular savior, or Christ figure, Mussolini.

---

[140] Benito Mussolini, "Discorso di Verona," in *Dal viaggio in Germania all'intervento dell'Italia nella seconda guerra mondiale.*, vol. 29, *OO*, 162–64.

Ritual as "Ordinary Life"

The story of fascist Verona amplifies the view of the fascist project seen through the lens of the March on Rome and suggests the extent to which fascism impinged on the texture of ordinary Italian life in the 1920s and 1930s. The March demonstrated how evolving ritual genres contributed to the developing fascist cultural project and documented the regime logic that underlay ritual actions. There was much in Veronese ritual that paralleled ritual life in the Roman center. The same enemies, heroes, events, and masses of fascist bodies established the boundaries of Veronese ritual. But the analysis of aggregate local ritual action juxtaposed against narratives of discrete time periods, such as the Catholic resistance in the 1930s, provides an alternative angle of vision that allows further nuancing of the process of fascist identity creation.

In Verona, the colonization of time itself was a measure of fascist imposition. The extent to which the Veronese Fascist Party managed to usurp hours, days, and months suggests the efficacy of fascist cultural and political practice. Colonization is a felicitous metaphor for the process of state identity creation, and recent students of the colonial process have identified spatial arrangements such as those found in public housing design or water supplies as potent vehicles of ideological communication.[141] Time, as encapsulated in the internalized rhythms of daily life, is as potent a vehicle of meaning as space, and the appropriation of the temporal patterns of daily life is a powerful political tool.[142] Repertoires of ritual actions, repeated symbolic and expressive action in public space, re-created or disrupted the texture of ordinary life in Verona. What political meaning Veronese ritual conveyed lay in the repeated social experience of recognizable ritual genres and not in the unique experience of single extraordinary ritual actions.

The repeated experience of ritual genres created patterns of familiarity that endowed public political ritual with meaning and communicative power.[143] The identification of genre patterns of ritual action over time in a specific political context, Verona during the fascist period, established what

---

[141] See for example, the discussion of landscape in Jean Comaroff and John Comaroff, *Of Revelation and Revolution* (Chicago: University of Chicago Press, 1991), 200–206; and Timothy Mitchell's description of colonial Egyptian model housing in *Colonising Egypt* (Berkeley: University of California Press, 1991), 44–48.

[142] Eviatar Zerubavel, *The Seven-Day Circle: The History and Meaning of the Week* (New York: Free Press, 1985), a comparative study of calendars and other temporal framing devices, addresses the meaning of temporal patterns and the sense of social habituation they create.

[143] See Mabel Berezin, "Cultural Form and Political Meaning: State-Subsidized Theater, Ideology, and the Language of Style in Fascist Italy," *American Journal of Sociology* 99 (March 1994), 1237–86.

was ordinary, customary, and recognizable in fascist political ritual. The mapping of the familiar had the added advantage of leading to a plausible story of political meaning that does not assume that representations of power equal realities of power.

The clearly observable genre patterns, as well as patterns of size of events and local/national interaction, suggest that ritual can serve as a vehicle of political learning or socialization. Further, the variation in these patterns in apparent response to national and international political occurrences indicates a political logic to ritual action. For example, the inverse relation between commemoration and celebration suggests that as the regime was crumbling, the emphasis on the future and the present was accelerated. This trend mirrors the evolving orchestration of the anniversary of the March on Rome. Similarly, the inverse relation between purely local events and those with national leaders present reveals that the regime most firmly imposed itself on local events, when it was in jeopardy at home and abroad.

Fascist ritual, which served as a vehicle of the regime's identity project, was a set of cultural actions that adapted to advance ideological ends. In and of themselves, the March on Rome and ritual life in Verona do not tell us how the fascist project imprinted itself on the minds of Italians, fascist or otherwise. This requires a rank-and-file fascist "voice," and it is to this voice that we now turn.

CHAPTER 6

Dead Bodies and Live Voices:
Locating the Fascist Self

Narrative Identity and Felt Identity

In 1944, when the Allied armies landed in Italy and the Axis powers were sliding toward defeat, a U.S. Army lieutenant entered the house of Giuseppe Bottai in Rome to requisition it as living quarters for American officers. Bottai, who has figured in other parts of this narrative, was a fascist of the "first hour," a leading architect of regime cultural policy and a man who had held several high-ranking posts in the regime such as minister of corporations and minister of education. Bottai had voted against Mussolini in the Grand Council meeting of 1943 which led to the king's request that Mussolini resign and to the dissolution of the Fascist Party. With Il Duce firmly ensconced in Salo under Nazi protection and the outcome of the war uncertain, Bottai had fled to North Africa to escape fascist wrath.[1]

When the American lieutenant entered Bottai's apartment, the Signora Bottai greeted him. Somewhat surprised at the civility and cultivation he encountered, he announced himself as part of the Allied forces and apologized for the confiscation of the property. The signora said, "But Lieutenant, you know, we *were* fascists." To which the lieutenant replied, "Thank you, Madame. I have been in Italy for six months and you are the first fascist I have met!"[2]

The American lieutenant drafted to fight the fascist enemy must have been surprised to have found a compliant Italian populace. Twenty-two years of social and cultural policies aimed at creating new fascist men and

---

[1] Bottai's fear was well founded. Mussolini's son-in-law Galeazzo Ciano had also voted against him, and Mussolini ordered his execution at the first available opportunity.

[2] Personal communication, Magali Sarfatti Larson.

women produced fascist identities that were fragile and crumbled readily before the invading Allied forces. If there were committed fascists in Italy in 1944, they were not advertising their identities.

Any Italian citizen born between 1910 and 1935, who would have attended school during the fascist era, experienced at least one fascist institution first hand, yet even today in Italy one is hard pressed to find an eighty-year-old or sixty-year-old who admits to having espoused a fascist identity. Even Gianfranco Fini, the leader of the new National Alliance, identifies himself and his party as "post-fascist." Is this forgetfulness simply an example of an Italian tendency to ideological expediency or does it suggest a failure of the fascist cultural project? As in all questions of ideology, identity, and culture, the answer lies between the cynicism of expediency and the utilitarianism of political failure.

Identity formation is difficult to reconstruct historically, and it is particularly difficult to reconstruct when the identity in question has become, until the 1994 elections, the object of moral sanctions. Memory is always selective, especially when morally questionable attachments are involved.[3] Narratives of fascist identity formation are fascist in origin, so they too are not useful, in and of themselves, as a measure of fascist attachment.

The fascist regime's penchant for self-commemoration left behind a dusty collection of testimonials that provide a window on what fascism meant to its most committed adherents. Spurred by the success of the 1932 Mostra della Rivoluzione Fascista, the regime decided on a repeat performance to celebrate its twentieth anniversary.[4] The organizers of the new Mostra asked the federal secretaries of the Fascist Party to contribute obituary biographies, pictures, and general memorabilia, including personal letters, of fascist "heroes" for the exhibit room that would honor the fascist war dead.[5]

---

[3] On research in the field of oral history pertaining to Italian fascism, see Alfredo Martini, "Oral History and Fascism," in *Memory and Totalitarianism*, ed. Luisa Passerini (New York: Oxford University Press, 1992), 17–183. Narrative as a social analytic form has begun to capture the imagination of social scientists. For a summary of this literature, see Margaret R. Somers and Gloria D. Gibson, "Reclaiming the Epistemological 'Other': Narrative and the Social Constitution of Identity," in *Social Theory and the Politics of Identity*, ed. Craig Calhoun (Cambridge, Mass.: Blackwell, 1994), 37–99. For a discussion of the role of narrative and politics that is germane to the issues explored here, see Janet Hart, "Cracking the Code: Narrative and Political Mobilization in the Greek Resistance," *Social Science History* 16 (Winter 1992), 631–68.

[4] See Roberta Suzzi Valli, "Riti del Ventennale," *Storia Contemporanea* 24 (1993), 1019–55.

[5] These materials are available at the Archivio Centrale dello Stato Rome in the Partito Nazionale Fascista, Mostra della Rivoluzione Fascista [PNF, MRF], I Carteggi Amministrativi, bustas 1–12. The archive also contains photographs of fascist public works in all provinces and clippings from the local party presses. See Ministero per i beni culturali e ambientali, *Partito nazionale fascista: Mostra della Rivoluzione Fascista* (Rome: Archivio Centrale dello Stato, 1990), 43–48, 59–60, 77–91.

The letters of the fascist heroes, written from the battlefields and sent to wives, mothers, and friends, are voices from the grave that are the best available articulations of an authentic and spontaneous fascist consciousness. The letters reveal a private understanding of the fascist self that permit us to explore the multifaceted manner in which individuals internalized fascist identity.[6] In contrast to the letters, the obituary biographies are public representations of the fascist self. When the local secretary possessed even rudimentary literary skills, the biographies read as dramatic moral narratives of ideal fascist lives.

This chapter juxtaposes private understandings of the fascist self, what fascism meant to those who were arguably the most committed to it, against public representations. Unlike Giuseppe Bottai, Margherita Sarfatti, and many of the other regime intellectuals and architects of fascist policy who had the luxury of rationalizing their involvement with the regime after the war, the "fascist heroes" were for the most part rank-and-file fascists.[7] They were schoolteachers, surveyors, shopkeepers, peasants; the more elite among them were university graduates, and there was an occasional local *literato*, but in general, they represented a fascist constituency, not leadership, and provide insight into fascism as felt experience.[8] The letters, which expressed hope for the future of fascist Italy, have an added poignancy because many

[6] Letters as a source of historical evidence must be used with some caution. Although I know of no work on surveillance of Italian war letters, evidence exists from France during the First World War. Ioannis Sinanoglou, "The Third Republic at War on the Home Front: Postal Surveillance as Social Diagnosis, 1914–18" (unpublished manuscript, 1993), describes how the French censored soldiers' letters for discouraging content. In a different context, Reid Mitchell uses soldiers' letters written during the American Civil War to explore the relation of gender, war and memory (*The Vacant Chair: The Northern Soldier Leaves Home* [New York: Oxford University Press, 1993]).

[7] Giuseppe Bottai was not permitted to return to Italy from Africa until 1949. During this period, he wrote his reflections on his involvement with the regime, *Vent'anni e un giorno*. Margherita Sarfatti wrote her autobiography, *L'acqua passata* (Water under the bridge), while she was in exile in Argentina, where she had fled with her family to escape the racial laws. Its title summed up her feelings about Mussolini and his regime. For a discussion of Sarfatti's forgetfulness, see Philip Cannistraro and Brian Sullivan, *Il Duce's Other Woman* (New York: Morrow, 1993), 558.

[8] The Florentine party head included the fascist leaders Italo Balbo and Nello Quilici in its obituaries, but these were exceptions. Including Balbo in this catalog is somewhat ironic as he met his death when his airplane was accidentally shot down by Italians over Africa. The story of the attraction that Italian fascism held for the lower middle classes has yet to be written. For a general overview, see Mabel Berezin, "Created Constituencies: Fascism and the Italian Middle Classes," in *Splintered Classes: Politics and the Lower Middle Classes in Interwar Europe*, ed. Rudy Koshar (New York: Holmes and Meier, 1990); for the beginnings of a history, see Jonathan Morris, *The Political Economy of Shopkeeping in Milan, 1886–1922*, (New York: Cambridge University Press, 1993), and Mariuccia Salvati, *Il regime e gli impiegati: La nazionalizzazione piccolo-borghese nel ventennio fascista* (Rome: Laterza, 1992).

of the writers died on the Greek-Albanian front, where Italy suffered its most crushing defeats.[9]

The juxtaposition of letters and obituaries reveals the intertwining of fascist rhetorics, popular cultural frames, and preexisting cultural schemata. Read against each other, they suggest a fascist reality that melded with the representation of that reality. The ensuing exegesis of the letters and obituaries completes an expository circle by returning to the issues of identity, state, and culture introduced in Chapters 1 and 2. When we speak of identity, we are speaking of individual or collective conceptions of the self that influence social actions—of both the public and private sort. Persons experience multiple identities as hierarchies, that is, some identities are felt as more important than others. The fascist cultural project aimed to create "new" Italian citizens who would experience fascism as a noncontingent identity.

New identities, even new political identities, rely on the repertoire of contingent and noncontingent identities available for transposition and rewriting. The preceding chapters focused upon the ritual dramatization of the fascist identity project. Underlying these dramatizations were public narratives of collective identity—Mussolini's speeches, the *Labor Charter*, newspaper accounts of ritual events. Additional public narratives of the fascist self found in obituaries, party handbooks, and popular culture existed beside the national identity narratives examined thus far. The obituaries and the self-representations of the "heroes" narrated and personalized themes that the fascist public rituals dramatized. The distinction between these public narratives of fascist selfhood and felt identity—between public representation and private emotional attachment—shapes the text that follows. Fascism, as regime and ideology, aspired to fuse the Italian public and private self in the new fascist nation-state; the question remains to what extent it succeeded. In an attempt to answer that question, I begin by discussing the status of death in Italian popular culture, the end of the self, and move on to the obituaries and letters.

The Cult of Commemoration

The end of the First World War initiated a virtual cult of commemoration in Europe and America.[10] Nation-states established veterans' days as legal

[9] On the frequently neglected Italian fighting in the Balkans, see James J. Sadkovich, "The Italo-Greek War in Context: Italian Priorities and Axis Diplomacy," *Journal of Contemporary History* 28 (1993), 439–64.

[10] There is a large and growing literature on the iconography of the First World War and its diffusion to popular culture. See, for example, Modris Eksteins, *Rites of Spring* (Boston:

holidays and built tombs for unknown soldiers, war memorials, and military cemeteries.[11] A panoply of veterans' organizations arose to support this commemorative activity and to provide bodies for the ritual events that public commemoration required.[12] Italy did not escape this general trend, although commemorative ceremonies organized around fascist heroes decreased as the regime started to move again toward war.

The dead soldier's body became the principal icon that carried the meaning of the war to the individual country. Tombs and war cemeteries were the tangible remains of the cult of commemoration. Italy along with other European countries contributed to the post–World War I boom in cemeteries.[13] Cemeteries were part of the fascist infrastructure along with trains, hospitals, and dams. The province of Verona, the matrix of small towns that surrounded the city of Verona, reported "forty ceremonies to inaugurate Monuments to the Fallen" in 1926.[14] The report on public works in the province of Modena that the Fascist Party federal secretary filed in preparation for the 1942 version of the Mostra suggests the extent to which the cemetery boom was a feature of national honor:

> In the very first years of the Regime worthy and even valuable Monuments to the Fallen from 1915–1918 World War were erected in the centers of all the provinces.
>
> In the Provincial Center, . . . a Memorial Temple dedicated to the Fallen of all wars, a majestic and imposing work, and a Painting of the Heroes in

---

Houghton Mifflin, 1989); Paul Fussell, *The Great War and Modern Memory* (New York: Oxford University Press, 1975); and Eric J. Leed, *No Man's Land: Combat and Identity in World War I* (Cambridge: Cambridge University Press, 1979). For the Italian case, see Mario Isnenghi, *Il mito della grand guerra* (Bologna: Il Mulino, 1989).

[11] On the modernity of the idea of the unknown soldier, see Benedict Anderson, *Imagined Communities: Reflections on the Origin and Spread of Nationalism*, rev. ed. (London: Verso, 1991), 9–10; on the commemoration of the dead, see George L. Mosse, *Fallen Soldiers: Reshaping the Memory of the World Wars* (New York: Oxford University Press, 1990), 70–106, and K. S. Inglis, "The Homecoming: The War Memorial Movement in Cambridge, England," *Journal of Contemporary History* 27 (1992), 583–605.

[12] The literature on veterans' organizations is sparse. Antoine Prost, *In the Wake of War*, trans. Helen McPhail (Oxford: Berg, 1992),examines French World War I veterans' war experience and postwar political proclivities. For Italy, Giovanni Sabbatucci, *La stampa del combattentismo (1918–1925)* (Bologna: Cappelli, 1980),studies the veterans' press and its opinions on events that led to the rise of fascism.

[13] On the war memorial movement in Italy, see Patrizia Dogliani, "Les monuments aux morts de la grande guerre en Italie," *Guerres Mondiales et Conflits Contemporains* 167 (July 1992), 87–94. On the significance of visiting the cemetery in Italian culture, see Jack Goody and Cesare Poppi, "Flowers and Bones: Approaches to the Dead in Anglo-American and Italian Cemeteries," *Comparative Studies in History and Society* 36 (1994), 146–75.

[14] See Associazione Nazionale Combattenti, *Relazione sul lavoro compiuto dalla Federazione Provinciale di Verona nell'anno 1926* (Villafranca di Verona: Massagrande, 1926), 33.

the Cemetery of Saint Cataldo, with marble statues consecrated to the bodies of the Fallen in the War and the [Fascist] Revolution.

In Modena, the Cemetery was enlarged, modernized, and refurbished and in the province eleven new cemeteries were completely constructed and numerous others were enlarged.[15]

The well-ordered rows of headstones in the Modena cemetery stand in sharp contrast to the chaos that brought the bodies to the cemetery (see Figure 16). The cemeteries, tombs, and monuments would have been ideologically useless if no one visited them, so local fascist parties added pilgrimages to former battlefields to their repertoire of ritual practices. The pilgrimages sought to build solidarity and fraternity among party members, a purpose made explicit in a 1933 provincial report:

> Associative spirit is maintained among our session with the organization of pilgrimages to former war locations.

Figure 16. Modena cemetery. *ACS, PNF, MRF,* b. 5 (Modena).

---

[15] Relazione sulle opere pubbliche realizzate nel ventennio di Regime Fascista nella provincia di Modena, *ACS, PNF, MRF,* b. 5 (Modena).

Almost all our sessions this year were taken to Carso or Pasubio or Grappa [battlefields] to relive again the passion of war to strengthen in our soul the memory of our Fallen brothers.

The cult of our Dead is very much alive in our sessions and among our members: the maintenance of Monuments to the Fallen and of Parks of Remembrance even in minor centers is the object of vigilant attention and fraternal spirit.[16]

Popular culture from cinema to religious postcards idealized the dead soldier and his noble sacrifices.[17] The fascist militia published anthologies commemorating the dead and disseminated them to local party headquarters and public libraries. *The Fallen of the Milizia* (*I caduti della milizia*), for example, offered brief biographies and pictures of 370 Black Shirts who "had fallen for the Fascist Revolution" between 1923 and 1931. The book opens with an invocation to the fascist dead that blends Catholicism and fascism. The church and the party coupled with the altar and the Patria underscore the sacred and secular imagery that dominated fascist discourse. A simple pen-and-ink drawing with a flaming cross surrounded by standing muskets with their knives pointed to the heavens adorns the invocation that blurs the boundary between God and the fascist heroes (Figure 17):

> God, that lights every fire and guards every heart, revive every day my passion for Italy.
> Make me always more worthy of our Dead so that they themselves—the strongest—respond to the living: PRESENT!
> Nourish us at the book of Your wisdom and our muskets at Your will.
> Make my glance sharper and my foot more secure on the sacred crossings of the Patria.
> On the streets, on the coasts, in the forests, and on the beaches that already was Rome.
> When the future soldier marches in rank beside me, I feel the beating of your faithful heart.
> When the banners and flags pass that all persons recognize as those of the Patria: The Patria is the Stone foundation that will carry us to greatness.
> God! Make Your Cross the insignia that proceeds the banner of my Legion.
> And save the Italy of the DUCE always and in the hour of our beautiful death. So be it.[18]

[16] Associazione Nazionale Combattenti Federazione Provinciale di Verona, *Rapporto provinciale—15 ottobre 1933—XI* (Verona: Arena-Verona, 1933), 8.

[17] On this tradition, which dates to the early eighteenth century, see Alberto Vecchi, *Il culto delle immagini nelle stampe popolari* (Florence: Olschki, 1968).

[18] Ufficio Storico della M.V.S.N., *I caduti della milizia* (Rome: Libreria del Littorio, 1932), frontispiece.

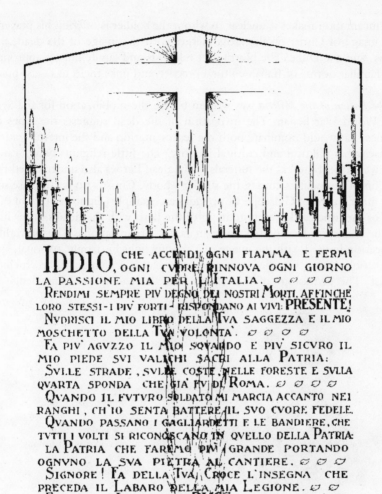

IDDIO, CHE ACCENDI OGNI FIAMMA E FERMI
OGNI CVORE, RINNOVA OGNI GIORNO
LA PASSIONE MIA PER L'ITALIA.

RENDIMI SEMPRE PIV DEGNO DEI NOSTRI MORTI. AFFINCHÉ
LORO STESSI - I PIV FORTI - RISPONDANO AI VIVI: PRESENTE!
NVDRISCI IL MIO LIBRO DELLA TVA SAGGEZZA E IL MIO
MOSCHETTO DELLA TVA VOLONTA'.

FA PIV' AGVZZO IL MIO SGVARDO E PIV' SICVRO IL
MIO PIEDE SVI VALICHI SACRI ALLA PATRIA:
SVLLE STRADE, SVLLE COSTE, NELLE FORESTE E SVLLA
QVARTA SPONDA CHE GIA' FV DI ROMA.

QVANDO IL FVTVRO SOLDATO MI MARCIA ACCANTO NEI
RANGHI, CH'IO SENTA BATTERE IL SVO CVORE FEDELE.
QVANDO PASSANO I GAGLIARDETTI E LE BANDIERE, CHE
TVTTI I VOLTI SI RICONOSCANO IN QVELLO DELLA PATRIA:
LA PATRIA CHE FAREMO PIV' GRANDE PORTANDO
OGNVNO LA SVA PIETRA AL CANTIERE.

SIGNORE! FA DELLA TVA CROCE L'INSEGNA CHE
PRECEDA IL LABARO DELLA MIA LEGIONE.

E SALVA L'ITALIA NEL DVCE SEMPRE E NELL'ORA
DI NOSTRA BELLA MORTE.
COSI SIA.

Figure 17. Invocation to the fascist dead. Ufficio Storico della M.V.S.N.,
I caduti della milizia (Rome: Libreria del Littorio, 1935).

The incantation makes it unclear to whom the soldier is offering his prayers. The image of Christ on the cross merges with the image of the dead, the Patria, and the Duce. The blurring of religious and family images appropriates familiar norms of Italian cultural practice and links them to fascist practice.

The Fallen of the Militia was written before the mobilization for the Second World War began. The invocation of the dead suggests the types of themes that would dominate both the representation and the internalization of fascism as political and cultural identity. The little religious prayer cards that were distributed at the funerals of the dead heroes also underscored the erosion of boundaries among the soldier's body, Christ's body, and fascism. The funeral card of Giuseppe C. provides an example (Figure 18).[19] On one side of the little card is a photograph of the hero with the details of his life, death, and record of participation in fascist organizations. The prayerlike invocation headed with the image of a crucifix links his family, national, and fascist obligations. On the cover of the booklet is a picture of the crucified Christ. The mythology of Catholicism, the day-to-day local knowledge of

Figure 18. Funeral prayer card. *ACS, PNF, MRF,* b. 4 (Grosetto).

[19] *ACS, PNF, MRF,* b. 4 (Grosetto). I have changed the names of the heroes to protect their heirs against possible violations of privacy.

popular Italian Catholicism, offered a ready-made set of symbols and daily practices that the regime, as well as Fascist Party members, could draw on to craft and interpret a fascist ethos and conception of the self.

The imagery of death and the cult of commemoration tapped a European, and not specifically Italian, ennui in the post–World War I period that the fascist movement and later regime exploited. Margherita Sarfatti argued that the idea of an unknown soldier captured the imagination of a generation that had lost direction and was seeking heroes.

> We all sought to create heroes for ourselves, worthy of our worship, but in vain.
>
> It seemed as though materialism were in the ascendant, with its negation of free will and its belief in blind chance, when suddenly there came an awakening of the spirit. Had not all men alike been in the trenches? Had not one and all been moved by the same instincts to face death for the common cause? Would not one stand for all? Thus musing, the nations singled out for their ideal of heroism the humble figure of the Unknown Warrior. He stood for the millions who had promised nothing but who gave everything, selfless, untiring, ubiquitous. In all lands the whole army saw itself in him, every mother mourned in him her own son. In him the obscure, antlike fighters in the trenches found at once their symbol and their apotheosis.[20]

The dead soldier's body represented more than social ennui. Cemeteries were the architectural icons of the fallen; public funerals and commemorative ceremonies, from the highly public reburying of the fallen in Santa Croce to the most obscure local events, were the ritualistic celebrations of death in the cause of the Patria. Local fascist parties publicly commemorated heroes to remind the populace of the glory and honor of offering one's life to the Patria.[21] Live bodies gathered in public space to commemorate dead bodies. Commemorative events for dead fascist heroes reinforced the linking of Italian political generations and ritually attacked all enemies of the Patria—liberals, bolsheviks, and capitalists.

For example, the weekly bulletin *La Fiamma*, of the Fighting Fascists of Foligno, devoted an entire issue in 1942 to the commemorative activities it staged to honor the third anniversary of the bestowing of a gold medal on a fascist hero. The plane of Alfonso D. was shot down in 1936 in Spain, where he had volunteered to fight the "Communist enemy." Over a picture of the

[20] Margherita Sarfatti, *The Life of Benito Mussolini*, trans. Frederic Whyte (New York: Frederick A. Stokes, 1925), 18.

[21] For example, in the city of Verona there were twenty-seven commemorative events of persons in twenty-two years; *ACS, PNF, MRF*, b. 12 (Verona).

deceased in his uniform, *La Fiamma*'s headlines read, "Foligno will worthily celebrate the Gold Medalist Alfonso D." The paper announced the celebration as "another epochal day of pure fascist faith, exalting the heroic figure of citizen and comrade, Captain and pilot of the Armed Forces Alfonso D., volunteer for Spain, in whose memory was awarded the Gold Medal of Military Valor."[22]

Alfonso died in 1936; his commemorative ceremony was staged six years after his death during the height of Italian fighting in the Second World War. The ceremony took over the small town of Foligno from morning until mid-afternoon. Unlike commemorative events staged in Rome, local events worked themselves into the fabric of a small social milieu and brought the fascist mission closer to the capillary cities of Italy. The ceremony began with a parade of local military organizations and concluded with a ceremony in the mayor's quarters. The principal street in Foligno was renamed after Alfonso and a commemorative stone was laid. The parade ended in the central piazza of the town where the bishop and military chaplain celebrated a mass. They blessed the stone and presented commemorative heraldry to Alfonso's family.

Commemoration as an overall proportion of ritual events declined during the war years. It did not disappear, however, and the events in Foligno suggest that it served a clear symbolic purpose. The local parties consciously resurrected fascist heroes during the war years to rally their publics around local figures whose deaths would serve as emblems of fascist victory over liberal and communist enemies.

The newspaper narrative of Alfonso's commemoration service began with a mass in the "extremely vast" central piazza of Foligno, which was "packed" for the occasion with an "imposing crowd of people" whose "souls" "vibrated" to the "sweet notes" of Gounod's *Ave Maria*. The diocesan bishop gave a "vibrant and fervid" speech in which he stated that the "youthful spirit of the volunteer and fighter was fused" in death "with his ardent fascist faith and his high apostleship of the devotee, in a magnificent exaltation of the heroic virtues of the Italian soldier, called by Divine Providence to perpetuate the civilization of Rome against the horrors and barbarisms of bolshevism." The bishop equated the Spanish communists Alfonso fought with the barbarians who sacked Rome in the fifth century. If it were not for heroes such as Alfonso D., the new barbarians, the communists, would sack Rome once more.[23]

The bishop went to the past to inscribe Alfonso's death in a pantheon of

[22] *ACS, PNF, MRF*, b. 7 (Perugia).
[23] Ibid.

heroism and sacrifice for the Patria. The federal secretary's representative linked Alfonso's death to the present war and noted:

> But Alfonso D. is not dead: his spirit, together with those of the purest heroes, lives among us to guide us on new paths and to vindicate the generous sacrifices of so many heroes and so many martyrs; and as He following the example of the martyrs of the Italian Risorgimento melded patriotism and combativeness within his consciousness, so we must follow his illustrious example to make us ever worthy of the imperial destiny of our Patria.

The bravery of 1936 must be repeated in the war of 1942, and in case the audience missed this point, the newspaper's commentary emphasized it. The local reporter stressed the party representative's "efficacious and expressive synthesis" that demonstrated that "our war" was "spreading out against all the cowardly and the profiteers," fascist code words for the twin enemies of communism and liberal capitalism, which aimed to "demolish the most sacred family and social institutions."[24] The war against the Allies was a war against communism and capitalism. The capitalization of the pronoun "he" when referring to the hero, a custom usually reserved for the Deity, wed the image of the sacred to the task of national aggrandizement. The cult of commemoration in its various manifestations used religious imagery to transform the dead bodies of the heroes; the hero's body evoked the transformed body of Christ, fusing the national and the religious.

The Fallen and Popular Culture

The glorification of the soldier's body was not limited to architecture and public ceremony. Cultural forms such as theater appropriated the dead as popular entertainment. For example, Antona-Traversi Grismondi Giannino's play *The Offering* (*L'offerta*), which debuted in Milan in November 1934, focused on the missing soldier's body. Missing bodies were a problem, because many soldiers died behind enemy lines and it was impossible either to find the bodies or to identify them properly. Many soldiers were buried in anonymous graves away from their homelands.

Giannino, a popular author of light comedies, turned to patriotic drama in the post–World War I years. Born in Milan in 1860, he wrote his first play in 1892. During the First World War, he became an ardent supporter of Italian intervention; in his late fifties, he volunteered for war service and achieved the rank of major. He received numerous military silver medals,

[24] Ibid.

and the Association of the Families of the Fallen of Rome, Bologna, and Padua awarded him a gold medal. After the war, he worked for the military office of propaganda at Innsbruck, where the bodies of presumably unknown Italian prisoners of war were buried in a large military cemetery. Giannino later joined the Office to Care and Honor the Corpses of the Fallen in War, where his particular duty was to give aid and comfort to the families of the fallen soldiers. In 1929, the regime honored Giannino by electing him to the Italian Senate.[25]

The Offering reflected Giannino's work with the families of the war dead. *La nazione operante*, the catalog of fascist bureaucrats, described the play, which was performed in more than "three hundred cities and small towns," as a "moving exaltation of the sacrifice of life, of blood and of sorrow for the Patria." Giannino called the play, which began with a dedication to the dead soldiers, "a rite in three acts."[26] The broken soldier's body, the focus of the dedication, emphasized the physicality of death and set the dedication apart from commemorative prose poems that centered on death's spirituality. In a series of incantations that begin "For you" (the "you" is plural, suggesting the community of the dead), Giannino described the dead as a group whose "blood" "bathes" the battlefields, whose extremities were ripped apart while their souls remained solid, and whose "nerves" and "muscles" were "bound as the fasces [sheafs of wheat] to reclaim a victory against the enemy."

The plot of *The Offering* was simple. In a local office of the National Association of Mothers, Widows, and Families of the Fallen and Missing in War, the clerk, a young woman named Bice, laments to her parish priest that her brother's body has never been returned from the front. A wealthy local youth, Filippo, who has also lost a brother in the war, courts Bice. She refuses his proposals of marriage because the death of her brother makes it necessary for her to care for her aging mother and to sacrifice the possibility of having a family of her own. This feature of Italian culture makes the family of origin take precedence to the family that might be created through marriage, underscoring the cultural domination of the mother.

Filippo, in contrast, believes that their common loss of a brother makes them ideal candidates for marriage to each other. After various plot twists and turns, the young people realize that their respective bothers' bodies have been confused. The young woman's brother is buried in the youth's

[25] On Giannino's military service, see Edoardo Savino, *La nazione operante*, 3d ed. (Novara: Istituto Geografico de Agostini, 1937), 273; his playwrighting career until 1934 is summarized in Societa Italiana Autori ed Editori, *Annuario del Teatro Italiano* (Rome: Societa Anonima Poligrafica Italiana, 1935), 7.

[26] Savino, *La nazione operante*, 273; Antona-Traversi Grismondi Giannino, *L'Offerta: Rito in tre quadri* (Milan: Novencentesca, 1934). Further quotations from *L'Offerta* are cited by page numbers in the text.

family tomb, and the brother of the wealthy youth is the truly missing body. Neither Bice nor Filippo has the heart to tell the mothers of the mistake. Instead, they agree to marry to unite the two families as the mistaken bodies have united them—they sacrifice their personal celibacy as another "offering to the Patria" and note, "Every fallen is the son of every mother" (142).

With the exception of the final scene, which occurs at the tomb where the incorrect body is interred, the action takes place in the association's office. This setting permits a group of characters to wander on and off stage and to raise issues about fallen soldiers for the priest to address. The range of situations is telling. For example, the entrance of a peasant woman whose son had received a gold medal for valor at the front but whose body was never returned provides a dramatic opportunity for the priest to lecture on the problem of the unknown soldier. The priest laments that this mother of a gold medalist was forced because of her ignorance and poverty to take a third-class train to the office—a mother of a gold medalist deserved better. He notes that while there is one Unknown soldier in Rome buried at the Altar of the Patria, at least three hundred thousand had been lost.

When Bice asks the priest why the number was so large, he lectures her on the realities of life on the battlefield, graphically describing the soldiers' shattered bodies. He rhapsodizes:

> But how many brave soldiers fell in the furor of the fighting, and remained entombed in the blood-drenched earth! How many others, on bad days, did we have to leave, with fraternal anguish, in enemy lines . . . or in our own, in those intermediate lines, battered by fire, that rendered useless the courage of their comrades. How many remained under the wreckage of shattered defenses, or under the rubble of fallen houses! How many were overwhelmed by avalanches, or drowned in the rivers! How many bodies, dismembered by grenades! . . . And on how many tombs weather has eroded the crosses, or rendered illegible the names! And how many small cemeteries, improvised behind the front trenches, were then destroyed by the explosion of artillery! There, signorina, the tragic sight of our three hundred thousand: Faceless Heroes. (40)

The priest's narrative was bivalent. On one level, it reflected the fascination with death and gore that George Mosse has labeled the "trivialization of death," which appeared regularly in popular depictions of war during this period.[27] On another level, it addressed the sacred character of the body in Catholic culture. Every Catholic body is sacred, as it partakes of the body of Christ; to desecrate the Catholic body is to desecrate the Christian community. Roman Catholicism, at least in the 1930s, forbade cremation and re-

---

[27] Mosse, *Fallen Soldiers*, 147–50.

fused the rites of Christian burial to Catholics who elected cremation. To the extent that the soldier's body, Christ's body, the nation, and the church were symbolically fused, the mutilation of the soldier's body that the missing bodies suggested pointed to the desecration of the Italian nation and demanded redemption or retribution.

If the Catholic soldier's body was sacred, the producer of new bodies was even more sacred. The discussions in the association's offices suggest the cultural salience of the mother as the producer of new bodies and the peculiarly Italian character of gender and family relations in fascist Italy.[28] Thus, the heroine of The Offering, Bice, felt free to marry only when she was able to join her marriage to her mother's sacrifice of a son. The cultural significance of the mother is dramatized when a widow walks into the association office and complains that she is not allowed to wear her dead husband's gold medal. A long discussion follows about the recent name change of the organization from the Association of "Mothers and Orphans of the Fallen" to the Association of "Families of the Fallen." Although Mussolini had approved of the name change, those present in the office were opposed, because the new name was disrespectful of mothers. A law decreed that a widow could wear her husband's medal only if there was no living mother to wear it. The rationale given was that mothers are faithful and wives are not. One of the characters puts it succinctly, if cynically: "Today there are very few women who know how to be faithful to the living; it would be ridiculous to believe that they could remain faithful to the memory of the dead" (72).[29]

The central "offering" of Giannino's play was the mothers' sacrifice of their sons to the Patria. When The Offering opened in Milan, drama critic Renato Simoni described it in religious terms, writing that the play demonstrated "the goodness of emotion . . . a simple, meek, profound emotion, that fuses piety and human tenderness and the religion of the cross, of the dead, of the Nation, of maternal sacrifice." The audience responded with

---

[28] Victoria De Grazia, How Fascism Ruled Women: Italy, 1922–1945 (Berkeley: University of California Press, 1992), devotes two chapters to motherhood and the family (41–115) but only partially alludes to the cultural significance of Italian family structure. On the latent connection between mothers and soldiers that takes issues of power and powerlessness into account, see Nancy Huston, "The Matrix of War: Mothers and Heroes," in The Female Body in Western Culture, ed. Susan Rubin Suleiman (Cambridge: Harvard University Press, 1986), 119–36.

[29] There was a more material issue at stake here than simply who would wear the gold medal. Widows received government pensions; mothers did not. On this issue with regard to the German case, see Karin Hausen, "The German Nation's Obligations to the Heroes' Widows of World War I," in Behind the Lines: Gender and the Two World Wars, ed. Margaret Randolph Higonnet, Jane Jensen, Sonya Michel, and Margaret Polling Weitz (New Haven: Yale University Press, 1987), 126–40.

"great emotion" and "immediate and sincere and intense" applause.[30] There were five curtain calls after the first act, seven after the second act, and six after the third.[31] "Offering" has another meaning in Roman Catholic liturgy which would not have been lost on the audience: the part of the Roman Catholic Mass in which the priest "offers" the bread and wine and transforms it into the body and blood of Christ. The offering of the liturgy ritually dramatizes the offering of Christ when he allowed himself to be crucified. In Roman Catholic doctrine, the broken and battered body of Christ redeemed the sins of mankind and brought the kingdom of God to earth. The broken and battered body of the dead soldiers will redeem the earthly kingdom of Italy and restore it to its rightful international position. The dead soldier's body in the play united the young couple, making a new Italian family, and the production of future Italian bodies, possible.

The Offering leaves us with three messages: first, the superiority of the sacrifice of the mother; second, the sacred quality of the soldier's body, which has the power to reunite families and re-create the nation; and third, the mediation by the church, as represented by the priest, of the diverse relations and interrelations between mother and soldier, family and nation. The same themes of the sacred body and the missing body dominate the obituaries.

Blood and the Dramaturgy of Death

The biography obituaries offer an insight into the ideal fascist life, or what the National Fascist Party wished to construct as the ideal fascist life. Obituaries are useful tools for cultural analysis because they provide representative idealizations of a life rather than the life itself.[32] Fascist Party handbooks and textbooks provided the rhetorical frames from which the local party heads inevitably crafted their descriptions of the fascist heroes. For example, a party handbook described "l'esprit de corps" as "sentiments of love and union and chains of strictest solidarity among all the members of a military body," and a few lines later, "camaraderie" as "sentiments of union and love

---

[30] R. S. [Renato Simoni], "'L'Offerta' rito in 3 atti di G. Antona-Traversi Gismondi," *Corriere della Sera* (Milan), 20 November 1934, 6.

[31] Scholars have argued that audiences were not receptive to fascist plays and films. On this point, see Gianfranco Pedulla, "Teatro e fascismo in Italia," *Passato e Presente* 10 (1991), 145–56; Victoria De Grazia, "Mass Culture and Sovereignty: The American Challenge to European Cinemas, 1920–1960," *Journal of Modern History* 61 (1989), 53–87; and Berezin, "Cultural Form and Political Meaning," 1237–86. The lack of hard evidence regarding the popularity of *The Offering* has more to do with the peculiarities of Italian theatrical culture than popular taste.

[32] The literary qualities of the obituaries depended on the literacy levels of the local party chiefs who wrote them. The range of variation in their length and prose style was wide.

that ought to reign among all parts of the armed forces."[33] The obituary narrative of Giovanni E. captured the flavor of the fascist definition of military solidarity. Giovanni E. was

> a complete leader. Of a very solid moral rectitude, of fairness that he displayed not only toward his closest friends but also toward those further away from his students, of a cordiality made of affectionate interest and sincere and profound will to be of use, he made all those who came near him love him. His university students found in him an example of a life lived with virility and humanity, a dispassionate faith, a goodwill that was not simply a rhetorical exercise, but was dictated from an instinctive need, from a profound interior conviction.
>
> He was still young, he was only twenty-nine years old. But already in his spirit and his physique was the vigor of complete maturity, exuding passion and enthusiasm, sustained by an extremely refined equilibrium. A generous promise for the Patria, one of the purest examples of our race.[34]

Giovanni E. was a university graduate with a bachelor's degree in jurisprudence. The descriptions and voices of the heroes varied somewhat depending on their level of education: complexity increased with educational level. For example, one hero, a peasant, an unusual social category for a Fascist Party devotee, was described as "an authentic rural."[35]

Obituary narratives that praised stoicism, bravery, and fidelity to fascist duty suggested party proscriptions on discipline and obedience. For example, the same party hand book cited earlier defined military discipline as "the habit of fulfilling all military and civic duties, exactly and conscientiously, not for fear of punishment or hope of recompense, but for the deep belief in their necessity." According to the handbook, obedience and subordination were linked and entailed the qualities of "readiness, respect, and steadfastness,"[36] which, translated into obituary form, yield the following descriptions. One hero died "calm and serene" "without a lament uttered from his mouth." Another was noted for his "purity of soul and the passion with which he performed his duty in the skies for the Patria." Another was an "intrepid squadrista, extremely fierce in his faith who never knew how to bend to compromises."[37]

---

[33] PNF—Comando Federale di Verona, *Elementi di cultura politico militare* (Rome: Partito Nazionale Fascista, 1939), 15.

[34] *ACS, PNF, MRF*, b. 12 (Verona).

[35] *ACS, PNF, MRF*, b. 4 (Grosetto).

[36] PNF—Comando Federale di Verona, *Elementi di cultura politico militare*, 12.

[37] *ACS, PNF, MRF*, b. 4 (Forli); *ACS, PNF, MRF*, b. 4 (Grosetto); *ACS, PNF, MRF*, b. 1 (Ascoli).

Umberto F.'s obituary blended elements of the military, the civic, and the fraternal that characterized the ideal fascist hero.

Young, courageous, enthusiastic of a bellicose life sacrificed to the Patria, a fascist of the purest faith, from youth Umberto F. had manifested his sentiments of profound patriotism. . . . Conceived and lived his life as a duty: studious at school, a model son, exemplary fascist and soldier. Umberto F. frequented with enthusiasm the official school for tank infantrymen. Discharged [the obituary does not suggest the reason], he dedicated the better part of his energies to the organization of the Fighting Fascists of Scopoli, trying with tenacious will to obtain an exemption that he would have easily obtained, welcomed with genuine enthusiasm and pride, the notice of his recall.[38]

The obituary narratives provide a window on the cultural capacities of the party chiefs and underscore the authenticity of this form of evidence. In this case, the party chief's writing skills and command of the Italian language were limited. For example, the chief used the word *combattuta* instead of the correct word, *combattivo*, to describe Umberto's life. The error is telling, as *combattuta* connotes "troubled," whereas *combattivo* means "fighting," which is the idea the party chief wished to convey.

The listing of fascist virtues paled before their enactment in the death scenes, dramatic tableaux that were an obligatory part of the lengthier biography obituaries. The death scenes displayed a remarkable similarity of narrative structure, suggesting that they were fictions created from the scraps of historic detail. The biographer was rarely present at the death, and for the most part, he relied on the testimony of the field doctor and other available witnesses.

The death scenes were structured around final acts in the battlefield where the hero frequently and defiantly threw his last grenade before his own immolation. Heroes refused medication and returned to fight after they were mortally wounded; one died singing the fascist anthem, "Giovinezza." A hero who received the gold medal of honor was in the hospital with a fever and refused to remain there. He returned to the battlefield with grenades and bayonets in hand and engaged in hand-to-hand combat as he walked through the battlefield over "bloody" bodies that were piled on top of one another. Wounded for the third time in the chest, he continued "to struggle with indomitable lionlike energy at the head of his heroic alpines; finally, mortally wounded, he flung with supreme force his bloody helmet against an enemy bursting on the scene hurling him with the tricolor in hand down

---

[38] *ACS, PNF, MRF,* b. 5 (Perugia).

into a ravine."[39] If the hero survived the battlefield and was taken to the camp hospital, the narrative shifted to focus on the last words of the deceased and his stoic refusal to surrender his fascist will in the face of his coming death. The broken, bloodied body of the hero was the dominant pictorial image. The doctor's testimony frequently transformed the body into an image of holiness.

Two representative death scenes capture the narrative structure of the story. Marzio G. was a medical student at the University of Padua when he volunteered for service in the war.[40] He died at the age of twenty-six while engaged in combat on the Greek Albanian front and was awarded a silver medal of honor. From his youth, he was actively involved in fascist organizations, and while he was a medical student he volunteered for military training. By July 1940, he was a sublieutenant in an infantry corps and wore the "gray-green" uniform of an "Italian soldier." This is an important distinction, because it means he did not wear the fascist black shirt. Stationed on the Greek-Albanian front, "he left with his beautiful faith intact, with the youthful ardor of his twenty-five years full of the very noblest ideals, secure of victory, with his beautiful, serene, and faithful smile that knew how to hide deep within his soul the secret that no one ought to see, the yearning that he felt at the farewell of his dear ones." The language displays the sentimentality that characterized the simple prose of the party chiefs as they sought to depict the personality of the pure innocent hero who will soon sacrifice his life for his patriotic ideals.

Marzio G.'s soldiers "loved" and "admired" him for his "strong and generous spirit," his "humanity," and his "lively intelligence." Marzio always insisted on fighting on the front lines, and his soldiers described him as "extremely courageous. Too courageous!" He was a father figure to his soldiers even though they frequently were older than he was. On Christmas Day 1940, he volunteered for an especially difficult mission. Although he was gravely wounded, and as a medical student he understood the seriousness of his wound, he remained on the battlefield:

All the time his soul remained firm, and he wanted to give all of himself, until the end.—He continued to stay near his soldiers and by his example encouraged them in combat.—Then, no longer able to hold himself up, he asked to take care of the numerous wounded, holding himself upright like a tree trunk.—He continued for hours, conquering with a supreme force of will his mortal spasm, and nourished with the flame of Faith and generous Christian Love [Carita] that came to him even while the blood was gushing from his open wound.—Finally, resistance was superior to every human

---

[39] ACS, PNF, MRF, b. 5 (Perugia).
[40] ACS, PNF, MRF, b. 2 (Bolzano). All quotations about Marzio G. are from this source.

possibility. He gave himself to others, raising the most noble virtue of a generous and pure soul to a heroic light.

From the zone of military operations, one of Marzio's comrades wrote a small literary piece, "The Heroic Christmas of Marzio G." transforming him into a Christlike fascist martyr. Written a year after the death, it began with the mythic incantation "Once upon a time." Marzio's men were as brave as "lions." Following much the same story line as the account of the federal secretary, the comrade explains that Marzio was engaged in a particularly dangerous and important maneuver and that it was during ground combat that he was "gravely wounded." Exalting Mario's courage and character, the comrade recounts how the hero volunteered for the mission:

> The purest figure of the hero, Marzio G., had participated voluntarily in the action.—He was a "Balilla" of Battaglione, the most sought after among his colleagues, the most loved among his superiors and inferiors.—

After volunteering, Marzio

> enjoyed the great faith of his inferiors, who admired him for his virile will.—He knew how to capture the soul of his soldiers, speaking purely to their frequent sentiments.—His voice penetrated into the depths of the hearts of his *ragazzi* [kids]—as he called them, even those who were older than he was—and they found a strong impression in his virile purity.

After two attacks, during which Marzio fought like a "lion," his men realized that he had been wounded:

> His [men] saw him fall to the ground.—Wounded? . . . Dead? . . . An act of uncertainty and then away, all, like a flame, above the enemy to vindicate the Hero.—But he rose again shouting energetically, "Forward," and then continued to incite with his voice while throwing his grenades.—

A "burst from a machine gun" had struck Marzio in the "groin," but despite his grave injury, he medicated himself and then went on to treat his soldiers. By the end of the day, he died, finally giving out on the battlefield in the snow.

> His last thought was to give recognition to his Mother for having worthily educated him in the cult of the Patria, to all his dear ones, and to his fiancée far way.—

The comrade's narrative concludes:

On the night of 25 December, a Christmas doubly holy, the elected figure
of Marzio G., luminous example of high military virtue, human generosity,
indomitable courage, will be numbered among the many other heroic
Fallen.

The narrator imbues the sanctity of Marzio's death on the day of Christ's
birth with double meaning. Marzio joins the other fallen and joins Christ;
his "offering" foreshadows the "offering" of Christ, born on Christmas.

Marzio G. died on the battlefield, and except for his decision to go forward in the face of his mortal wounds, the narrative of his sacrifice was given
voice by others. In contrast, Marcello I., who died in a field hospital, articulated the meaning of his own death in a little death-bed drama.[41] Marcello, a
state employee who worked as a geometer, had missed out on participation
in the First World War because he was too young. He compensated by
volunteering for the Ethiopian campaign, where he was awarded a bronze
medal. He volunteered for the second time in the Italian assault against the
"Bolshevik order in Russia," where he met his death. A member of the
Fascist Party since 1921, he had participated in the March on Rome. According to his biographer, the narration of his life was a "small thing" in
comparison to his "glorious holocaust." Marcello was wounded on the Russian front when a "bullet exploded in his abdomen." Taken off the battlefield wearing his bloody black shirt, he refused to allow the field chaplain to
summon a physician. Lying in the camp, he demonstrated his "unshakable
faith and will."

To the Chaplain who wished to bring him to a physician, soon after the
mortal wound, He responded: "If you wish me well, I beg you, leave me
here. I want to die with my black shirt. I feel so much that no doctor would
be able to do anything for me, instead these kids have more need than me."

Then . . . he made a speech . . . he called Officials and the noncommis-
sioned officers, a few at a time, and gave them advice and orders. To those
Black Shirts that were near him with tearful eyes, He, the dying, was courageous and said: "Strength, kids [*ragazzi*], do not worry yourself about me.
Be hard yet a little more; if they do not succeed now, the Reds will never
return. Stay calm at your posts, then surely we will push back the enemy."

Continuing the last dialogue with his chaplain, who assisted him lovingly,
the hero said:

"With God I am already in accord, this you know. Their mamma and Providence will guide my children . . . I believe much in Providence. And then I
believe also that I will follow him equally, also soon I will be dead. . . .

[41] *ACS, PNF, MRF*, b. 9 (Piacenza). All quotations about Marcello I. are from this source.

"No, I assure you that I am not mistaken. I know that I am dying. You know how much I have loved Italy and our Cause. I have already given my blood to the Revolution and I am content to have given it. Now I die . . . I am content to die."

The chaplain asks Marcello if he is truly content to die, to which Marcello responds:

"Yes, for this war, yes. Because I am certain that we have to do it; I am certain that it will go well. Also here the Reds will not pass. It is best to resist a little. And for this I want to remain here with my men, where I will be able to guide them for yet a little more. Then also my death will serve some cause."

Marcello receives the last rites of the Catholic Church and requests that his men do not come to see him because he wants them at their posts. He is finally taken to the "infirmary," somewhat against his will, where the physicians confirm they can do nothing for "his intestines ripped apart in many pieces." A friend comes to see him, and Marcello has a premonition that they will be "joined in death." The friend indeed appears later as another fascist hero. Finally, as death nears, Marcello prepares his final speech, which he delivers to the chaplain: " 'I am in accord with God and with men. I die for Italy, I die for the Duce.' He called an attendant, and with a glance that reminded them of the recommendations he had made, he said to the physician: 'Doctor, I am no longer able to speak.' " The biographer concludes:

Those were his last words. His last thought was, yet, for the Patria, for the Duce, for the family.
    The spirit of Marcello I. had left his material body and entered the field to pluck the palm of glory among his Black Shirts that were turning the outcome of hard battle in their favor, animated by His spirit, His sublime example.

Marcello's final words echo the last words of the crucified Christ, and the biographer capitalizes the pronoun "His" to strengthen the suggestion of deity.
    The drama of the death scene and the image of the broken, bloodied body has sacred and secular antecedents in Italian cultural life. Death scenes were staples of operas, the popular and familiar nineteenth-century Italian cultural form. The standard plot of the repertoire of Italian dramatic operas usually culminates in a death scene where the hero or heroine lies dying, frequently by stabbing, and cries out, or rather sings out, his or her final words. In a note entitled "The Operatic Conception of Life," Antonio Gramsci observes

that an attachment to opera on the part of the quasi-educated introduced artificiality into social life. He argues:

> "Artificial" is perhaps not the right word because among the popular classes this artificiality assumes naive and moving forms. To many common people the baroque and the operatic appear as an extraordinarily fascinating way of feeling and acting, a means of escaping what they consider low, mean, and contemptible in their lives and education in order to enter a more select sphere of great feelings and noble passions. . . . But opera is the most pestiferous because words set to music are more easily recalled, and they become matrices in which thought takes shape out of flux. Look at the writing style of many common people: it is modeled on a repertory of clichés.[42]

Gramsci's comment applies equally to the popular idiom of sentimentality that permeates the letters and obituaries, as well as the emotionally charged discourse of newspaper accounts of fascist spectacle.

Blood was as highly a charged symbolic entity as opera in Italy.[43] There were three cultural resonances of blood in wartime Italy: the act of giving blood in Red Cross drives; the fascist appropriation of blood in race theory that was becoming prominent in the late 1930s; and the imagery of blood in Catholic culture. The iconography of Christ and the saints was focused on their bloodied bodies.[44] There was a clear attempt to link the soldiers to religious imagery in their death scenes as they were compared to saints. The obituaries used the Italian popular idiom of sentimentality and emotion to meld fascist virtues to Italian images of family, God, and Patria. Their rhetorical style was only one step below many of the newspaper narratives I cited. If it were not for the quasi-educated prose style, however, Mazzini himself could have authored these narratives.

Voices from the Grave

The obituaries created narratives of identity that relied on a blend of fascist and Christian iconography. The heroes' letters narrated felt identities that wed their private to their public selves. These voices from the grave

---

[42] Antonio Gramsci, "The Operatic Conception of Life," in *Antonio Gramsci: Selections from the Cultural Writings*, ed. David Forgacs and Geoffrey Nowell-Smith, trans. William Boelhower (Cambridge: Harvard University Press, 1985), 377–78.

[43] On the general social significance of blood during this period, see Richard Titmuss, *The Gift Relationship: From Human Blood to Social Policy* (New York: Pantheon, 1971).

[44] I am indebted to Mary Vogel for first pointing this out to me.

articulated a fascist identity that suggested a collage of deeply held private attachments to family and church and public attachments to country.[45]

"La Mamma" and "La Patria"

The biography of Franco L. and his self-representation in his letters displayed the merging of family and country, public and private that threads through the consciousness of the dead heroes.[46] Franco L.'s principal identities, as son and as fascist, dance through his letters.

Franco L. died in Greece in 1940 at the age of twenty-seven. He was awarded the silver medal of honor. The Fascist Party in Grottazzolina commemorated his life and death in a bound azure-blue pamphlet that they distributed to local party members. In the front was Sublieutenant Franco's picture in his military uniform. He is blond, thin, and almost fragile looking and stares off into the distance as if he were gazing wistfully at some more desirable locale (Figure 19). What is striking about this photograph and so many of the others is that often the fascist heroes do not fit either the fascist construction of the "hard" fascist or standard popular cultural notions of fascists as thugs.

Franco was a university student who received the *laurea*, the Italian version of the baccalaureate degree, in philosophy. In contrast to many of the other heroes, his family belonged to the educated Italian middle classes. The letters that Franco's commanding officers wrote to his parents offering condolences on his death addressed his father as "Dottore," suggesting that he had a university education. Franco's biographer attempts to reconcile the cerebral nature of Franco's academic pursuits to his life as a fascist man of action. The biographer begins by saying that a biography of Franco would be "perfectly useless," because he "wrote" his own life "with an unmistakable style: from his smile in life, from his blood in death."

As his photograph suggests, Franco's body joined "physical elegance" and "spiritual elegance." The author makes much of the fact that despite studying philosophy, Franco was still able to be a fascist man of action who reconciled the disjuncture between a life of thought and a life of action.[47] The

---

[45] The only comparable study I am aware of is Klaus Theweleit's work on the memories and diaries of the German Freikorps, *Male Fantasies* (Minneapolis: University of Minnesota Press, 1987). As my text displays, the Italian fascists and the Germans had very different fantasy lives.

[46] *ACS, PNF, MRF,* b. 1 (Ascoli). All quotations about and by Franco L. are from this source.

[47] Many young fascists, and the regime itself, faced the dilemma posed in the reconciliation of thought and action. The protagonist of Mario Carli's *L'italiano di Mussolini* (Milan: Mondadori, 1930) spends an entire chapter of this propagandist novel musing on how he resolved these two dimensions of his personality.

Figure 19. Franco L. *ACS, PNF, MRF*, b. 1 (Ascoli).

author tells us that Franco was not a "melancholy person" and that the study of philosophy had not transformed him into a cerebral person; rather, "young, good-looking, exuberant, and dynamic, he went to meet life passionately." Franco, the philosopher who had a "body well molded by gymnastics," represented the perfect "compromise between thought and action."

The biographer cannot imagine that after death Franco would remain "inert" in the "kingdom of the spirits." Rather, he would transform heaven with "magnificent violence, in throbbing action." And what would Franco do? In his domestic quarters he would erect "an altar, to adore an idol that had a boundless name:—MAMMA," and at the "light of his ideals" he would erect another altar "to adore another idol that called itself:—PATRIA."

The biographer concluded with a vision of Franco's death that is both ethereal and religious. In this description, which may have been excerpted from a colleague's letter, Franco takes on the persona of a Christ figure that is being raised to heaven and becomes a Christian icon.

It is a night of November. Devoured by the battle, the earth of Kalibaki is in flames. . . . In half-finished yearning, among the flashing lights, we sight (heavenly visions) the glorious figure of a young Hero. "IT IS FRANCO."

A frank face, "a sublime and definitive gesture," He goes to meet death, as he went to meet life. But he is taller than everyone: he surpasses everyone.

Hero among Heroes, already we see you sculpted in the most pure Carrara marble.

The prose style of the biographical section of the commemorative booklet was characteristic of the language of emotion that permeated fascist discourse and Italian melodramatic writing in general. The operatic tradition translated to ordinary Italian semiliterate prose became simply sentimental. Aside from the string of adjectives describing Franco, the reader has no sense of the dead man's personality. Rather, the adjectives assume a human shape, and emotion becomes a substitute for personality.

The letters of sympathy that Franco's commanding officers and comrades at arms wrote to his parents reiterate the pamphlet narrative of his patriotism and virtues. Franco met his death while leading his platoon into action; like the fascist heroes who populated the obituary narratives, he died while throwing a bomb at the enemy. mortally wounded, he "tried to draw from his energy the force and will to crown his life with an expression of the most pure military values: 'Comrades, avenge me! Long live Italy.'" And throwing his last bomb, "he accomplished the greatest honor for a fighting commander: to sway his dependents with his example." Other descriptions of the death scene repeated the same story: Franco died at the head of the unit; he threw his last bomb while he was already wounded. A friend narrates, "Dear Franco L., Hero among Heroes, I see you yet again when gripping the last bomb in your hand, wounded for the second time by enemy fire, sacrificing your glorious youth for the greater destiny of our beautiful Italy." Two cruel truths circumscribed his death: first, his body was missing behind enemy lines, and second, he could not receive the gold medal of honor because his captain died moments before him and fascist hierarchy demanded that Franco receive a silver medal.

Franco's self-presentation was rhetorically more compelling than his biographical one. More literate than his biographers, his letters displayed confidence and commitment to the Italian cause without being overly sentimental. In "The Last Words of Franco L. to His Mother," printed after his biography, he told his mother not to cry because it would disturb the serenity that he needed to do his job well on the front, and he enjoins her: "If tomorrow you read in the newspapers: 'Franco L. has died heroically for his beautiful Italy' neither you nor papa should shed a tear. It should be enough to have given a son to the Patria, worthy also of the compassion of Heaven."

Franco's letters, written to his parents between August and November 1940, reflected exhilaration at being at the front and continual reassurance that he was not in danger. He described himself as in the "highest spirits" and stated, "I am very well in all and for all, and this quasi-nomadic existence does not bother me and I am able to endure it without weakness and sacrifice." In trying to assure his parents of his well-being, he compared going to war with going to a party: "*For me it is like going to a dancing party* : I have soldiers who are brave, trained, and full of courage who adore me." Franco's conception of war as a party is a somewhat more astute observation than the mere tossed-off remark it immediately suggests. Parties, theaters of war, rallies in public spaces share a formal property. They all create transient communities and bonds of solidarity that exist only in the liminal space between social and political structures. War is as exhilarating as a party because it is supposed to be a temporary condition.

Franco L. was the only voice that spoke of war as a party. Yet all the voices conditioned by continual exposure to the staged exhilaration of fascist public ritual exhibited a confidence in the Italian future belying the fact that Italy was suffering huge losses and that fascism itself was on the way to defeat. Franco's last letter displayed the blend of confidence, dedication, and oblivion that makes all the letters ultimately rather poignant: "I am serving the Patria with all my ardor, and I am secure that soon our armies will be victorious. . . . I know how to bear whatever sacrifices the war imposes on me."

The mother and the Patria were connected in the obituary narrative that proceeded the reproduction of Franco's letters in the commemorative pamphlet. His letters to his parents and the continual reassurances he offers his mother underscore the fascist commitment to family. In general, his language was calm and measured. With the exception of the war-as-party metaphor, the idea of duty governed his letters home. Franco wrote, "I know how to do my duty in the understanding of everything and everyone, especially toward my subalterns, marked by the principle of justice and reasonable goodwill." His conception of duty was linked solely to country, and his conception of emotion was linked to his family, particularly his mother. Franco was a bachelor, and his demographic status circumscribed his notion of duty. His married counterparts displayed a notion of duty that wed the family to the nation and juxtaposed the competing demands of both.

"The Patria is our greatest family"

The letters to wives, in contrast to the letters to parents, portrayed a fusion of public duty as fascist citizen and private duty as husband and father.

The reflection of duty in the letters of married men suggested that they had merged their public and private identities. A fascist hero from Cremona wrote a letter to his wife that was emblematic of this merging. The author, pictured working diligently at his desk, had received a *laurea* in law and volunteered for combat duty in Africa and later Greece. He wrote from the front:

> The Patria is our greatest family and the adopted mother of our children: the hope for the future; the certainty of our glory. . . . I am well enough.— The battle still rages on: we ought to cede on numbers alone.—We have done all that is possible not to say impossible.—Rina, my love, how sorrowful it is, after a victorious day, to leave the embankment of the earth bathed in the blood of our colleagues, of our soldiers. Do not humble yourself, though; remember that we have done our duty.[48]

The tension between public and private duty emerges in a series of letters written on the Greek front between July 1940 and February 1941. Michele M., the author of the letters, was an accountant who had received a *laurea* in economics and commerce.[49] Married and the father of two children, he had participated as a fascist squad member in the March on Rome and had been active in fascist organizations from his youth. Although his date of birth is not given, his biography suggests that he was too old for conscription in the war effort and that he volunteered for the Ethiopian campaign. We can infer that he may have been called up for the fighting in 1940, because he admonishes his wife, who seems to be trying to petition the Minister of War to obtain his release from service. He writes that he "would never forgive her" if she were to take this action, because he feels that is necessary to "bear arms against the extremely hateful English, who recently killed one of the best men of the Regime: Italo Balbo."[50]

In contrast to images from popular culture, Michele M.'s photograph, like those of the other fascist heroes, suggests a mild-mannered person who looks more like a local business-man than a hard-edged fascist. His letters reflect a sober and sometimes stern commitment to his duty as a fascist and a faith in Italy's victory in the war, perhaps because his wife was not as committed to fascist ideals as Michele was. He reminds his wife that she knows "his enthusiasms and ideals" for the nation and the idea of going to war and that they should unite in joint sacrifice for the "supreme ideals of the Patria." While he has deep hopes for the future of his children, especially his son, he can return home only after "having completed his duty entirely,

---

[48] *ACS, PNF, MRF*, b. 2 (Cremona).
[49] Ibid. All quotations from Michele M.'s letters are from this source.
[50] As noted earlier, Balbo was mistakingly shot down by Italian troops.

in the manner that he intends." This last phrase is underlined in his letter, and the wording he uses for "intends," *intendo io*, is more emphatic than its English translation. For Michele, fascism was the "great faith that for twenty years has sustained me and illuminated me like an incandescent beacon." He considers it a "*privilege*" to "bear arms" for the "*unfailing Victory*" in which he has "absolute trust."

Michele sees no disjuncture between his ideals and the sacrifices they demand. His last letter written from the front incorporates his belief in duty and weds his faith in God to his faith in fascism. It is one of the few letters that admits to the discomforts and dangers of war, and its poignancy comes from his joy in view of his impending death.

> 13 February 1941
>> Terrible night from the 17th to the 18th. . . .
>> Now that it is passed I can tell you.—In that night, which I will remember for all my life, which I would pass entirely on foot under the snow and rain that soaked my shoes, as if my feet were in a hip bath and froze three toes.—To tell the truth it was not so much the cold or the water that made me unable to take weight off my mind, but not knowing where I will be from one day to the next.—With all this I would not abandon the front line, and my doctors at best made me take care of myself with anticoagulant and camphor massages. I do not want to say that I have suffered.—The only thing that keeps me always on my feet and always ready: faith in God and in the Duce.

Michele's idea of duty was limited to the success of fascism. Some fascist heroes were able to conceive of a notion of fascism and duty that incorporated a complicated vision of the future. Claudio N., a fascist hero from Cuneo, a small city in Piemonte, linked his vision of fascist duty to a vision of a fascist future.[51] His principal concern, both on the battlefield and off was the "education of youth," the next generation of fascists. He transformed his vision of fascism and his fascist identity into a life ethic. *La Stampa*, the Torinese daily newspaper, published Claudio's biography and letters in a full-page obituary, which the local party chief clipped and sent on to the Mostra della Rivoluzione Fascista. Because Turin was an anti-fascist stronghold and *La Stampa* had never been particularly sympathetic to fascism, Claudio's full-page treatment was remarkable.

Claudio N. was born in 1907 of what Italians would term a "good family." His father was a colonel in the Italian army, and the obituary describes the family as "bourgeois." As a student, Claudio participated in many fascist

---

[51] *ACS, PNF, MRF*, b. 3 (Cuneo). All quotations from Claudio N.'s letters and obituary are from this source.

youth organizations and was a *squadrista*. He spent fifteen years in the fascist militia. He received a *laurea* in law and won a *concorso* that permitted him to enter legal practice for the government. Married and the father of two children, he was happy to go off to war at an unknown destination even at the "cost of sacrifice," if it meant the "conquest of Empire and the defense of Fascism." He was sent to the Russian front, where he wrote a series of letters to his wife and kept a diary. After he died, his wife struck out the personal parts of the letters and the diaries and sent them to the editors of *La Stampa*.

The newspaper editor described the collection as an "archive of moral probity, noble humanity, and fascist consciousness." Claudio's writings berated the weakness of the bourgeoisie and the facile certainties of irony, yet there is a kind of irony in his biography in that the virtues the obituary writers ascribed to him are rather typically bourgeois. Claudio was "modest, extremely disciplined, scrupulous in the fulfillment of his duties (but for Claudio N., duty has no limits; he does with maximum simplicity also those acts that no rules prescribe), adored by his machine gunners, . . . usually silent . . . he loved intelligent conversations, fecund exchanges of ideas." When Claudio died, the doctor attending him testified, "He was transfigured; I felt that I had assisted at the death of a Saint." His last words uttered with "extreme certainty and an extreme invocation" were "I die for my Country."

Claudio's letters reveal an almost religious awareness of the toll of war combined with a conviction of its necessity. Writing to his wife, he noted that glorifications of war are "fantasies of romance writers," whereas the truth was somewhat less glowing. Yet he was happy to serve the fascist revolution, asserting, "What times we live in! Hard, but worthy to have lived." According to Claudio, life was a "divine gift" that "imposed responsibilities, duties, and sacrifices." His favorite phrase was "Life is a mission." The "olympic Claudio N." was so committed to the fascist cause that after marching in the "dust, mud, and snow," he felt "fresh as a rose" because of the good he was doing.

Claudio's major preoccupation, differentiating him from the other heroes, was his concern for the future and the education of the young. In his diary, he meditated on the bourgeoisie and its failures. Sounding as much like a socialist as a fascist, he mused that the bourgeoisie was in "substance" full of "errors, of ambitions, of greed for the few." The fascist solution to the problem of bourgeois society lay in the merging of public and private spheres; the family hand and hand with the state would create the new fascist future: "The [fascist] Revolution has to isolate it [bourgeois society], strike it, eliminate it. It is a problem of education that ought to join fathers and mothers of families in the work of the State." Irony, which he views as a particular cultural gift of the bourgeoisie, should be avoided at all costs for its facile solutions to difficult problems. Claudio's letter echoed fascist family policy and evoked Giacomo Acerbo's speech at the first anniversary of the March on Rome and Augusto Turati's speech in Verona in 1926.

In his final letter to his wife, Claudio exhorted her to take care of the children and to make them aware of the virtues of a fascist life. His children represented the future of Italy as well as his personal future. Producing children was a duty of a fascist man that was consonant with the duty to fight the enemy.[52] Having fulfilled both duties, Claudio was sanguine about his fate on the battlefield:

> I do not know what destiny will bring. I do not dare to predict the end from now because it is not necessary to abuse good fortune. . . . But we are spiritually prepared, is not that so? I feel that if am doing all my duty as an Italian man, that this is my post. God willing that I will be able to help you to raise our two children in a healthy and good manner; it is the greatest task of our two lives; and also for them that lie here wounded I want on the delicate subject of example that our little children always have respect for their papa. And you too—also when you see other tranquil and happy youth—do not think that in these great times, that I would be content at home and do not ever doubt the honor and affection of your Claudio.

"Educate our children in the faith of their father"

The twin themes of education and family appeared in letters that lacked Claudio's breadth of vision. Among the less formally educated, these themes emerged as a chant, suggesting that education and family were deeply embedded in fascist consciousness. For example, Roberto O., an elementary schoolteacher, and Luigi P., a land surveyor, merged the idea of education with distinctly fascist organizations and symbols. Roberto was thirty-eight years old when he died in Albania in 1940. Married with one child, he had volunteered for combat in Spain, where he had received military honors, and volunteered again to go to Albania.

Roberto O. was sentimental and sentimentalized in his obituaries. His letters reveal a simple belief in Mussolini and fascism. His concept of educating his children consisted of admonishing them to learn appropriate fascist words and to repeat them in chantlike fashion. He tells his wife: "Educate our little son in the faith of his father. Teach him to spell at the same time the first names: Virgin, papa, mamma: Italy, Italy."[53] When Roberto was wounded, he "shouted," "Good-bye to all, long live the Duce, long live Italy!" As he lay on his deathbed, he kissed the picture of his wife and child and again cried out, "Long live Italy!" His biographers described him as the "purest soul among believers and heroes" and continued in this sentimental vein: "He was always the best among us; he who had always a smile on his lips, serenity of heart; we have always admired in him his great faith in God, his overflowing, ardent love of Patria, the goodwill of his soul, his courage."

The love of country and devotion to fascism of Roberto is elegiac in contrast to that of the university-educated heroes. He uses the language of romance and emotion and speaks of Italy as one would a lover. He tells his wife that although he feels a certain "nostalgia" for home, he has to confess that he experiences a stronger attraction to the demands of the Patria.

But a grander duty, a more ardent love in addition to my love for you and my son and that shares with that love in the same time and with the same sentiment of passion. This love of Patria, this sentiment of Italianness, which helps me bear every inconvenience, every sacrifice, for the good, the grandness of Italy, and which ties us like a pure golden thread to you far away, to the family.

His love of country and his identity as a fascist superseded his identity as a husband and father. Unlike other fascists, Roberto was able to link this identity to his participation in fascist organizations and activities. He continued to his wife:

I repeat to you until infinity, my affection is tied to another noble and grand sentiment: love of Patria. You know, Clara, when I spoke to your fascist women and *massaie rurali* and to my fascists, you learned this affection, this passion that vibrated in my every word, and in every rally I saw you cry, Clara, your ROBERTO did not feel alone, but carried out, I was carrying out, have carried out such words in a life lived in trenches and ditches. I love, Clara, my Italy, a grand, free, independent Italy, lord of its seas and of its own life, not a servile Italy. I wish yet again to shout it in the piazza.

Roberto clearly links his love of Italy to his activities in fascist organizations and events. His position as secretary of his local *fascio* and his public activities as head of that organization reinforced his identity as a fascist, which superseded his concern for his wife's tears when he addressed local fascist

---

[53] *ACS, PNF, MRF*, b. 9 (Pesaro). All quotations from Roberto O.'s letters are from this source.

groups. Italy as an imperial entity was a future reality that surpassed the present reality of his wife and child. Roberto accepted the myth of Italian servility that Mussolini used to justify military aggression.

If assembling the masses in the piazza fueled Roberto O.'s love of country and fascist identity, Luigi P., the surveyor, articulated his patriotism in terms of the fascist black shirt. Luigi P. was born in 1902 in a small village near the city of Asti in Piemonte.[54] He died at the age of thirty-nine in Greece, making him somewhat older than the other heroes. He was a fascist *squadrista* from 1921, which meant he was part of fascism from its pre-regime days. His biographer uses the language of religion to describe Luigi's devotion to fascism, noting that Luigi had the "most ardent faith" and that "for every day of his exemplary life, comrade LUIGI P. remained faithful to the principles of our doctrine, intransigence itself, loyal to and consistent with the commandments of Mussolini. One can well affirm that his existence constituted a daily ascent toward the highest and noblest values of a life that cherishes Fascism."

God, family, and country dominated Luigi's cultural frame of reference. A series of letters to his wife merged his religious and fascist identity. Luigi "confides" in "GOD" and "asks" "GOD" for victory for the Patria and the strength to do his duty. He reports on the religious life of the battlefront, recounting how the field chaplain created a little chapel to keep the soldiers "near to GOD and to receive in any moment the Confirmed in our Religion." In his "spiritual" last will and testament, Luigi exhorts his wife to make "GOD" and "PATRIA" the basis of his children's education and cautions her that they should not become "cowardly" or develop an "overly bourgeois spirit." For Luigi, the consolation of being with old friends, comrades in the fascist struggle, and a belief in God overcomes the hardships of life at the front. He links the idea of duty to the common struggle: "I think that I will do my duty to the utmost and when I return I will be satisfied. . . . I have found myself among old friends. These friendships are living moments and create ties that will remain throughout life."

The symbols of fascism and religion embodied Luigi's devotion to God and country and provided frames for articulating the importance of these intertwining identities. In a letter to his wife dated March 23, 1941, he recounted how the anniversary of the founding of the Fighting Fascists was celebrated on the battlefield. This was one of the legal holidays the regime had created, and memorial services were held throughout Italy. Luigi tells how Roberto Farinacci, a member of the Grand Council noted for his propensity to violence and intransigence, visited the camp to speak to the Black

---

[54] *ACS, PNF, MRF*, b. 1 (Asti). All quotations from Luigi P.'s obituary and letters are from this source.

Shirts about military virtue. The traditional mass in the field was celebrated to commemorate the dead. Luigi discussed the event in terms of the wearing of the black shirt: in Italy, he mused, all fascists were required to wear the black shirt on this date, but on the battlefield "we wear it day and night. Certain that here fascists (in a manner of speaking) disgust [the enemy]. And in comparing the difference of sentiment of those who live a life of war and those who live in tranquility, it is marvelous to observe the faith that always accompanies a fighter in the victory of our Patria and DUCE."

On April 17, Luigi wrote his last letter to his wife. He equated the exhilaration he felt at the beginning of the Easter holiday with the exhilaration he felt in anticipation of a fascist victory. For Luigi, the Christian redemption at the death and resurrection of Christ suggests the redemption of the fascist nation through military victory.

Dear Nina,
Finally the hour of advancing begins and it will conclude with the total destruction of the Greeks and English.
What a magnificent Easter! In the morning we began our movement with a sign of indescribable joy.
Everything embraces us. Easter has been our redemption.
Believe me, dear Nina, that if a desire to cry from emotion overtakes you, I am content, even extremely happy to be able to continue this march of victory.
. . . And now to us!

The phrase "to us" (*a noi* in Italian) was the fascist victory chant in 1922. Luigi deliberately conflated it in his letter with his personal relationship with his wife. The victory over the English will at once establish fascism as a world power and provide a personal family victory.

"There will not be a human force"

The commentary on the letters and life of Pietro S. conflated God, faith, and fascism, and this fascist hero was represented as a divine force.[55] Pietro S. was born in 1905 in a small village near Verona and died in 1941 in Africa. His involvement in the early fascist movement is described in terms of a religious vocation. In 1920, at the age of fifteen, he heard the "voice of the Patria" calling him, and at the "dawn of resurrection" that the fascist revolution promised, he joined the "fascist apostolate." "From that moment, he served Mussolini's idea, professing it with absolute coherence, his life grow-

---

[55] *ACS, PNF, MRF,* b. 12 (Verona). All quotations from Pietro S.'s obituary and letters from this source.

ing with the growing fortune of Fascism." The narrative structure of point-counterpoint that interspersed details of Pietro's biography with his letters suggested an image of fascism as religious practice and war as its principal rite of purification.

Pietro S. was described as a fascist monk. He entered the fascist militia at the age of fifteen and distinguished himself by being a "team member" who displayed "perfect obedience." As he advanced through the ranks of the local fascist paramilitary organizations, his capacity for "discipline" grew and he developed an "exquisite fascist sense." "Serene" and "indefatigable," Pietro put his apostolic zeal into the education of youth, which he approached with "force of faith" and "passion of action." He was remembered for leading his youth squads with "pride" as they marched through the town and for his presence at sports competitions.

War was a source of joy for Pietro, and he eagerly enlisted in the army when Italy declared war. Like any Christian saint, he was willing to shed his blood for the fascist cause. The Fascist Party chief drew on religious metaphors to describe Pietro's commitment to fascism:

> Convinced that the sacrifice of blood was necessary to the fulfillment of Italian claims, when Italy decided to enter in struggle with the magnificent weight of its warlike power, he enlisted content and happy to share his regiment's fate. . . . He wanted ardently to participate in the struggle against the enemy and when his regiment was designated to participate in the operations on African soil, it proved a great joy, feeling that all his desires were finally fulfilled and granted.

In a letter to his wife, Pietro's own voice provides the counterpoint to that of the party chief: "Do not cry, you know that it has always been the goal of my life; you know that I have waited always for this day, that today, more than ever, the Patria remains deeply in my heart and above all in my thoughts." His secular faith in fascism united with his sacred faith in God transcends and reinforces his duties as husband and father: "I also unite my prayers with yours and those of our children and I pray fervently to God that he give me the strength to carry out completely until the end all my duties." The party chief commented that, these words "in their sublime simplicity reveal the complete heroism of a soul nourished and raised in ideals that have given his entire life a magnificent synthesis."

In a letter to his local Fascist Party head, Pietro described his faith in his mission:

> In these last days, we have advanced much in the firing zone. . . . My spirit and that of my "infantrymen" is always very elevated, we are animated by

the same will: "WIN"; the radiant spring promised us by our DUCE, advances and with it our wonderful Victory. This is the certainty of everyone, this is the reality that leads the way. The DUCE's memorable speech of a few days ago was heard and read by all with the most vibrant attention and the most indescribable enthusiasm. I send an embrace accompanied by a formidable "TO US."[56]

The Fascist Party chief responded:

His infantrymen were ready! his company was all covered. "Feathers to the wind, enemy in flight," this was the motto. To his soldiers he had given all of himself and they believed in him, they returned his love equally. Because his was not only team spirit, but the instinctive need to nourish those around him, proselytizing the miracle that faith can fulfill in the field of action. Like an apostle, he carried to his men the ardor that totally consumed him internally; life and victory had formed in him an indissoluble couple: he could not sustain one without the other.

The metaphor of the body and the spirit governs the biographer's interpretation. His gloss of Pietro's animation plays with images of the body and the spirit in a way that invokes the secular and sacred and merges the boundary between the physical and the spiritual, between fascist ideals and the fascist body. The English translation "team spirit" does not do justice to the fact that the Italian, like the French, phrase is translated literally as "spirit of bodies" (*spirito di corpi*), suggesting the solidarity that emerges from bodies being physically proximate in pursuit of a common goal. Indeed, Pietro nourished his men with his ideals.

But Pietro is also an "apostle" consumed with the burning desire to advance the fascist cause on the battlefield and to shed his own blood if necessary. The leap from apostle to Christ figure is not far. In Christian iconography, the twelve apostles gathered around Christ at the Last Supper, an extremely popular religious image in Italy. In glossing this letter, the fascist biographer rhetorically transforms Pietro into a saint; his body, which will soon be mangled by enemy bullets, as Christ's was by Roman nails, is transformed into a spiritual entity.

When Pietro wrote his last letter to the federal secretary, his mental transformation was complete, and he defined himself in spiritual and superhuman terms:

[56] Pietro's letter is dated March 4, 1941. The speech of Mussolini to which he is referring was made on March 2, 1941, while the leader was reviewing troops on the Albanian front. See Benito Mussolini, "Colloquio con Il Generale Geloso al posto tattico trentaquattro in Albania," in *Dall'Intervento dell'Italia nella seconda guerra mondiale al discorso al direttorio nazionale del P.N.F. dell 3 gennaio 1942*, vol. 30, *OO*, 60–64.

This simple wartime postcard brings you not only my affectionate greeting but also wants to tell you about the spirit of those that have the great honor to bear arms for the Patria against the enemy. Distance no longer exists. We are awaiting the order to attack, we are impatient, but we know how to conserve our strength. And the conviction deeply rooted in all of us that once the way is given we will never stop. It is necessary to hear the speeches of our soldiers to convince us that *there will not be a human force* [emphasis added] that will stop the fascist youth of Mussolini's Italy.

The biographer's gloss on Pietro's words, "the purest heart of this hero felt the victory that nourished him daily," combined the hero's body and soul in one image. Pietro S. died in Tobruk at the head of his troops, "falling with a great vision of the enemy in flight."

"Finally I feel a man"

Pietro S. self-consciously merged devotion to fascism with an ascetic discipline that transcended family obligation. The party chief's representation underscored this fascist asceticism by transforming him from fascist saint to Christ figure. War was the fulfillment of the fascist mission for Pietro, the end point of his life and devotion to the fascist cause. For Pietro, who died at age thirty-six, the war was the end of the fascist journey. In contrast, for Carlo T., a bachelor who died at the age of twenty-four, war was a rite of purification and the principal vehicle for initiating him into manhood and adult responsibility.[57]

Carlo T. was one of the more educated of the fascist heroes, and his letters are more evocative of those of the bachelor Franco L. than of his older and less intellectual married compatriots. Carlo attended a *liceo classico*, the top tier of the Italian secondary school system, dedicated to broad humanistic learning, and received a bachelor's degree in law. From his adolescence, he was active in fascist cultural organizations and wrote on art and the cinema for several local fascist periodicals. His articles bore such titles as "Youth in the Present Hour," "The New University Spirit," and "Youth and Culture."

Unlike the other fascist heroes, he left an "extremely noble war diary, which was a sublime life lesson," from which the party chief extracted key letters. The chief described a letter Carlo wrote on the death of a colleague as a "superb document, worthy of being handed down to generations of Italians." History has made moot the chief's hyperbolic assessment; nevertheless, Carlo exhibited literary gifts. He rendered his emotions in a more powerful and cogent manner than his less educated comrades, and as a result

[57] *ACS, PNF, MRF*, b. 9 (Ravenna).

what appears sentimental and naive in the other letters is more urbane and intellectual in his.

The classic letter written to his friend Paolo on the death of his comrade Marco articulated religious themes that his diary reiterated. Carlo described combat as "primordial cruelty," and this is the closest any of the heroes came to the war-is-hell metaphor. He says he "does not know how to cry on the destiny of our friends. Their heroic death arouses me and increases my impatience. Perhaps I would not believe my own words, but I think that our mediocrity is preferable to the light of their heroism." Comparing the love of country to a love affair, he says: "It is beautiful to give freely, to give all for one's love: They [the fascist dead] are in love with our Patria and with consciousness, they are dematerialized to be with Their Spirit, Idea." He invokes the image of Saint Frances, whom he "understands and reveres." Saint Frances apparently died without speaking, as did Marco, which kept him from making the ultimate fascist "offering"—to die shouting "Viva l'Italia!"—and barred him from receiving the military honor of the gold medal.

On the death of another comrade, Carlo articulates the religious meaning of the "offering" and merges it with the image of blood that dominated Pietro S.'s letters and obituaries. In writing of his dead colleague, Carlo notes, using the capital usually reserved for the Deity, "His offering assumed the value of a symbol, His blood left a trace to follow," and remembers the Duce's words that "only the sacrifice of blood is truly great and worthy." All fascist martyrs participated in the secular sacrifice for their country and in the sacred sacrifice of Christ—the offertory of the Catholic Mass, in which blood and heroism merge.

In contrast to the condolence letters, Carlo's occasional letters to Paolo reveal a vision of war as a masculine rite of purification. Unlike Franco L., who viewed war as a party, Carlo's liminal space suggests the cult of virility.[58] In a series of letters from Christmas 1941 to the spring of 1942 written principally to male friends, Carlo tried to reconcile the discipline that war required with the hedonistic pleasures of youth. War becomes a vehicle of personal purification and a bridge to responsible adulthood as well as a

[58] George L. Mosse's discussion of "manliness" juxtaposes the idea of homosexuality and the cult of the Virgin. Mosse argues that manliness represented a return to aristocratic knightly virtues. See *Nationalism and Sexuality: Respectability and Abnormal Sexuality in Modern Europe* (New York: Fertig, 1985), 23–47. Although there was plenty of manliness in the exploits of both Mussolini and his predecessor Gabriel D'Annunzio, and "manliness" and "virile" appear regularly in Italian fascist tracts, it is not clear that one can apply the same arguments to Latin Italy that one applies to northern Europe, particularly Germany. On this issue, see Barbara Spackman, "The Fascist Rhetoric of Virility," *Stanford Italian Review* 8 (1990), 81–102.

method of international purgation. On the eve of his departure for the African front, he wrote to his "dearest" friend:

> I am happy, Paolo. Now I am no longer ashamed of my small past, but I see a perfect continuity between my fascist faith and my soldier's faith. I would have a thousand things to tell you, but today, who knows why, the pen refuses to serve me.
>
> I seem to have lost the agility of my hands.
>
> But you imagine and know. You know how proud and content, you know that *finally I feel a man* [emphasis added].
>
> When you receive this, I will be already there. I will have taken the plunge and touched the earth of our Africa.

The death of his comrade Marco pushes Carlo to articulate the full extent of his emotions over the war as a vehicle of masculine development. Again writing to Paolo, he says: "I feel a great need to purify myself in war, in this very beautiful war that seems to express the most ancient values of our race. I am tired of vanity, mediocrity. I want to live, live, live. Also in falling one lives. Maybe only then one plucks the values and the juice of all existence." Carlo also feels the need to use war as a patriotic means to rid the world of those who would hinder Italian grandeur. He expresses this idea before leaving for the front:

> But in Italy there is something that is absolute and pressing that animates it, dominates it, pushes it to fight for a higher idea. It is the future.
>
> I also will make war, if they will allow me, for a more just, more noble, and more clean future.
>
> To do a good cleaning it is necessary to become immersed in the brooms and the garbage.
>
> . . . I feel strong and ready as in June, last year, when in the piazza in Ravenna, under the rain, among the silent anguish of many, I would cry, Long live the war. I have the same animation as then. Because even then, I saw the filth and injustice.
>
> We ought not to look to the living but to our dead that have guided us and are guiding us.

Carlo's letters were filled with masculine bravado; his personal diaries were fraught with anxieties and visions of Catholicism and religion. In his diary, Carlo sounds like any sixteenth-century Protestant. He worries that his character needs "forging" and regrets his former life, which he characterizes as dominated by "hedonism and laziness." The experience of being at the front will discipline him and wipe out his former ways. In contrast to the talk of manhood, virility, and bravado that dominated the letters to his friend Paolo, the diary reveals a deep reliance on the mythology of Catholicism to sustain him at the front.

In an entry made shortly before Christmas, Carlo wrote that an "unknown world seems to be opening" before him and that his letters reveal only "a bit" of his "soul." He says, "I feel the need to recollect myself for a moment in church and to pray for Italy, for mine, for me. I ask strength and serenity. And that which is necessary for me." But he finds that the feeling of dislocation which comes from being on the battlefield has caused him to forget the "Our Father." On New Year's day, Carlo writes about his struggle to give up even the longing for the "hedonistic" life that the war has forced him to abandon:

> I passed the last night of the year in my tent, thinking of distant persons and things. It seemed impossible to me that someone would be able to find oneself in a well-heated, secure place with women and champagne [*spumante*]. Instead in Italy who knows how many partied. My infantrymen did not even wait for midnight. They slept soundly in their holes, accustomed by now to ignore parties and holidays. Maybe they dreamed of family, home, friends. Home, they who for thirty months sleep on the bare earth, covered at most by the canvas of a tent.
>
> From the 24th to the 31st of December it rained. Raindrops on the canvas of my tent were the music of my solitary holiday. And it felt sweet and sufficient to feel the heat of the covers, while it rained outside.

Carlo seeks spiritual comfort in the mythology of Roman Catholicism. His diary displayed a familiarity with biblical lore that reflected twenty-four years of socialization in both Catholicism and fascism. For example, he exhibited deep knowledge of a Gospel story the chaplain recounted, the story of Christ calming a storm at sea. Christ is sleeping on a boat with his twelve apostles while a storm rages around them. The apostles, overcome by fear, wake him and exhort him, "Save us, Master!" To which Christ responds, "Men of little faith, why do you fear?" and then raises his hands and calms the storm. The army chaplain makes the connection:

> Also here, in Africa, a great tempest for our troops.
> Also here the invocation: "Save us, Master!" "Men of little faith, why do you fear?" Peace will come with the victory of the most just and the most strong. It will come because God is with us.

The differences among Carlo's three narratives—the commemorative letters, the letters to friends, and the diary entries—are striking and revealing.

The commemorative letters, like the party chiefs' obituaries, rely on the metaphor of the broken, bloodied body of Christ; the letters to Paulo represent a youthful bravado and desire to see war as a rite of passage and virility; and the diary reveals a genuine reliance on the myths of Catholicism.

"She fixed her beautiful luminous eyes on high peaks"

Carlo T.'s multiple voice is striking when juxtaposed against the fascist heroine who has no voice. Letitia M. was a twenty-six-year-old schoolteacher who died in a communist "terrorist attack" in the city of Fiume in 1942.[59] Fiume was border city that had been in dispute since the turn of the century, and the official obituaries are written in Italian and a Slavic language. The Fascist Party daily order sheet dated June 1942 bore a photograph of Letitia M. in her party uniform and described her as the director of the Rural Housewives' Organization (Massaie Rurali) of Lubiana.

The mourning flowers that were planted for the fascist heroine who was "cut off in the springtime of her life" are "full of passion" because they are "watered by tears and nourished by blood." The woman who heads the local fascist women's organization (Fascio Femminile) wrote an obituary that described Letitia as a fascist nun. Virility and Christlike grandeur dominated the male accounts of death; purity and virginity suffused the representation of Letitia M. She displayed "infinite goodness," "unstoppable faith," and "youthful enthusiasm" as she "consecrated" her life in the year proceeding her death to the "rural population," who viewed her as "the purest and highest expression of Fascism." Death may have "struck down a fragile life, but her soul was elected to ascend to shine in the heavens of Martyrs and of Heroes." Letitia "gave" to the "Revolution" until "her last breath . . . the best part of herself."

Letitia pursued one of the few careers open to women of lower-middle-class origin—life as a schoolteacher. It was membership and participation in the Fascist Party and its organizations that gave whatever social mobility was possible to a single woman in fascist Italy. At age twenty-six when she died, she was well on her way to spinsterhood.[60] Letitia belonged to fascist gymnastic, sporting, and cultural organizations from her youth. She was the first woman in Trieste to win a prize, the cross of merit. Despite her youth, she was a leader, and even those older than she in these organizations turned to her for guidance. In part, it was her religious commitment to fascism as a

---

[59] *ACS, PNF, MRF*, b. 4 (Fiume). All quotations about Letitia M. are from this source.

[60] For a comparative demographic analysis of spinsterhood, see Susan Cotts Watkins, "Spinsters," *Journal of Family History* (1984), 310–25, esp. 314. For a discussion of spinsters in modern Italy, see Maura Palazzi, "Female Solitude and Patrilineage: Unmarried Women and Widows during the Eighteenth and Nineteenth Centuries," *Journal of Family History* 15 (1990), 443–59.

style of life that gave her authority and distinguished her from her peers, who realized that she was "different" and "at a higher level because [she was] more intimately fused with that which [was] the faith that dominated the most alluring segment of Italians, the faith in Fascism and in its DUCE which she has served, in purity, until the last hour of her life."

She became a schoolteacher and received a bronze medal from the National Ministry of Education for her considerable work as "pioneer of Italianness [*italianità*] and fascist faith." During the summers, when school was not in session, she worked in fascist youth colonies where she became famous for singing patriotic songs to the children. The long description of her character and personality on the concluding page of her commemorative obituary portrays Letitia as a person who has no identity outside her commitment to fascism. This notion of a lack of identity beyond one's ideological mission is common to descriptions of the politically committed, but it is also a feature of the personality of the Catholic nun. The idea of personality is not even applicable, because it implies individuality, and Letitia, in contrast to her male counterparts, completely surrenders herself to her dedication to fascism.

In the last year of her life, Letitia worked for the Rural Housewives' Association. There is a certain irony in the ideal fascist spinster's helping rural women rationalize or fascisticize their gender roles as mothers and housekeepers. Letitia gave the rural housewives the "treasures of her intelligence, of her goodness and her limitless faith," yet in all this activity she kept her personality "hidden" "behind a smiling mask of joking conversations." Despite her hidden self, her dedication to office work, propaganda, and the problems of rural life was "prodigious" in a "thousand ways." Photographs of Letitia M. support this assessment of her character (see Figures 20 and 21). Pictured gazing adoringly at the local priest or rolling bandages with other fascist women, she seems to have walked two steps behind everyone else: she existed to labor and not to be the center of attention. What the fascist local chief does not add and that the pictures bear out is that, by the standards of 1940s Italy, Letitia is physically rather unattractive. Her soul may be beautiful but her person is not. Although her eyes stand out in the pictures, her plain appearance makes a sharp contrast to her fascist sisters, who work by her side for the local Red Cross. In fact, the more attractive women appear patently bored by their wartime activity while she is obviously engaged. In a culture where there was a clearly defined marriage market, Letitia seems to have had only her fascist organizations to give her life meaning.

The conclusion of the party chief's letter transformed Letitia into a fascist saint by offering a prayerlike incantation to her. In a culture where women marry and saints are virgins, Letitia achieved the pinnacle of cultural and

Figure 20. Letitia M. *ACS, PNF, MRF,* b. 4 (Fiume).

political success in her death, as the party chief said in closing, "And in everything that we do, You will be our small unforgettable one. Guide to our actions, comfort in our work, light of our souls, we only ask to imitate you, in the name of the DUCE and in the holy name of our Patria." The capitalization of "you" implies Letitia's secular canonization, and the form of the incantation suggests Catholic prayers to saints as models for future action. The ending evokes the words from the Sign of the Cross—"In the name of the Father, and of the Son, and of the Holy Ghost"—which is recited at the beginning and the end of all Roman Catholic prayers.

Letitia received a public funeral in Trieste which merited a page of reporting in the inside section of *Il Piccolo di Trieste,* the local newspaper. The headlines read in bold print, "Trieste Saluted the Corpse of Letitia M. with a Unanimous Demonstration of Fascist Faith."[61] Her death was used to dramatize the perfidy of the traditional fascist enemies, the communists. The

---

[61] *Il Piccolo di Trieste* (Trieste), 14 June 1942, 3.

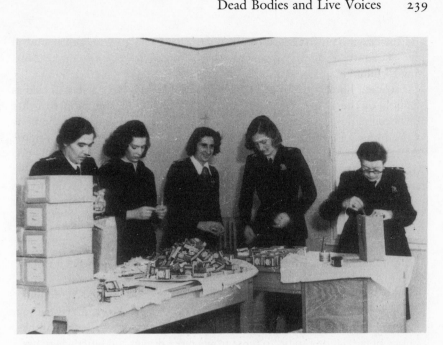

Figure 21. Letitia M. at work. *ACS, PNF, MRF,* b. 4 (Fiume).

funeral received national recognition in the form of the attendance of two dignitaries: the National Fascist Party secretary and Giuseppe Bottai, the national minister of education. The account suggests that Letitia is more an icon than a personality. The newspaper described the funeral with the emotional language that dominated all fascist discourse, but in a subtle shift in rhetorical style the feminine language of tears replaced the masculine language of bravado.

Letitia's funeral set off a "wave of collective emotion" in Trieste, where "thousands of tears streamed down the faces of the crowd as the white coffin in which the ripped flesh of the Martyr was arranged" passed by.[62] This is the only mention of her body, and from the account it becomes clear that she is invisible except as a rallying point for the devotion of fascist mothers and a symbol of political strife on the frequently contested Austrian-Italian border. The crowds that lined the street as the coffin was carried from the central train station to the cathedral, where the bishop officiated at a solemn high mass, was composed of "common faces" of "laborers, salesgirls, office workers, and above all good mothers; faces of simple and pure creatures, who in the morning hour have left their work and their hard

[62] Ibid.

and uncertain daily existence to create an act of solidarity in sorrow and in love of country as only a people and its most noble flowers, a woman, knows how to fulfill."

If women have a special gift for emotion, they also have a special role as symbols of the nation.[63] In Italy this secular tradition, common to other European nations, is lacking, but its sacred counterpart is found in the body of the Blessed Virgin Mary, the Mother of Christ, who is a virtual cult figure in Italian Catholic culture.[64] In the representation of the funeral of Letitia M., the mother and the nation come together in the same way as in the letters of the fascist heroes, the wedding ring campaign, and the numerous public ceremonies that made up the body of fascist ritual. The newspaper account argued that the sacrifice of Letitia's life would implant Trieste, a border city, in the Italian national struggle.

> But in addition to sentiment there is a political reality that merits medita-tion. And the political reality is represented in the full consciousness with which Trieste never so much as today is worthy to be called "a faithful follower of Rome" participating in this war on all fronts, from this closest to us, where this insidious, cowardly, and treacherous aggression has taken the place of fair fighting spirit, to those fronts more distant and bitter where her most stout-hearted and nobly daring children write pages of insurmount-able heroism.[65]

The death of Letitia M. at the hands of local terrorists was important because it placed Trieste in the Italian camp and created a symbolic bridge between the soldiers who gave their life in the war and the mothers of those soldiers.

> The mothers, the wives, the children that yesterday accompanied the corpse of Letitia M. with a Roman salute that formed a superb arch of force and human gentleness, are the mothers, wives, sisters of soldiers, of sailors, of pilots, and of Black Shirts laboring in the hardest struggle ever recorded in the history of our Patria. In their salute vibrated the will of victory of their

---

[63] There is no woman who stands as a national symbol of Italy, but it was quite common in other countries to use the woman's body to convey national solidarity; see, for example, Maurice Agulhon, *Marianne into Battle: Republican Imagery and Symbolism in France, 1789–1890*, trans. Janet Lloyd (rpt., New York: Cambridge University Press, 1981), esp. 122–34, on the connection between Marianne and the Blessed Virgin Mary.

[64] The cult of the Virgin Mary is deeply ingrained in Italian culture. The history of its significance for the modern period has not yet been written. For the premodern period, see Michael P. Carroll, *The Cult of the Virgin Mary* (Princeton: Princeton University Press, 1986), and *Madonnas That Maim: Popular Catholicism in Italy since the Fifteenth Century* (Baltimore: Johns Hopkins University Press, 1992).

[65] *Il Piccolo di Trieste*, 14 June 1942, 3.

sons, of their husbands far away; vibrated a faith that the enemy will never be able to conquer or scorn.[66]

Soldiers who give their lives in national war achieve importance by nature of their sacrifice. This is why the tombs of the unknown soldiers have achieved such prominence and also why it does not really matter who is in them. But even in a field where personality is secondary to membership in the community, Letitia M. is curiously invisible, in part because she belongs to a group—unmarried women—that ultimately had no place in either Italian or fascist culture.

Gender, Identity, and the Imagery of Death

In contrast to the fascist heroes, Letitia M. is rendered invisible, and her invisibility provides the link in the story between fascist political identities and long-standing cultural identities. Letitia M. has no voice, no body, and no family. She is completely a construction of others. Elaine Scarry makes the point that "to have a body is, finally, to permit oneself to be described."[67] As a spinster, Letitia M. was socially and culturally invisible; her body was beyond description. As Victoria De Grazia describes the condition of spinsterhood in fascist or even nonfascist Italy, to be a spinster was a fate worse than death:

> The *signorina* approaching thirty was fast becoming a *zitella*, haunted by the specter of spinsterdom, which in the public mind carried more than a social stigma. It denoted a moral and physical state, "an inability to inspire sentiments, because of physical defects, bad character, or lack of dowry." It signaled the arrival of an age in life when love was "no longer in season." The status of being single was made worse under the dictatorship. Fascism publicly stigmatized women who were not wives and mothers. Moreover, in urban areas, low pay and the lack of decent housing made it impossible to live outside the family residence. In rural areas . . . failing to marry meant "a life as spinsters, as maiden aunts, or as servants, which was more or less the same thing."[68]

Letitia M.'s death was passive, an accident of being in the wrong place at the wrong time. With the exception of the one newspaper reference to her torn-

---

[66] Ibid.

[67] Elaine Scarry, *The Body in Pain: The Making and Unmaking of the World* (New York: Oxford University Press, 1985), 216.

[68] De Grazia, *How Fascism Ruled Women*, 128. Quotations are from Anna Garofalo, *L'italiana in Italia* (Bari: Laterza, 1956), 50–51.

apart body (she was killed by a terrorist bomb), she was pure spirit; her soul and her intelligence, intangible qualities, were the only characteristics mentioned. Her body was sacred and invisible, except for her "luminous eyes" that gazed on the heavens. More strikingly, for a woman who spent her entire life in fascist organizations, where amateur writing was the norm and where it is hard to imagine that she did not write something down, there was not a letter or a written thought that the Fascist Party chief thought worthy of noting or saving.

In jarring contrast to the male heroes, she was portrayed as entirely without family. Letitia M. may have been an orphan, but we do not know that; in fact, we know absolutely nothing about her family background. Although she clearly merited attention, she was not important for herself; the self in Letitia's case was denied. This absence might be attributed to missing data or faulty evidence if the stories of the male fascist heroes were not available for comparison. The heroes had voice. Their bodies in their stricken and pre-stricken state were described, and they always, even the bachelors, had families, particularly mothers.

Letitia M. was depicted in virginal terms and as such evoked the Virgin Mary, not the Christ figure of the men. The Virgin Mary in Catholic iconography is important because of her role in giving birth to Christ, the Son of God. Letitia M. gave birth to nothing and thus serves only as an icon—an icon that reinforces the sacrifice of the mothers, the purveyors of cultural power. The mothers are sacred in the letters of the heroes, and when these men address their wives, it is in their roles as mothers. Sexuality of women was invisible until it resulted in fertility, but sexuality was quite visible in the language of virility and emotion that dominated the descriptions of fascist heroes and public events.

Letitia M. was important as a cultural cipher that forced the mothers into the streets to assert their solidarity with the regime. As a spinster, she achieved her only social importance by dying. Paradoxically, fascism provided women such as Letitia some economic and political power as they worked at jobs in the public sphere.[69] But social and cultural power was reserved for the mothers. The regime was somewhat schizophrenic in its position on women. On one hand, it wished women to work as part of the modernization project, and on the other, it initiated demographic policies that taxed bachelors and gave monetary rewards to mothers of large families. As disciplined fascist bodies lay in shambles on the battlefield, it was the mother as the producer of new fascist bodies that had power in this story. Thus, the offering of the mothers of their sons to the nation takes precedence to the death of the spinster.

[69] De Grazia, *How Fascism Ruled Women*, 166–200.

Fascist Identity and the Rules of the Cultural Game

In contrast to the preceding chapters, this chapter focused on the fascist body as emblematic of the fascist self. The obituaries and letters replaced the fascist bodies parading in public space; the fascist body torn apart by enemy grenades replaced the disciplined fascist body politic.[70] The transformed fascist body was a metaphor for the success and failure of the fascist regime as an international political actor. Nation as self and self as nation fused.

The representation of the dead body in the public narratives—obituaries, party handbooks, and even theater—merged political and religious meaning. The secular body of the fascist *squadrista* in death became the sacred body of the dead "hero."[71] The language that described the transformed bodies evoked the image of the ruined and battered body of the crucified Christ and underscored the power of Catholicism as popular cultural practice. The salience of mothers in public and private narratives reasserted the cultural importance of the cult of motherhood and raised issues of gender, sexuality, and power in Italian, and fascist, culture.[72]

The voices of the heroes suggest that they conceived of themselves as fascist to the extent that they could articulate this identity in terms of the two noncontingent identities they already possessed: their family and religious identities. In short, they conceived of their fascist selves as a melding of these prior and salient identities. To the degree that they could see the Patria as a family and church, the heroes were Italian and fascist. Although they readily railed against the socialist and liberal bourgeois enemy, they never articulated their selves as workers and citizens of a new corporativist fascist national state. The fascist project, anticlerical at heart, never stamped out attachment to the Catholic Church, and the Patria never truly replaced the family. The post-fascist period, in which political arrangements de-

---

[70] On images of war and the broken body, see Scarry, *Body in Pain*.

[71] Owing to the influence of Michel Foucault, the body is becoming an object of theoretical inquiry in social analysis. For a review of this literature, see Roy Porter, "History of the Body," in *New Perspectives on Historical Writing*, ed. Peter Burke (University Park: Pennsylvania State University Press, 1991), 206–32, and Bryan S. Turner, *The Body and Society* (London: Blackwell, 1984). In her discussion of pornography, Lynn Hunt observes that the sacralization of the body, and by extension the soldier's body, is an Enlightenment phenomenon. See "Introduction: Obscenity and the Origins of Modernity, 1500–1800," in *The Invention of Pornography* (New York: Zone, 1993), 9–45. Claude Lefort, *The Political Forms of Modern Society*, trans. John B. Thompson (Cambridge: MIT Press, 1986), 292–306, makes the point that totalitarian states offer a new image of the body politic which is somewhat suggestive of but not congruous with my notion of fascist community.

[72] De Grazia, *How Fascism Ruled Women*, the definitive work on women during this period, only partially discusses the cultural significance of motherhood. A comparable work on nazi Germany but less culturally nuanced than De Grazia's is Claudia Koonz, *Mothers in the Fatherland: Women, the Family, and Nazi Politics* (New York: St. Martin's Press, 1987).

pended on clientelism in both the north and the south, gives testimony to the general Italian failure ever to project the nation-state as an object of political attachment.

Universalism was one of the few "isms" that never captured the Italian imagination, fascist or otherwise. The fascist regime, that is, fascism as ideology coupled with state power, was the pillar of fascist identities. When the regime fell, fascism as a source of political, social, and cultural identity crumbled. The peculiar Italian iterations of Catholicism and family, however, buttressed by the strong institutional support of the church and particularist social arrangements, remained. In power, fascism could transpose the rules of the cultural game, but it never succeeded in rewriting them. Fascist identity withered with the fall of the regime. Thus, it was not surprising that the American lieutenant had not met many fascists until he encountered the Signora Bottai. Only the Italian elite, the architects of the fascist cultural project, enjoyed the luxury of commitment—and even Bottai was in Africa at the time.

CONCLUSION

Fascism/Identity/Ritual

Not a Parenthesis

Fascism is a peculiar political entity. Unlike liberalism or socialism, fascism has a commonsense definition that equates it with violence. In contrast to facile popular notions of fascism, definition has eluded scholarly exegesis. Confronted with a seemingly protean political entity, scholars have concentrated on explanations of particular instances of fascism generally situated in the European cases of the early twentieth century. Until recently, the coupling of a popular conception with scholarly ambiguity has produced a tendency to view fascism as a political aberration limited to a particular historical period and without contemporary political relevance.

I have argued that Italian fascism offered a competing model of modernity that was nonrational but not irrational. My analysis of ritual suggests that the "old fascism" is more fully understood if one turns to the cultural features of democracy it rejected. Italian fascism repudiated the split between the public and private self, the core of liberal democracy. This rejection was explicit and not accidental. My broader point is that at certain historical moments social groups perceive the bifurcation of a public and private self as untenable, and political movements, parties, and ideologies that reject this split on cultural grounds gain political ascendance. I suggest that we might gain analytic purchase on those movements, parties, and ideologies if we reconceptualize them as fascist—or anti-liberal.

My conclusion is a proposition that requires testing with additional empirically grounded historical and contemporary case studies. The reemergence of right-wing parties in contemporary Europe, the 1994 electoral success of the Italian "post-fascist" National Alliance, and even the rise of the American right suggest that the fascist impulse is not, as Benedetto Croce suggested, a "parenthesis." The 1990s are not the 1920s or the 1930s. Historical and cultural specificity matters. Black Shirts will not march on Rome; the Reichstag will not burn. A recent *New York Times* editorial ruefully begins, "Germany's New Right Wears a Three-Piece Suit." Fascism has always worn a three-piece suit, and its cultural and social dimensions must be taken seriously.

Mussolini's regime with its visions of nation and community spoke the language of social revolution. The new fascist political culture that merged public and private identities aimed to colonize the mind as well as the state. Public political spectacle was the favored vehicle of cultural persuasion and reconstruction. Scholars of early-twentieth-century "totalitarian" regimes, particularly nazism, equated the newness of this style of politics with the newness of mass politics and assumed that spectacle was a constitutive property of nondemocratic regimes.

In contrast, students of political ritual, who view aesthetics as a property of political regimes, tell us little about either the regimes they purport to explain or how ritual contributes to political practice. The logical weakness of the purely descriptive approach to political ritual is that it conflates intention, the public rhetorics and actions of regimes, with effects, the presumed response of publics to these rhetorics and actions. The elision of the distinction between observer and participant, intention and effect has analytic and methodological consequences. On the analytic level, it assumes, first, that regimes have total power and elides the process of regime choice, and second, that publics passively receive regime messages. Methodologically, it suggests, as in the Italian fascist case, that we can read fascist culture and meaning from fascist propaganda, images, and symbols without taking relevant context into account. In short, it assumes that representations of power equal realities of power.

I have taken a counterposition in this book which permits a nuanced account of, first, fascism as political ideology and practice and, second, of the process by which states attempt to create new political identities. In contrast to earlier studies of fascism that neglect its cultural dimension and more recent and reductionist studies of culture and power, my analysis suggests complexity. Rituals were vehicles of solidarity—communities of feeling—in an ideological project. Rituals multiplied in fascist Italy because they served as public dramatizations of the merging of the public/private self that characterized nonliberal ideology in an age of large nation-states. They were also particularly suited to a political ideology and Italian culture that eschewed text in favor of emotion.

Fascist Identity: Was Anyone Listening?

Ritual facilitates the creation of new identities and meanings to the extent that it articulates with prior identities. In fascist Italy, rituals served as expressive political arenas where Italian cultural meanings—Catholicism as popular culture and the cult of motherhood—were appropriated and reinvented. The interplay of schemata and resources shaped and limited the fascist cultural project. The identities that resonated with fascism were not simply free-floating, as the dead soldiers' voices suggest. The institutional buttresses of church and family continually reinforced the cultural meaning of Catholicism and motherhood. But this is only one part of the story. The performance aspects of ritual provide a permanent quality of indeterminacy. Ritual actions, existing in real time and space, are new with each enactment. This indeterminacy means that rituals are as capable of creating disorder as order. At any moment, a parade or rally may become a riot, a crowd may become a mob. It was no accident that the Ministries of the Interior and Public Security allocated a significant portion of their resources during the fascist period to guarding the piazza, where the ghosts of socialism lurked.

Fascist identities, like all political identities, are public in that they are constructed outside the realm of the private self although they may incorporate dimensions of the private self. Identity assumes community because it implies a group of others to whom one can feel similarity against a group of others to whom one is not similar. One both has an identity and identifies with. Crafted identities, such as those that political regimes attempt to create, demand that we pay attention to the receiving community—or, to put it in terms more commonly reserved for studies of aesthetics, they imply questions of audience and reception. In her 1991 study of symbolic politics in Nicolae Ceausescu's Romania, anthropologist Katherine Verdery raises, but does not answer, the question of reception and calls it the "is-anyone-listening problem."[1]

Verdery's question translated to the Italian fascist case becomes: To what extent was the fascist cultural project internalized by its citizens—the audience for symbolic practices—that is, to what extent did fascist identities form? This question, germane to all efforts at civic education whether the ideologies and practices at issue are liberal or totalitarian, is particularly salient in the instance of regimes that aim to construct a new ethos or culture, to merge the public and private self.

The fascist heroes forged their political identities in terms of their two

---

[1] Katherine Verdery, *National Ideology under Socialism* (Berkeley: University of California Press, 1991), 6.

non-contingent and private identities—as sons and as Catholics. The Italian devotion to Catholicism as a form of popular cultural practice and the dedication to family embodied in the cult of the mother limited what was ideologically possible on the part of the regime. The imposed fascist "identity" was a collage that, as the letters suggest, was the product of deeply held cultural beliefs supported by the particular Italian social iterations of the institutions of church and family. As Allied bombs fell along with the regime, fascist identity revealed itself as highly contingent.

The story I have told is a story of extremes. It has focused on the most public of spectacles and pronouncements and the most committed fascists, from the architects of fascist policy to the rank-and-file heroes. Extremes serve analytic and theoretical ends if we recognize them as such; in this case we have addressed a theoretical question regarding the nature of fascism and an analytic question concerning the state construction of identity. States can create public political identities, feelings of membership, only to the extent that these identities articulate with existing deeply held private identities with strong institutional supports. Or to put it even more telegraphically, social institutions organize communities of public and private identities. This is a conclusion and a hypothesis that demands further study in other contexts. The democratization and citizenship projects under way in central europe as well as other parts of the globe lend contemporary salience to this proposition. What remains is the issue of ritual itself as a vehicle of political meaning.

Ritual and the Political Meaning of Indeterminacy

Literacy and language were cultural problems in Italy. In the 1920s and 1930s, despite the best efforts of the regime, Italy still had higher rates of illiteracy than comparable countries, especially in the south. The north/south divide does not explain the problem of language, however. Dialect was the preferred form of communication among the populace, and standard Italian was limited to the educated few. In daily practice, even the educated might resort to a local dialect. This problem with text meant that the public sphere was rather restricted. Newspaper reading was not widely diffused (although surprisingly, there was an abundance of newspapers), and despite the increase in the number of propaganda tracts, Italy was not a country with a mass reading public. Communication was linked to physical action and to conversation, and not to the impersonal vehicle of print.

What most persons would recognize in terms of political meaning and communication were actions in public places. Italy as a social landscape combined the symbolic material of centuries with modern social spaces such as the elaborately designed train stations. The salience of social space and the political possibilities of parading through it were not lost on the planners of fascist spectacle. The maps of the parade routes the fascists left behind suggest that they paid close attention to space and hierarchy. The arrival of the leader is an archetypal form of public ritual, and the train stations modernized this traditional form. Many of the stations in Italy were redesigned or rebuilt during the fascist period, and the regime touted the trains (they ran on time!) as an exemplary feature of the new fascist infrastructure.

The train stations were located on the periphery of the center of many Italian cities, and the motorcade that carried the leader to the ritual event usually interrupted the flow of street life. The parade routes touched multipurpose parts of the cities—for example, the Corso Umberto in Rome contained shops, apartments, and government buildings. The Italian piazzas were the scene of battles between socialists and fascists in the postwar period, and a rhetoric and consciousness developed about who controlled these spaces.

When the fascists took over the piazzas for public spectacle, they aimed to create a community of feeling based on the emotion of solidarity and not a rhetoric of political persuasion. The problem with text in Italy to some extent determined this method of political communication. The reliance on spectacle also pointed to a core feature of fascist ideology. The rallying cry of fascism in the mid-1930s was "Believe, Fight, and Obey,"a call to action without an object, to a style of behavior without a goal. In contrast, "Liberty, Equality, and Fraternity" is a call to values and content. In democratic societies, discourse around ideas is theoretically central to political participation. In Italian fascist society, the text was secondary because the fascists wished to create a feeling of participation, not actual participation in the community. This feeling of community would presumably produce a disciplined fascist citizen who would subordinate his or her self to the organism of the state.

The fascist regime made crowds. Bodies transported by train from all parts of Italy populated fascist spectacle. The ordinary Italian citizen had limited access to these spectacles, which they were carefully policed. While the regime legally controlled public space, it could not control memory. The appropriation of time and space through the constant parading in public space and the frequent cessation of work for holidays were powerful vehicles of fascist social imposition. The landscape which provided the staging for fascist spectacle and which the regime restamped with its parades and rituals contained social memories not only of past glories of the Roman Empire or the Italian Renaissance but also of the daily activity of commerce and entertainment. Walking and talking in the historic centers was a principal feature of the social life of ordinary Italian men and women. Thus, the average citizen experienced fascist spectacle as disruptive of work and play.

Scholars tend to view parades as integrative social vehicles.[2] The question is, Integrative for whom? For the carefully selected groups of fascist squads, fascist spectacle might have been an identity-forming experience. For the persons who regularly used the social spaces that the regime appropriated, spectacle was at best a nuisance and at worst an object of ridicule. Fascist spectacle was an experience that sharpened divisions about who was in and who was out and made consensus problematic as the regime marched into the late 1930s, the pact with Hitler, and the war.

But if fascist ritual did not achieve its presumed purpose, the enduring creation of new identities and bonds of solidarity, the questions remain: what does political ritual do, and what did fascist political ritual do? Discursive ritual knowledge is, as I have suggested, ultimately indeterminate. But how does ritual mean if not discursively? And how does it contribute to a politics of identity if it conveys no narrative knowledge?

Ritual "does" three things that are germane to the construction of identities. First, it forces ritual actors, defined as both observers and participants, to engage in a process of repeated actions or performances. Repeated actions in time generate morphologies of meaning based on the familiarity that repeated exposure to ritual forms generates. The formal characteristics of ritual action establish what is ordinary, customary, and recognizable in public political ritual to ritual actors. My narratives of the March on Rome and ritual life in Verona support this contention.

Public political rituals serve as arenas of identity, bounded spaces where collective national selfhood is enacted. Ritual action communicates familiarity with form, and this familiarity may be as simple as the recognition that one is required to be present at an event. Familiarity and identity are coterminous. This brings us to the second of the three things that ritual does. The repeated experience of ritual participation produces a feeling of solidarity—"we *are* all here together, we *must* share something." Third, it produces collective memory—"we *were* all there together." What is experienced and what is remembered is the act of participating in the ritual event in the name of the polity.

Ritual temporarily eliminates material indeterminacy in bounded social spaces such as the piazzas of fascist Italy, but to say this is not to assume that ritual eliminates indeterminacy as to meaning. Ritual by acting out emotion includes indeterminacy. Public political ritual is a double-edged sword be-

---

[2] See Mary Ryan, "The American Parade: Representations of the Nineteenth-Century Social Order," in *The New Cultural History*, ed. Lynn Hunt (Berkeley: University of California Press, 1989), 131–53.

cause it creates an open interpretive space. Solidarities and memories—the identities of subjects who have gathered under similar circumstances—may be extremely fluid. Emotion may obliterate the old self, but there is no guarantee as to what form the new self or identity will assume. "We *are* all here together" may as easily become "Here we go yet again!"

Italian politics, fascist or not, is particularly suited to ritual as a form of political communication for all the reasons I have outlined. From the Renaissance state as work of art to the fascist state and to contemporary Italy, Italian political discourse has frequently been a conversation among diverse groups of ritual actions. In this restricted sense, ritual provides an alternative nondiscursive language of politics with a syntax of actions and a vocabulary of symbols. In fascist Italy, ritual genres that changed in response to shifting political imperatives suggested a logic to regime ritual action. Historically and culturally specific, the denotative meanings of fascist ritual were easily within public grasp. A regime event in the piazza was fascist power on display. The broader and deeper meanings of fascist ritual were indeterminate, but on the every-shifting terrain of symbolic politics indeterminacy is a virtue, not a vice.

Did the fascist regime create new political meanings around the piazza? In 1945, Italian resistance fighters executed Mussolini, his lover Clara Petacci, and a few remaining loyal fascists as they were trying to escape to Switzerland. Mussolini's wife, the mother of his children, and his family remained safely at a house on Lake Como under German protection. The partisans took the bodies to Milan. They hung Mussolini's dead body, with the body of his lover beside him, from its heels in Piazza Loreto—two blocks from the Central Train Station. Someone had been listening—to something.

Methodological Appendix

The footnotes to this book are substantive and exhaustive. They provide complete documentation of the primary and secondary sources from which I derived my arguments. In the place of a standard bibliography, I provide here a methodological appendix, which describes the archival sources I consulted and discusses the evidence I used to construct the three empirical cases.

Manuscript Sources

Police reports, public security memoes, Fascist Party manuals, plans for public events, memoranda from state meetings, and descriptions of legislation were located in the central state archives in Rome and the local state archive in Verona. The following is a list of the files I consulted. I have included where appropriate the principal number of the file. This is somewhat deceptive for those unfamiliar with these archives, as it does not capture the extent of the raw mass of material I sifted through to find useful evidence. Each file has several subfiles. For example, in the archive of the Presidenza del Consiglio dei Ministri, where I systematically searched each year from 1922 to 1941, there are hundreds of subfiles for each year.

A. *Archivio Centrale dello Stato (Rome)*

Mostra della Rivoluzione Fascista:
Bustas 1–13, 50, 53, 89. Bustas 1–12 contained the soldiers' letters and obituaries as well as the Fascist Party log for the city of Verona.

Segretaria Particolare del Duce, Carteggio Riservato:
Bustas 31 242/R 10C; 32 242/R 8B; 42, sf. 22.

Presidenza del Consiglio dei Ministri (1922–41):
Bustas:

1923	2.4–1/f. 2680
1924	2.4–1/f. 2654
1926	2.4–1/f. 3904; 1.3–3/f. 1710
1927	2.4–1/f. 4060
1931–33	3.3.3/f. 2754 (sf. 1–19); 14–1/f. 890 (sf. 1–23), 5754/1; 3.3.12/f. 7257; 3.3.9/f. 1962
1934–36	3.3.3/f. 2344 (sf. a–c)
1937–39	14.2/f. 3546 (sf. 1–3); 3.3.3/f. 1558 (sf. 1–8); 3.3.9/f. 3202/sf. 1; f. 2422 (sf. 1–21)

Partito Nazionale Fascista Direttorio Serie I:
Bustas 1202–05. Veronese Fascist Party reports to national headquarters.

Ministero della Cultura Popolare:
Busta 241.91. Local propagandists.

B. *Archivio di Stato di Verona*

Gabinetto della Prefettura (1922–40):
Bustas 1923/135, 1924/141, 1934/487
Regia Questura di Verona—Relazione Mattinale del Giorno, 1933/480.

Dono Frediani (1936)—I Ritagli Stampa del Periodo fra 15/7/34 e 12/31/35.

Newspapers

I consulted the following newspapers selectively for the years between 1922 and 1940. I have included the city and first year of publication in the citation.

L'Arena (Verona), 1866.
L'Assalto (Perugia), 1921.
La Corriere della Sera (Milan), 1876.
Cremona Nuova (Cremona), 1922.
Il Messagero (Rome), 1878.

La Nazione (Florence), 1859.
Il Popolo d'Italia (Milan), 1914.
Il Resto del Carlino (Bologna), 1895.
La Stampa (Turin), 1866.
La Tribuna (Rome), 1882, originally *L'Idea Nazionale*.

National Fascist Party Sources

Folgio d'Ordini di Partito Nazionale Fascista (Rome), 1926–40.
Opera Omnia di Benito Mussolini. Florence: La Fenice, 1956.

Case Construction

The cases in this book posed two challenges: first, the data themselves, and second, the historical representation of performance. I have addressed these issues in the text, including my conceptualization of ritual action. I turn here to the mechanics of case construction.

In general, for the March on Rome (Chapters 3 and 4) and Verona (Chapter 5), I tracked events in party, police, and government files and tried to locate newspaper descriptions of the events I chose to focus on. Collecting systematic evidence on the fascist period is difficult, because gaps frequently appear in the data. Even finding the newspapers that provide a large part of my empirical evidence required trips to National Libraries in Rome, Florence, and Verona to trace particular issues. The juxtaposition of three cases was part of the logic that entered my research design—in part, to compensate for limitations in the data and, in part, to achieve my purpose of re-creating felt experience.

The March on Rome

I constructed Chapter 3 from a planning commission report on the design of the holiday found in the archives of the Presidenza. I then traced the event in local newspapers supplemented with Mussolini's speeches as recorded in the *Opera Omnia*. The newspapers that provided the evidence for this chapter were *Il Popolo d'Italia* (Milan), 2, 17–19, 24–31 October and 1–7 November 1923; *Cremona Nuova* (Cremona), 24–28 October 1923; *L'Assalto* (Perugia), 27, 29 October 1923; *Il Resto del Carlino* (Bologna), 24–30 October 1923; *Il Messaggero* (Rome), 28, 30, 31 October and 1 November 1923; *La Nazione* (Florence), 30, 31 October and 1 November 1923; *La Tribuna* (Rome), 28, 30 October and 1 November 1923; *La Corriere della Sera* (Milan), 28 October and 1 November 1923.

These were the major Italian newspapers of the period as well as the local newspapers from specific cities that were part of the first anniversary commemorations. Of these eight newspapers, the first three were explicitly fascist and the next four were nationalist and sympathetic to fascism. The *Corriere della Sera* was the only one that could be considered mildly dissenting in that its reporting was neutral and unemotional and it frequently did not give first-page coverage to the commemorations. Socialist newspapers were published during this period, but they were not germane to my analysis. I checked *L'Avanti*, which did not cover the ceremonies.

The story of the March in the post-1923 commemoration (Chapter 4) was mapped from party documents in the archives of the Presidenza and the *Foglio d'Ordini*. I supplemented these descriptions with material from *Il Popolo d'Italia* and selected local newspapers where appropriate.

Verona

The historical source that formed the basis of Chapter 5 was a typewritten calendar of all public events run by the local Fascist Party in Verona. The calendar entries began before Mussolini came to power and continued through the beginning of World War II (PNF [Partito Nazionale Fascista]. Federazione dei Fasci di Combattimento di Verona. Documentario Manifestazioni della Federazione Fascista dal 23 Gennaio 1922 al 19 Luglio 1942–xx. PNF. MRF [Mostra della Rivoluzione Fascista]. I Carteggi Amministrativi. BB. 12. Rome: Archivio Centrale dello Stato). A description of how this archive was assembled is provided in Ministero per i beni culturali e ambientali, *Partito Nazionale Fascista: Mostra della Rivoluzione Fascista* (Rome: Archivio Centrale dello Stato, 1990), 43–48, 59–60.

As I was interested in quantifying the material on the calendar to generate my "ritual waves," I systematically checked its reliability. I matched the events recorded on the log to descriptions in the Veronese newspaper *L'Arena*. The large number of events and the unavailability of complete issues of *L'Arena* in the National Libraries in both Rome and Florence for the 1930s made it impossible to check every entry. *L'Arena* was available on microfilm for 1922 to 1931. For those years, I was able to locate a newspaper account ranging from a notice to a front-page story for virtually every log entry, suggesting that the log was a reliable source of information on local fascist events. For example, in 1926 the log listed thirty events. I located twenty-six of them in *L'Arena*; the other four were not locatable owing to gaps in the microfilm. Similarly, in 1931 the log listed thirty-three events. I located twenty-six of them, and there were seven gaps in the microfilm. For 1933, I cross-checked log entries with the Veronese police chief's daily report, and I located eight of forty-seven events. This finding supported my contention that many of these events were considered sufficiently routine so as not to require police surveillance.

As I had reconceptualized ritual as cultural action, I viewed the calendar as an opportunity to generate diachronic data that would visually capture the formal dimensions of ritual action. To code the calendar, I borrowed a methodology developed by Charles Tilly (and elaborated by Sidney Tarrow and numerous students) to study collective action.[1]

I coded all 727 events in Verona. My unit of analysis was a "public political event," which I defined as a bounded action on a discrete calendar entry. I coded a series of descriptive variables (partially reported in Chapter 5, Table 1) and a series of constructed variables: genre, local/national interaction, and period (reported in Chapter 5, Table 2). The content of the calendar entries varied from single lines to descriptive paragraphs. Short entries permitted me to code date and type but not much else.

A typical short data entry was:

21 April [1929]. Celebration of Labor Day.

I coded this event as "celebratory" and a "national event with local leader present," noting also that it occurred on a Sunday. Another example of a short entry was:

24 August [1938]. The federal secretary [of the Fascist Party] gave the party's salute to one hundred Veronese colonists leaving for Libya.

This event was coded as "celebratory" and "national event with local leader present."

Longer entries permitted more detailed coding. For example:

24 May [1935]. For the XX anniversary of the entrance into war, a mass in honor of the glorious soldiers immolated on the battlefield was celebrated in the Church of the Cemetery under the auspices of the Association of the Families of the Fallen, and afterward on the historic stage of the Piazza dei Signori the honorable Alessandro Dudam, designated by the party secretary, gave a celebratory speech and followed the ceremony of the Leva Fascista with the symbolic rite of the passing of the ranks.

I coded this mass as "commemorative" and "national event with local leader present." The additional information of the lengthier entry allowed me to

---

[1] For examples, see Charles Tilly, *The Contentious French* (Cambridge: Harvard University Press, 1986), and more recently, "Contentious Repertoires in Great Britain, 1758–1834," *Social Science History* 17(2) (1993), 253–80; Sidney Tarrow, *Democracy and Disorder: Protest and Politics in Italy, 1965–1975* (New York: Oxford University Press, 1989).

code location ("church"), ritual action ("mass"), and participants ("veterans" and "clergy"). The speech was coded as a separate event under the rubric of "symposia." Because party designates were sent from Rome, I coded this occasion as "national event with national leader present." The notation of location of the event in the Piazza dei Signori permitted me to code for type of public space.

There were no observable differences in the length of entries between years.

Obituaries and Soldiers' Letters

The data for Chapter 6 are taken from PNF.MRF (Mostra della Rivoluzione Fascista). I Carteggi Amministrativi. BB. 1–13. Rome: Archivio Centrale dello Stato. This archive, assembled for the 1942 edition of the Mostra della Rivoluzione Fascista, was the result of a national party call to the local party secretaries to provide information on the fascist war dead. The federal secretaries responded with reports from sixty-five Italian cities and created an archive of biographies of six hundred fifty-nine dead fascist heroes.[2]

The men and one woman spanned a fascist generational divide. The younger "heroes" had experienced fascism as an ideology from youth and had been active members of fascist organizations. The older "heroes" claimed to have fought in the fascist revolution or participated in the March on Rome. The response was varied and selective. Some local party heads responded to the federals with only the most perfunctory of biographies on all Fascist Party members who had given their lives in Spain, Africa, or the Balkans. Others, depending on their energy and literary ability, responded with full-length obituary biographies that extolled the virtues of their local fascist heroes. The more creative party heads included excerpts from the personal letters and diaries of the dead.

As I make a claim that we can read identity from the letters, a question emerges as to how representative they were. These data have limitations that must be acknowledged; nevertheless, I believe the letters remain the best available representation of an authentic fascist voice. Some local party leaders sent only the minimum information—names and dates of death. Among those who sent information, the response varied enormously. I could find no trends in the data that suggested systematic bias due to location; for example, region did not seem to make a difference.

The thoroughness of response, to the best that I could determine, seemed

[2] There was a fascist federation for each province in Italy. Mussolini chose the federal secretaries, who reported directly to the head of the National Fascist Party. For an English-language description of Fascist Party organization and hierarchy, see *The Fascist Party* (Florence: Vallecchi, 1937), 77–86.

entirely random. For example, no other local federal prepared a calendar of events such as the one I found in Verona. The constant effort of the Veronese Fascist Party to demonstrate its commitment most likely contributed to the completeness of its file. The rhetorical style of both the letters and the obituaries displayed the predisposition to sentimentality which, as I have argued, is attributable to Italian culture, and not fascism. Close reading of the letters, however, reveals enough difference, enough roughness at the edges, to suggest that they were indeed what they claimed to be: excerpts from soldiers' letters written from the front.

As for representativeness, the question remains, Representative of what? I make no claims that the letters represent all Italian soldiers on the front or all fascists. As I noted in the text, this is a story of extremes. The letters cited have gone through two filters. First, a local party chief decided which ones to include in the archive; and second, I decided, of the hundreds that I read (I read all the files from sixty-five cities), which ones to focus on. My task here was essentially ethnographic and interpretive, that is, I made selections. The letters represent my "clinical" feeling for what was important; in that sense, they are representative of what I learned in the course of my study. I suspect a more "scientific" sample of committed fascists would yield similar results. Second, there is no way to account for the selection mechanisms, literary abilities of local party heads, or internal organization of local parties without a full-length study like Chapter 5. Acknowledging these limitations supports my claim that the letters provide the best available evidence of a fascist voice.

Index

The Wilder House Series in Politics, History, and Culture

Mabel Berezin teaches sociology at the
University of California, Los Angeles.